Connections
Essentials

Empowering College and Career Success

Paul A. Gore
Xavier University

Wade Leuwerke
Drake University

A.J. Metz
The University of Utah

bedford/st.martin's
Macmillan Learning

Boston | New York

For Bedford/St. Martin's

Vice President, Editorial, Macmillan Learning Humanities: Edwin Hill
Senior Program Director for Communication and College Success: Erika Gutierrez
Senior Development Manager: Susan McLaughlin
Marketing Manager: Kayti Corfield
Director of Content Development: Jane Knetzger
Senior Developmental Editor: Christina Lembo
Assistant Content Project Manager: Emily Brower
Senior Workflow Project Supervisor: Joe Ford
Production Supervisor: Robin Besofsky
Media Project Manager: Sarah O'Connor
Editorial Assistant: Kathy McInerney
Copyeditor: Mary Lou Wilshaw-Watts
Editorial Services: Lumina Datamatics, Inc.
Composition: Jouve
Permissions Editor: Angela Boehler
Photo Researcher: Richard Fox
Permissions Manager: Kalina Ingham
Senior Art Director: Anna Palchik
Text Design: Maureen McCutcheon
Cover Design: John Callahan
Cover Art: paprika/Shutterstock
Printing and Binding: LSC Communications

Manufactured in the United States of America.

2 1 0 9 8 7
f e d c b a

For information, write: Bedford/St. Martin's, 75 Arlington Street, Boston, MA 02116

ISBN 978-1-319-03082-7

Acknowledgments

Acknowledgments and copyrights appear on the same page as the text and art selections they cover; these acknowledgments and copyrights constitute an extension of the copyright page.

brief contents

1 Building a Foundation for Success   *1*

2 Thinking Critically and Setting Goals   *13*

3 Motivation, Decision Making, and Personal Responsibility   *33*

4 Understanding Learning   *49*

5 Organization and Time Management   *69*

6 Reading for College Success   *87*

7 Taking Effective Notes   *105*

8 Memory, Studying, and Test Taking   *125*

9 Information Literacy and Communication   *147*

10 Connecting with Others   *163*

11 Personal and Financial Health   *185*

12 Academic and Career Planning   *203*

GLOSSARY   *227*

ENDNOTES   *229*

INDEX   *235*

brief contents

1. Building a Foundation for Success

2. Thinking Critically and Setting Goals   13

3. Motivation, Decision Making, and Personal Responsibility   33

4. Understanding Learning   49

5. Organization and Time Management   69

6. Reading for College Success   87

7. Taking Effective Notes   101

8. Memory, Studying, and Test Taking   125

9. Information Literacy and Communication   141

10. Connecting with Others   163

11. Personal and Financial Health   183

12. Academic and Career Planning   202

GLOSSARY   221

ENDNOTES   225

INDEX   235

contents

BRIEF CONTENTS *iii*
PREFACE *xiii*

Commercial Eye/Getty Images

1 Building a Foundation for Success 1

Why Go to College? 2

Education: Good for Society, Good for You 2

What It Means to Be in College 2

Learn about Yourself 3

Discover Your Values 3

Follow Your Interests 4

Embrace Your Strengths — and Learn from Your Weaknesses 5

● **Getting to Know *You*: ACES and Other Tools** 6

● **Student Voices of Experience: Finding Your Purpose** 7

Feel the Power of Positive Psychology 8

Build Self-Efficacy 8

Be Resilient 8

Keep Hope Alive 9

Take Personal Responsibility for Your Success 10

● **Recruit Help** 10

College Success Leads to Career Success 11

CHAPTER SUMMARY 12 **/** **CHAPTER ACTIVITIES** 12

Peter Cade/Getty Images

2 Thinking Critically and Setting Goals 13

Build Your Critical-Thinking Skills 15

The Higher-Level Thinking Skills behind Critical Thinking 15

How to Use Your Higher-Level Thinking Skills 15

- **Compare and Contrast: Critical vs. Creative Thinking** 18

Use Bloom's Taxonomy 19

- **Those Blooming Test Questions!** 21

Think Critically to Set Goals 22

Step 1: Gather Information (about *You*) 22

Step 2: Set a SMART Goal 22

Step 3: Make an Action Plan 23

- **Got Goals? They're Your Path to Academic Success** 24

Step 4: List Barriers and Solutions 25

Step 5: Act and Evaluate Outcomes 25

- **Student Voices of Experience: Focusing on Solutions** 26

Create Your Personal Success Plan 27

The PSP in Action 27

Create Your First Personal Success Plan 28

- **Employers Value Goal Setting** 30

CHAPTER SUMMARY 32 / **CHAPTER ACTIVITIES** 32

Don Mason/Getty Images

3 Motivation, Decision Making, and Personal Responsibility 33

What Keeps You Motivated? 35

Self-Efficacy 35

Relevance 35

Attitude 37

- **You're Good Enough *and* You're Smart Enough** 37

Tap into Your Internal Motivation 38

- **Student Voices of Experience: Staying Motivated in College** 39

Make Good Decisions 40

Take Personal Responsibility for Your Education 42

Develop a Growth Mind-set 42

Take an Active Approach to Your Learning 42

- **Active Learning, Personal Responsibility, and Belief Lead to Success!** 43

Navigate the Transition to College Life 44

Think about Thinking and Learning 45

- **My Personal Success Plan** 46

CHAPTER SUMMARY 48 / **CHAPTER ACTIVITIES** 48

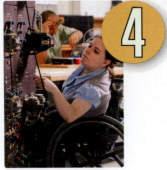

Huntstock/Getty Images

Understanding Learning *49*

Learning That Works: What the Research Tells Us *51*

Test Yourself *51*

Space Out Your Studying *52*

Change Up Your Material *53*

Make Connections So Learning Lasts *53*

Use Verbal *and* Visual Information *54*

● **Your Brain Is Required for Learning!** *55*

Make Learning Personal *56*

Use the Myers-Briggs Model *56*

Use the VARK Model *58*

● **Student Voices of Experience: Using Learning Strategies in College** *62*

Succeed in Different Learning Environments *63*

Work in a Group *63*

Make Sure You're Multimodal *64*

● **Seek Help for Learning Challenges** *65*

● **My Personal Success Plan** *66*

CHAPTER SUMMARY *68* **/** **CHAPTER ACTIVITIES** *68*

Westend61/Getty Images

Organization and Time Management *69*

Get Organized *71*

Create a Clean Study Space *71*

Organize Your Documents *71*

● **What's in a Name? How to Label Your Files and Folders** *72*

Take Control of Your Time *73*

Step 1: Track Your Time *73*

Step 2: Identify Your Priorities *75*

Step 3: Build Your Schedule *75*

● **Manage Time When You Learn Online** *77*

Step 4: Use Tools to Track Progress on Your Projects *78*

● **Student Voices of Experience: Tools for Time Management** *80*

Overcome Procrastination and Minimize Distractions *81*

Beat Procrastination *81*

Minimize Distractions *82*

● **Find Your Flow** *83*

● **My Personal Success Plan** *84*

CHAPTER SUMMARY *86* **/** **CHAPTER ACTIVITIES** *86*

olaser/Getty Images

6 Reading for College Success 87

Embrace Reading! 89
Read Actively in College 89
Connect Reading with Other Study Skills 89

Prepare to Read 90
Preview the Material 90
- **Make a Plan for Your Reading** 90
Identify Purposeful Reading Questions 91

Read with Focus 92
Mark Up Your Reading Material 92
Think Critically about What You Read 92
- **Student Voices of Experience: Gaining Confidence in Reading** 94
Clarify Confusing Material 95
Boost Your Reading Efficiency 95
- **Reading: It's Good for You!** 95

Review What You've Read 97
Recite 97
Summarize 97
Review and Study 97

Read Different Types of Materials 98
Read for Math and Science Classes 98
Read Journal Articles 98
Read Online Course Materials 100
- **Ask for Help with Reading Challenges** 100
- **My Personal Success Plan** 102
CHAPTER SUMMARY 104 / **CHAPTER ACTIVITIES** 104

UpperCut Images/Getty Images

7 Taking Effective Notes 105

Supercharge Your Note Taking with a Four-Step Strategy 107
Step 1: Prepare to Take Notes 107
Step 2: Actively Listen, Watch, Read, and Participate 108
Step 3: Record Information 109
- **Taking Notes? Grab a Pen and Paper** 111
Step 4: Review Your Notes 111

Experiment with Note-Taking Methods 112
Outlining 112
- **Student Voices of Experience: Outlining and Other Note-Taking Strategies** 114
Charting 115
Cornell System 116
Mapping 116

Note-Taking Tips for Math, Science, and Online Classes 119
Taking Notes in Math and Science Classes 119
Taking Notes in Online Classes 119
- **Take Notes like a Professional** 121
- **My Personal Success Plan** 122
CHAPTER SUMMARY 124 / **CHAPTER ACTIVITIES** 124

Jacob Lund/Shutterstock

8 Memory, Studying, and Test Taking *125*

Learn How Your Memory Works *127*

Sensory Memory *127*

Short-Term / Working Memory *128*

Long-Term Memory *128*

Putting It All Together *128*

● **Why You Forget** *129*

Study Basics: Set Yourself Up for Success *130*

Manage Your Time Wisely *130*

Join a Study Group *130*

Make Connections *131*

● **Remember Material with Mnemonics** *131*

Create Your Own Study Tools *132*

Study for Math and Science Classes *132*

Study for Online Classes *133*

Prepare for Tests *134*

Know the Exam Format *134*

Review Previous Exams *134*

Stay Healthy *134*

Talk with Your Instructor *135*

Manage Test Anxiety *135*

● **Think Good Thoughts** *136*

● **Student Voices of Experience: Preparing for Tests and Overcoming Test Anxiety** *137*

Learn Test-Taking Strategies *138*

Start Smart *138*

Answer Common Question Types *138*

Take Math and Science Tests *141*

Take Tests Online *141*

● **You've Got Integrity** *142*

Follow Up after Tests *143*

Evaluate Your Approach *143*

Get Hard Evidence *143*

Learn from Your Mistakes *143*

● **My Personal Success Plan** *144*

CHAPTER SUMMARY *146* **/** **CHAPTER ACTIVITIES** *146*

Digital Vision/Getty Images

9 Information Literacy and Communication 147

Develop Information Literacy *149*

Find the Information You Need *149*

Evaluate the Information You've Found *150*

- **Wikipedia: Friend or Foe?** *151*

Communicate Information through Writing *152*

Prepare to Write *152*

Write Your First Draft *153*

Revise and Polish Your Paper *155*

Write in Online Classes *156*

- **Avoid Plagiarism** *156*
- **Student Voices of Experience: Getting Feedback on Your Writing** *157*

Present in Class with Confidence *158*

Know Your Purpose — and Your Audience *158*

Craft Your Presentation *158*

Present like a Pro *159*

Harness the Power of Technology: Present Online *159*

- **Practice, Practice, Practice!** *159*
- **My Personal Success Plan** *160*

CHAPTER SUMMARY *162* / **CHAPTER ACTIVITIES** *162*

Sam Edwards/Getty Images

10 Connecting with Others 163

Enhance Your Communication Skills *165*

Become a Better Listener *165*

Become a Better Speaker *166*

Build Emotional Intelligence *167*

Recognize Emotions *167*

Understand Emotions *168*

Manage Emotions *169*

- **The Dangers of Suppressing Your Emotions** *170*

Resolve Conflict *171*

Be Assertive *171*

Use "I" Statements *172*

- **Don't Be a Doormat** *172*

Use All Your Skills to Resolve Conflicts *173*

Grow and Sustain Healthy Relationships *174*

Connect with Classmates *174*

Connect with Instructors *174*

Connect with Your Campus Community *175*

- **There's More to College than the Classroom** 175
  - Connect with Others Online 176
  - Stay Connected with Friends and Family 176
  - **Student Voices of Experience: Maintaining Relationships** 177

Embrace Diversity 178
- Recognize Differences 178
- Respect Differences 178
- Think Critically about Differences 180
- **My Personal Success Plan** 182

CHAPTER SUMMARY 184 / CHAPTER ACTIVITIES 184

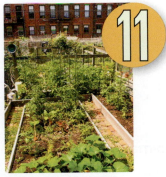

145/Eunice Harris/Ocean/CORBIS

Personal and Financial Health 185

Stress Less, Feel Better 187

Physical and Mental Health 188
- Eat Right 188
- Stay Active 189
- Don't Skimp on the Z's 189
- **Healthy Behavior Is Good for Your Grades** 190
- Take Care of Your Mental Health 190
- **Student Voices of Experience: Staying Healthy and Coping with Stress** 191
- Don't Abuse Alcohol and Drugs 192

Sexual Health 193
- Avoid Sexually Transmitted Infections 193
- Practice Birth Control 194

Financial Health 195
- Create a Budget 195
- Reduce Your Spending 196
- Get a Job to Boost Your Income 197
- Navigate Financial Aid 197
- **I've Got Financial Aid — Now How Do I Keep It?** 198
- Control Your Credit Cards — So They Don't Control You 199
- **My Personal Success Plan** 200

CHAPTER SUMMARY 202 / CHAPTER ACTIVITIES 202

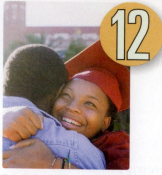
Kevin Dodge/Corbis

12 Academic and Career Planning *203*

Know Yourself *205*
  Explore Your Interests *205*
  Explore Your Values *206*
  Explore Your Skills *207*
  • **Understand Yourself through Campus Engagement** *207*

Develop an Academic Plan *208*
  Choose a Degree or Certificate *208*
  Choose a College Major *208*
  Choose Your Courses *209*
  Get Help from an Academic Adviser or a Counselor *210*
  • **Know Your Milestones** *210*
  • **Student Voices of Experience: Selecting a Major and Choosing Classes** *211*

Investigate Career Options *212*
  Get to Know the O*NET *212*
  Talk with Experts *212*
  Get Experience *214*

Launch Your Job Search *215*
  Write a Résumé *215*
  Find Job Opportunities *217*
  Write a Cover Letter *217*
  Interview Effectively *219*
  • **Be Ready for Behavioral Interview Questions** *219*

End-of-Term Reflection: Assess Your ACES Progress *221*
  • **My Personal Success Plan** *224*

CHAPTER SUMMARY *226* / **CHAPTER ACTIVITIES** *226*

GLOSSARY *227*
ENDNOTES *229*
INDEX *235*

preface

We've had the great privilege of interacting with students throughout our careers as instructors at two- and four-year schools, as advisers and mentors, as student success administrators, and as researchers in the area of student transition and success. It's because of our fascinating and fulfilling experiences with students of all kinds that we knew we wanted to write a textbook for the college success course: It would be an amazing opportunity to put in one place the combined knowledge, experience, and expertise we'd garnered over many years of working with college students and studying the different factors that impact their success.

We were thrilled to publish the first edition of *Connections: Empowering College and Career Success* in 2016, along with an accompanying student self-assessment tool called ACES (the Academic and Career Excellence System) that we built to help increase student satisfaction, retention, and completion. Creating *Connections* and ACES together was a wonderful, rewarding five-year journey, and one of our favorite parts of the process has been speaking with instructors across the country about their students, the challenges they face, and how our resources can help with these challenges.

It is from these many conversations that the idea for this new text, *Connections Essentials*, was born: We saw that, while a comprehensive, fourteen-chapter textbook is a perfect fit for some programs, there are other programs for which a **briefer, more streamlined approach** works best. For these programs, we set out to create a version of *Connections* that upholds the defining principles of the comprehensive text, but does so in just twelve chapters.

What are those defining principles? First and foremost, as counseling psychologists, we've come to believe—and have seen the research to support—the idea that there's more to student success than academic achievement alone. That's why we use a **holistic, strengths-based approach** in *Connections Essentials* that integrates a balance of motivational skills, study skills, and life skills—and does so in a concise, streamlined way that focuses on the most essential information students need to succeed in college. Our goal is to help students understand themselves as individuals who appreciate their own strengths, acknowledge where their challenges lie, and work to strengthen current skills and build new ones. Our experience has shown us that one of the best ways to accomplish this is through an emphasis on personal reflection and self-assessment—an emphasis that has its **foundation in positive psychology,** concepts of which are woven throughout this text. While research has shown us that past academic performance is a good predictor of future academic performance, recent and compelling research also clearly establishes the role of motivational—*noncognitive*—factors in promoting college and career success.[1] These noncognitive factors include attitudes, behaviors, and skills—such as critical thinking, self-efficacy, resilience, and working with others—and they form the scaffolding for achievement.

Because we believe that noncognitive skills, in concert with cognitive skills, are crucial to student success, we jumped at the chance to create an online student self-assessment platform, **ACES, the Academic and Career Excellence System**, which can be packaged with *Connections Essentials*. ACES is a powerful, norm-referenced self-assessment that helps students pinpoint their strengths and challenges. Students can take ACES at the start of the course to better understand their own abilities and attitudes in twelve critical areas, both cognitive and noncognitive, that correspond to specific chapters in the book. They can then use the information in *Connections Essentials* to help them develop and strengthen their skills in each area.

The idea to pair *Connections Essentials* and ACES comes from our shared experience in counseling and assessment. Rather than a self-assessment that serves as an "add on," we wanted to develop one that was woven into the fabric of the book, thereby providing two valuable resources that are even more beneficial when used together. Our goal was to ensure that information would lead to action. We achieved this goal by creating a powerful and easy-to-use assessment, along with tools and guidance that students can use to act on their results.

The idea of translating information into action also prompted us to develop another one of the key features of this book: the **Personal Success Plan (PSP)** goal-setting tool. It has been our experience that the act of responding to questions has zero value in and of itself. What *does* have value is what you *do* with or how you *act* on that information. And that's where the PSP comes in. Students learn about themselves through ACES and then can apply that knowledge in each chapter using the PSP to create SMART goals and purposeful, personalized action plans to achieve those goals. Students can track their PSPs throughout the term, helping them document the action steps and goals they've achieved and demonstrate the specific ways they're building important skills for college, career, and life.

As crucial as self-reflection and self-assessment are to the identity of *Connections Essentials*, there is another driving force behind the text that is just as crucial: making the **connection between college and career success** meaningful to today's students. Throughout the book we emphasize specific ways that the attitudes, habits, and skills needed to succeed in college—such as persistence, communication, and critical thinking—are the exact same attitudes, habits, and skills needed to succeed in the workplace. Our goal is to help students see how the material they are learning now can be applied directly in any work environment.

Our work on *Connections Essentials* and ACES has been rewarding and invigorating, and we've been gratified by the positive feedback we've received from instructors around the country. We hope that *Connections Essentials* and ACES prove as meaningful and effective for you and your students as they have been for us and for our reviewers. We hope that you, too, find this program a powerful mix of essential content, effective activities, thought-provoking research, and useful self-assessment data that will help students build the skills they need to succeed in college, in their careers, and in life.

---

[1] S. B. Robbins, K. Lauver, H. Le, D. Davis, R. Langley, and A. Carlstrom, "Do Psychosocial and Study Skill Factors Predict College Outcomes? A Meta-analysis," *Psychological Bulletin* 130 (2004): 261–88; W. J. Camara, "Broadening Predictors of College Success," in W. J. Camara and E. W. Kimmel (Eds.), *Choosing Students: Higher Education Admissions Tools for the 21st Century* (Mahwah, NJ: Erlbaum), pp. 81–105; N. Schmitt, J. Keeney, F. L. Oswald, T. J. Pleskac, A. Q. Billington, R. Sinha, and M. Zorzie, "Prediction of Four-Year College Student Performance Using Cognitive and Noncognitive Predictors and the Impact on Demographic Status of Admitted Students," *Journal of Applied Psychology* 94 (2009): 1479–97.

Using ACES with *Connections Essentials*

ACES gives students, instructors, and administrators the data they need to succeed. Available to be packaged with *Connections Essentials*, the ACES (Academic and Career Excellence System) online self-assessment helps students develop a thoughtful, strengths-based understanding of themselves. ACES measures student strengths in twelve critical areas, both cognitive and noncognitive. Norm-referenced reports indicate whether students are at a high, moderate, or low skill level in these areas, as compared to students in other schools across the country.

- **Students** take ACES at the start of the term to get a snapshot of their own attitudes, skills, habits, and opportunities for improvement. Throughout the book, students reflect on their results, which they can use to set and achieve goals with the Personal Success Plan.
- **Instructors** can use ACES data to start conversations with students—individually and as a class—about how to achieve excellence in college and in their careers. ACES data can also help instructors prioritize the topics they teach, highlight relevant programs or events outside of class to provide additional support for addressing students' weaknesses, and identify strong students who might be willing to report on the ways they practice a skill.
- **Administrators** can use aggregate information about student performance from ACES to track progress within the program and individual classes and to determine the type and level of resources needed to help students succeed.

ACES has been designed with ease of use in mind. It takes students about 20 minutes to complete and offers intriguing questions in a clean, appealing interface, helping ensure high student satisfaction and participation rates.

ACES works in concert with *Connections Essentials*. Students answer questions about twelve areas, or scales, that match the chapter topics in *Connections Essentials*. They reflect on their results throughout the book and use what they've learned to strengthen their strengths and to approach challenges as opportunities for growth.

Students respond to 80+ empirically reliable statements. Questions have been thoroughly tested in a national pilot study and are organized to obtain the clearest possible picture of students' attitudes and skills. Reverse scoring on select questions helps ensure that students are honest in their responses.

Targeted, thorough feedback helps each student take his or her own next steps. Students get feedback on their responses in each of the twelve skill areas. Each area is correlated as higher, moderate, or lower compared with the national sample. Feedback offers students an assessment of their current skills, encouragement to improve, and concrete suggestions for activities and resources to help them achieve their goals.

Individualized and class-level reports give students and instructors the information they need to understand student strengths and weaknesses and to formulate realistic plans for improvement. Data can be organized in several ways and be output for use in standard quantitative programs like Excel and Qualtrix.

ACES is available in LaunchPad Solo for *Connections Essentials*. To give your students access to ACES, assign the text with LaunchPad Solo for *Connections Essentials*—which includes ACES. LaunchPad Solo brings together all the media content for the textbook, curated and organized for easy assignability and assessment and presented in a powerful yet easy-to-use interface.

- LaunchPad Solo is available at a significant discount when packaged with the book. To package the text with LaunchPad Solo, use ISBN 978-1-319-16725-7.

Key Features in *Connections Essentials*

All the essential information is included in one easy-to-use resource. Brief and to the point, each of the text's twelve chapters focuses on the most important concepts and skills for student success. Coverage starts with the motivational skills and mind-sets necessary for college success (critical thinking, goal setting, decision making, personal responsibility, and understanding learning) and then moves on to academic and life skills.

An appealing, engaging layout keeps students reading. The book's magazine-style format, pop-out articles, and attractive visual program make it a fun read for students. Material is presented in an accessible and interesting manner that helps students stay focused and engaged.

The holistic, strengths-based approach is designed for a broad range of students and institutions. Firmly rooted in positive psychology, *Connections Essentials* encourages all students to develop their strengths, celebrate progress, and use setbacks as opportunities for growth. With coverage and examples drawn from a diverse group of students and institutions, the text is designed for an audience with a wide range of experiences—including recent high school graduates, returning adult learners, commuters, and students living on campus.

Prominent coverage of critical thinking and goal setting helps students develop key skills necessary for success. Chapter 2, Thinking Critically and Setting Goals, presents these essential skills up front, and self-assessments and activities throughout the text encourage students to think critically about their work and themselves. Included at the end of Chapters 2–12, the **Personal Success Plan (PSP)** goal-setting tool provides students with a structured platform for SMART goal setting and action planning. It encourages students

to think metacognitively about the skills they develop as they set and achieve goals.

An emphasis on college and career connections points students in the right direction. A full chapter on academic and career planning (Chapter 12) helps students begin creating their own personal roadmaps to success, and career-focused examples throughout the text illustrate how a wide range of topics apply to the world of work.

Student "Voices of Experience" narratives are included in each chapter. These first-person stories show the real-world effects of chapter concepts in the lives of college students across the country.

Research backs the authors' guidance to students throughout the book; articles and features throughout the text introduce original research in an accessible way that helps students connect the findings to their own experiences.

Chapter Activities reinforce key themes, prompt self-reflection, and strengthen skills. At the beginning of Chapters 2–12, an **ACES Journal** prompt invites students to reflect in writing on the skills being spotlighted in the chapter. Each chapter then concludes with two activities that instructors can assign as homework or use to prompt class discussion: **Adopting a Success Attitude** activities focus on positive psychology concepts, while **Applying Your Skills** activities help students practice the skills they've learned in the chapter.

Key Chapter-by-Chapter Content

Chapter 1, Building a Foundation for Success, introduces the text's unique themes using a clear and approachable narrative style. It makes a strong case for the benefits of a college education for students in our society and lays the foundation for the book's balanced emphasis on motivational, academic, and life skills. Topics include the benefits of personal reflection, the power of positivity, and the strong connection between skills needed to succeed in college and in one's career.

Chapter 2, Thinking Critically and Setting Goals, presents these essential topics earlier than most competing texts do and prompts students to focus on them as they read the chapters that follow. The chapter examines what it means to be a critical thinker and covers higher-level thinking skills, critical-thinking processes, and Bloom's taxonomy. The chapter then shows how critical thinking connects to goal setting, gives step-by-step goal-setting guidance, and introduces the powerful Personal Success Plan (PSP) goal-setting tool.

Chapter 3, Motivation, Decision Making, and Personal Responsibility, offers a strong emphasis on noncognitive skills, ensuring that students explore key motivational topics early in the term. Students learn concrete ways to stay driven and focused; make effective decisions; adopt active learning and metacognitive principles to take responsibility for their success; and develop a growth mind-set.

Chapter 4, Understanding Learning, introduces the concept of learning science and presents five evidence-based learning strategies that are useful for all learners. Students then consider their own preferences for learning via an introduction to the Myers-Briggs Type Indicator and VARK models and discover techniques for excelling as multimodal learners in all environments—even those that don't match their preferences.

Chapter 5, Organization and Time Management, helps students take ownership of their time and use this valuable resource in a way that fits their priorities and allows them to meet their very personal goals. The chapter also includes a unique section on strategies for getting (and staying) organized and examines ways to beat procrastination and deal with distractions.

Chapter 6, Reading for College Success, introduces a three-step process for getting the most out of college reading—preparing to read, reading with focus, and reviewing what's been read. This chapter illustrates the relationship between reading and other key study skills and also includes specific suggestions that students can use to excel in math, science, and online classes.

Chapter 7, Taking Effective Notes, introduces note taking not as a mechanical activity but as a method of working with—and mastering—information. In addition to presenting a clear, four-step strategy for participating in class and recording information effectively, the chapter presents methods and strategies students can use to take notes in a variety of settings.

Chapter 8, Memory, Studying, and Test Taking, spotlights strategies students can use to remember what they've learned, study effectively, and perform well on exams. This cohesive chapter discusses memory basics, including the processes of encoding, storing, and retrieving information; introduces a wide variety of study strategies that students can use to stay focused and productive; and provides students with the information they need to take tests successfully.

Chapter 9, Information Literacy and Communication, connects these key academic skills to broader approaches to critical thinking and explores three essential components of information literacy—locating information, evaluating its quality, and communicating that information through writing and speaking. The chapter also discusses how to navigate the writing process, avoid plagiarism, and give strong class presentations.

Chapter 10, Connecting with Others, focuses on key skills that students need to build and sustain relationships, with special emphasis on active listening and effective speaking. The chapter explores how to strengthen emotional intelligence and manage conflict and examines how connecting with others can help students enhance existing relationships, build new ones, and develop relationships with people from different backgrounds.

Chapter 11, Personal and Financial Health, draws important connections between the discrete but closely related topics of stress, personal health, and financial health. Through a self-management lens, the chapter introduces strategies that students can use to promote physical well-being and mental health, maintain sexual health, and take control of their finances—all of which can help them manage stress and live happier, more fulfilled lives.

Chapter 12, Academic and Career Planning, provides information students need to think critically about their academic and career options—whether they've chosen a major or not. The chapter helps students personalize academic and career planning by considering their own interests, values, skills, and goals as they make an academic plan, conduct career research, and search for a job. The chapter concludes with a special end-of-term reflection in which students assess how they've changed since the start of the course—and update their ACES scores in response.

Instructor Resources

LaunchPad Solo for *Connections Essentials* with ACES and LearningCurve

LaunchPad Solo for *Connections Essentials* is home to high-quality digital content and ready-made assessment options, including the ACES student self-assessment and LearningCurve adaptive quizzing. Prebuilt units are easy to assign or adapt to your material, such as readings, videos, quizzes, discussion groups, and more. LaunchPad Solo also provides access to a gradebook that provides a clear window on performance for your whole class, for individual students, and for individual assignments.

- **Included in LaunchPad Solo: ACES (The Academic and Career Excellence System).** See the earlier discussion of ACES for more details.

- **Included in LaunchPad Solo: LearningCurve.** LearningCurve is an online self-quizzing program that quickly learns what students already know and helps them practice what they haven't yet mastered. LearningCurve motivates students to read and engage with key concepts before they come to class so that they are ready to participate, and it offers reporting tools to help you discern your students' needs.

- **Ordering information.** Please note that *Connections Essentials* is not automatically packaged with LaunchPad Solo. To package the text with LaunchPad Solo, use ISBN 978-1-319-16725-7.

Instructor's Manual

The Instructor's Manual, available online, is packed full of activities and resources. Content includes sample syllabi; chapter objectives and summaries; class activities, topics for discussion, and writing assignments for each chapter; and a guide to using the ACES self-assessment in class.

Computerized Test Bank

The computerized test bank contains 600 multiple-choice, true/false, short-answer, and essay questions designed to assess students' understanding of key concepts. A midterm and final exam are included. A digital text file is also available.

Lecture Slides

Available online for download, lecture slides accompany each chapter of the book and include key concepts and art from the text. Use the slides as provided to structure your lectures, or customize them as desired to fit your course's needs.

Curriculum Solutions

Our new Curriculum Solutions group brings together the quality and reputation of Bedford/St. Martin's content with Hayden-McNeil's expertise in publishing original custom print and digital products. With our new capabilities, we are excited to deliver customized course solutions at an affordable price. Make *Connections Essentials* fit your course and goals by integrating your own institutional materials, including only the parts of the text you intend to use in your course, or both. Please contact your local Macmillan Learning sales representative for more information and to see samples.

CS Select Custom Database

The CS Select database allows you to create a textbook for your college success course that reflects your course's objectives and uses just the content you need. Start with one of our core texts; then rearrange chapters, delete chapters, and insert additional content—including your own original content—to create the book you're looking for. Get started by visiting **macmillanlearning .com/csSelect**.

TradeUp

Bring more value and choice to your students' first-year experience by packaging *Connections Essentials* with one of a thousand titles from Macmillan publishers at a 50 percent discount off the regular price. Contact your local Macmillan Learning sales representative for more information.

Student Resources

LaunchPad Solo for *Connections Essentials* with ACES and LearningCurve

LaunchPad Solo is an online course solution that offers our acclaimed digital tools, including the ACES self-assessment, LearningCurve adaptive quizzes, and videos. For more information, see the Instructor Resources section.

- **Included in LaunchPad Solo: ACES (the Academic and Career Excellence System).** See the earlier discussion of ACES for more details.
- **Included in LaunchPad Solo: Learning-Curve.** LearningCurve is an online, adaptive, self-quizzing program that quickly learns what students already know and helps them practice what they haven't yet mastered.
- **Ordering information.** Please note that *Connections Essentials* is not automatically packaged with LaunchPad Solo. To package the text with LaunchPad Solo, use ISBN 978-1-319-16725-7.

E-book Options

E-books offer an affordable alternative for students. You can find e-book versions of our books when you shop online at our publishing partners' sites. Learn more at **macmillanlearning.com/ebooks**.

Bedford/St. Martin's Insider's Guides

These concise and student friendly booklets on topics critical to college success are a perfect complement to your textbook and course. One Insider's Guide can be packaged with *any* Bedford/St. Martin's textbook at no additional cost. Additional Insider's Guides can also be packaged at additional cost. Titles include *Insider's Guide to Academic Planning*; *Insider's Guide to Beating Test Anxiety*; *Insider's Guide to*

Career Services; Insider's Guide to Getting Involved on Campus; Insider's Guide to Time Management, Second Edition; and many more. For more information on ordering one of these guides with the text, go to **macmillanlearning.com/ collegesuccess**.

About the Authors

Paul A. Gore

Christina Rodriguez

Paul's efforts to promote college and career readiness, high school and college student persistence, and academic success are informed by more than twenty years of research, program development, implementation, evaluation, consulting, and teaching. Paul currently serves as the dean of the College of Professional Sciences at Xavier University in Ohio. Paul earned his Ph.D. in counseling psychology, with an emphasis in student career development, academic success, and transition, from Loyola University–Chicago. He has held academic and administrative responsibilities at the University of Missouri–Kansas City, Southern Illinois University–Carbondale, ACT, Inc., and the University of Utah.

Paul's work focuses on noncognitive and motivational determinants of academic and career success. In particular, he is interested in how secondary and postsecondary institutions use data describing the noncognitive strengths and weaknesses of their students to promote student success and retention. He regularly consults with secondary and postsecondary institutions in the United States and abroad on developing and evaluating student academic and career success programs.

Paul has authored more than fifty peer-reviewed journal articles and book chapters. He is the past chair of the Society for Vocational Psychology and served as an advisory board member and journal editor for the National Resource Center for the First-Year Experience and Students in Transition. He is a fellow of the American Psychological Association and was the recipient of a 2013–2014 American Council on Education Emerging Leadership fellowship.

Wade Leuwerke

MRogalla Photography

Wade is an associate professor of counseling at Drake University. He earned his Ph.D. in counseling psychology from Southern Illinois University–Carbondale. Wade has authored over fifty journal articles and book chapters, as well as national and international conference presentations. One of his areas of research is the assessment and development of student and employee noncognitive skills. He cocreated the Student Strengths Inventory, a measure of noncognitive skills used with secondary and postsecondary students to identify students' skills and drive interventions for students at risk of academic failure or dropout. Wade also studies the factors that predict college retention, the impact of computer-assisted career guidance systems on academic planning and career exploration behaviors, and the role of technology in career development processes.

Wade has experience examining school counselors' roles and working with professional school counselors to positively impact students' academic development, career and college exploration, and acquisition of personal and social skills that will prepare them for college and life beyond. He has worked with dozens of secondary and postsecondary institutions on a range of factors related to student success and persistence, including evaluation of institutional practices, use of data to drive student interventions, creation of individualized student success plans, training, strategic planning, resource allocation, and collaboration to promote student success. He has also worked as a research project manager focusing on academic and career development research for Kuder, Inc.; ACT, Inc.; Career Cruising; and intoCareers. Wade provides executive and career coaching for corporations and the federal government.

A.J. Metz

A.J. is an associate professor in the Department of Educational Psychology at the University of Utah and serves as director of the master's program in school counseling. She earned a M.Ed. in rehabilitation counseling in 1997 and a

Photo courtesy of Andy Brimhall

Ph.D. in urban education (with a specialization in counseling psychology) in 2005 from the University of Wisconsin–Milwaukee. Her research examining factors related to academic success and career development in underrepresented and underserved student populations has led to numerous journal articles, book chapters, conference presentations, workshops, grant proposals, and faculty in-service training sessions.

A.J. has extensive teaching, counseling, consulting, and career advising experience in high schools, community colleges, and four-year public and private institutions of higher education. Her passion for teaching motivates her to experiment with innovative teaching methods and develop new and engaging activities and instructional materials. In 2015 she received the University of Utah's Early Career Teaching Award, and in 2017 she received the College of Education Teaching Award. She is the past president of the Utah Psychological Association and serves on multiple state-level task forces and advisory councils promoting school counseling, college access, and career readiness.

Acknowledgments

We wish to express our gratitude to all the people who have helped make this book a reality. Paul would like to thank his parents, who taught him balance between critical reflection and creativity; his mentors Waded Cruzado, Steve D. Brown, Virginia Rinella, and Michael Anch, who have supported his personal and professional development for almost thirty years; and the staff of the National Resource Center for the First-Year Experience and Students in Transition for embracing his passion for promoting student success. Wade wishes to thank his wonderful partner, Lesley, and his three great yahoos at home. They put up with a lot over the past few years, and he couldn't have done this without their support. A.J. wishes to thank her parents (Kay and Jerry), brothers (Mike and Dave), and extended family (Christine, Joe, and Kayden) for their continuous interest, support, and encouragement through the course of writing this book. We'd also like to thank all the students who shared their stories with us and made the "Voices of Experience" feature possible. The richness and variety of their stories helps bring the book content alive, and we hope that you find their wisdom and advice as helpful as we do.

At Bedford/St. Martin's, thanks to Edwin Hill, vice president, editorial; we wouldn't have gotten this project off the ground without your support. To Simon Glick, formerly senior executive editor for College Success, thank you for providing insight and encouragement as we worked on this edition. To Christina Lembo, senior editor, thank you for steering us through this process. The book is a testament to your guidance, patience, and skill at helping us make our vision a reality. Our appreciation also goes out to Deb Baker, senior content project manager, and Emily Brower, assistant content project manager, for their invaluable attention to detail; to Erika Gutierrez, senior program director, and Susan McLaughlin, senior development manager, for their ideas and leadership; to Tom Kane, senior media editor, for his work on ACES; to Kathy McInerney, editorial assistant, for managing the accompanying ancillaries; and to Kayti Corfield, marketing manager, for her enthusiasm in sharing this book with instructors across the country.

Finally, we would like to thank the reviewers who took the time to provide detailed, thoughtful feedback on the book throughout the development process. Your comments and suggestions were instrumental in creating *Connections Essentials*:

Pamela Bilton Beard, Houston Community College – Southwest
Michelle Buggs, Texas Woman's University
Colin Charlton, University of Texas Rio Grande Valley
Erika Deiters, Moraine Valley Community College
Barbara Garrett, Pikes Peak Community College
Vanessa Haddad, Erie Community College
Michele Jenkins, Radford University
Benjamin Johnson, Utah Valley University
Elizabeth Kennedy, Florida Atlantic University
Anne Lehew, North Central Texas College
Stacey Macchi, Western Illinois University
MaryAnn McGuirk, North Lake College
Patricia Missad, Grand Rapids Community College
Rachelle Powell, North Lake College
Rebecca Samberg, Housatonic Community College
Sarah Shutt, J. Sargeant Reynolds Community College
Amy Townsend, Pearl River Community College

M. David Williams, The Community College of Baltimore County
C. James Wong, San Jacinto College

Thank you, too, to the reviewers, survey participants, and focus-group attendees for *Connections*, First Edition, who offered many helpful suggestions and creative ideas that ultimately informed the development of *Connections Essentials*:

Sandra Albers, Leeward Community College; Fred Amador, Phoenix College; Holly Andress-Martin, Culver-Stockton College; Bonnie Bailey, Central New Mexico Community College; Christopher Barker, Miami Dade College; Wesley Beal, Lyon College; Jennifer Beattie, Tri-County Technical College; Ashley Becker, Florida Institute of Technology; Sheila Bedworth, Long Beach City College; Kristine Benard, Bryant & Stratton College, Eastlake Campus; Edie Blakley, Clark College; Dustyn Bork, Lyon College; Jennifer Boyle, Davidson County Community College; Beverly Brucks, Illinois Central College; Alim Chandani, Gallaudet University; Rebecca Coco, Massasoit Community College; Colleen Coughlin, University of Massachusetts; Melanie Deffendall, Delgado Community College; Erika Deiters, Moraine Valley Community College; Susan Delker, The Community College of Baltimore County; Bob DuBois, Waukesha County Technical College; Denise Dufek, Bay de Noc Community College; Kim Dunnavant, Martin Methodist College; Darin Eckton, Utah Valley University; Carly Edwards, Campbell University; Shawna Elsberry, Central Oregon Community College; Annette Fields, University of Arkansas at Pine Bluff; Stephanie M. Foote, Kennesaw State University; Karen Frost, University of Arkansas at Little Rock; Kate Frost, Arizona State University; Susan Gaer, Santa Ana College; Cathy Gann, Missouri Western State University; Linda Gannon, College of Southern Nevada; Margaret Garroway, Howard Community College; Nicole Gilbertson, Mt. Hood Community College; Carlen Gilseth,

Minot State University; Tracey Glaessgen, Missouri State University; Joselyn Gonzalez, El Centro College; Tymon Graham, Coker College; Barbara Granger, Holyoke Community College; Laurie Grimes, Lorain County Community College; Betsy Hall, Illinois College; Timothy Hare, Morehead State University; Angie Hatlestad, Ridgewater College; Robin Hayhurst, Western Nebraska Community College; Teresa Hays, DeVry University; Lorraine M. Daniels Howland, NHTI, Concord's Community College; Cedric Jackson, University of Arkansas at Pine Bluff; Barbara Jaffe, El Camino College; Jody Kamens, Jacksonville University; Kim Keffer, Ohio University Southern; Alice Kimara, Baltimore City Community College; Stacy Kirch, Orange Coast College; Ray Korpi, Clark College; Fatina LaMar-Taylor, Prince George's Community College; Teresa Landers, Lee College; Christopher Lau, Hutchinson Community College; Kristina Leonard, Daytona State College; Andrew Logemann, Gordon College; Judith Lynch, Kansas State University; Malinda Mansfield, Ivy Tech Community College; Melanie Marine, University of Wisconsin Oshkosh; Lisa Marks, Ozarks Technical Community College; Mickey Marsee, University of New Mexico–Los Alamos; Patrick McConnell, Rio Hondo College; MaryAnn McGuirk, North Lake College; Maureen McMahon, Paul Smith's College; Ryan Messatzzia, Wor-Wic Community College; Pat Missad, Grand Rapids Community College; Pamela Moss, Midwestern State University; Jodi Murrow, Fort Scott Community College; Tami Mysliwiec, Pennsylvania State University Berks; Nicole Nagy, Madonna University; Chaelle Norman, Cedar Valley College; Scott O'Leary, University of Saint Mary; Ellen Oppenberg, Glendale Community College; Taunya Paul, York Technical College; Elizabeth Price, Ranger College; Cynthia Puckett, Eastern Florida State College; Linda Refsland, William Paterson University; Leigh-Ann Routh, Ivy Tech Community College; Danielle Rowland, University of Washington Bothell and Cascadia College; James Rubin, Paradise Valley Community College; Carolyn Sanders, University of Alabama in Huntsville; Sarah Sell, Wichita State University; Mark Shea, Buena Vista University; Barbara Sherry, Northeastern Illinois University; Sarah Shutt, J. Sargeant Reynolds Community College; Cheryl Spector, California State University Northridge; Charlene Stephens, Wesley College; Pamela Stephens, Fairmont State University; Chris Strouthopoulos, San Juan College; Brenda Sudan, Georgia Perimeter College; Susan Sullivan, Louisiana State University Alexandria; Ricardo Teixeira, University of Houston–Victoria; Kim Thomas, Polk State University; Virginia Thompson, Grayson County College; Althea Truesdale, Bennett College; Adanta Ugo, San Jacinto College; Dominick Usher, University of Massachusetts Amherst; Sherri VandenAkker, Springfield College; Jodie Vangrov, Chattahoochee Technical College; Angela Vaughan, University of Northern Colorado; Melanie Wadsworth, Western Nevada College; Jacob Widdekind, Miami Dade College; Cheryl Wieseler, Luther College; Margaret Williamson, Dillard University; Cornelia Wills, Middle Tennessee State University; Leslie Wilson, Chestnut Hill College; and Marguerite Yawin, Tunxis Community College.

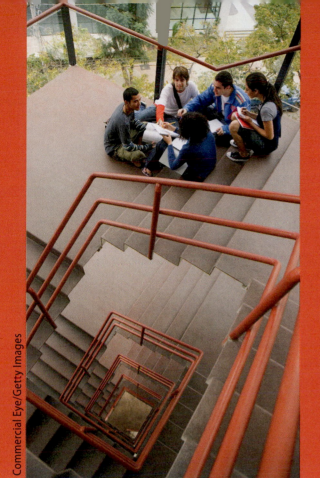

1

Building a Foundation for Success

Why Go to College?

Learn about Yourself

Feel the Power of Positive Psychology

College Success Leads to Career Success

Welcome to college! Are you a recent high school graduate? Did you put your education on hold to raise a family, and now you're returning to school? Are you a veteran beginning college after a tour of duty in the military? Regardless of your personal situation, congratulations! Starting college is a huge accomplishment that you can be proud of. And it's a major step toward your future success.

Getting through college requires effort and persistence. That's why so many schools have developed courses like this one to equip you with the attitudes and skills you need to achieve your goals. With the help of your instructor, this book, and other resources on your campus, you'll develop the tools you'll need to excel in college and embark on a satisfying and successful career.

Keep in mind that successful people draw on connections to advance toward their goals—

connections with other people, with new knowledge, and with their own strengths and intentions. By making similar connections, you'll maintain your motivation in school. For example, if you connect the skills you learn now with those you'll use in your career, then your courses will have more value. And if you connect with the people around you, then you'll build a network of supporters who can help celebrate your successes.

Connections are a big theme in this book— and in this course. As you'll discover, *nothing* you do or learn is isolated: Topics you read about in one chapter relate to topics in other chapters; what you learn in this class will be useful in other classes; and the skills you build here will help you excel at work.

In this chapter, you'll get an introduction to the critical components of your success: recognizing why college is important, understanding yourself, learning the power of positivity, and connecting college and career. Let's get started!

Why Go to College?

Life is full of choices, and you've already made an important one: to attend college and further your education. Now that you've made this choice, ask yourself a basic question: Why are you here? All students have their own reasons for going to school, whether it's training for a specific occupation, pursuing a love of learning, or searching for their life's purpose. You may not even be sure why you're here, other than to give yourself a chance for a better life.

No matter what your reasons, it's crucial to understand one thing: By pursuing your education, you're making a smart investment in your future.

Education: Good for Society, Good for You

Half a century ago, fewer than 50 percent of adults in the United States had a high school diploma.[1] Today, that number has risen to 88 percent, and 42 percent of all adults have an associate's degree or higher.[2] What prompted the change? Think of everything that's happened in the past fifty years: We've landed on the moon, sent scientific equipment to Mars, invented the Internet and smartphone, advanced civil rights, and made countless gains in medicine, communications, agriculture, and energy. Improving any society in these ways requires education, and the more sophisticated our society becomes, the higher the demand will be for educated people—people like you.

Education not only strengthens societies but also pays off for individuals—and in more ways than one. For example, a recent report by the College Board suggests that compared to high school graduates, college graduates

- are more engaged in their communities
- lead healthier lifestyles
- participate more actively in their children's education
- earn higher salaries (as much as $20,000 more a year)
- are more likely to have jobs[3]

In fact, by the time you graduate, more than 60 percent of all jobs will require some form of college education.[4] As you can see, you're in the right place at the right time.

What It Means to Be in College

So now that you're in college, what should you expect? And what will be expected of you? First and foremost, you'll encounter challenges. More so than in high school, your instructors will expect you to participate actively in your learning, not just look to them for all the answers. They'll expect you to figure out *how* and *what* to study, to determine how to apply what you've learned to new situations, and to think carefully about concepts you might have just accepted as fact in high school. They'll also assume you'll ask for help when you need it, schedule your own study time, and keep up with your assignments.

If this responsibility feels difficult at times, that's okay. College is designed to push you out of your comfort zone. It's about growing intellectually and personally so that when you graduate, you're ready to launch a career that meets your needs and lead a fulfilling life that you can be proud of. Fortunately, this book is packed with tips that can help you become an active, successful learner. So as you progress through this class and others, remember that you're in college for great reasons and that the rewards of completing your education will make all that hard work worthwhile.

Learn about Yourself

Though everyone's path to success looks different, there's one skill that we all need to succeed: critical thinking. When you engage in *critical thinking*, you consider information thoughtfully, understand how to think logically and rationally, and apply those methods of thinking in your classes and your life.[5] Critical thinking helps you examine information in a careful, unbiased way so that you can use that information to make good decisions.

In college, academic success and critical thinking go hand in hand. You can use critical thinking in your classes to analyze information, answer questions on exams, and write papers, among many other pursuits. But you can also use it in a more personal way, to better understand yourself. This kind of critical thinking involves reflection, which is a time for *you* to think about your hopes, your wishes, and what you're looking for from college and from life. Reflection helps you pinpoint your goals (what you want to achieve) and your motivations (what drives you to keep working toward your goals). When you recognize your goals and motivations, classes have more meaning and you feel more confident when

you're making important decisions, such as what major to declare or certificate to pursue.

Over the course of this term, you'll have many opportunities to learn more about yourself. To get started, think critically about several personal attributes that powerfully influence your goals and motivations: your values, your interests, and your strengths and weaknesses.

Discover Your Values

Your values are what you consider important—really important. They stem from your experiences with your family, your community, or your faith. For example, your values may include getting a good job, taking care of your family, or playing an active role in your community. Values are essential because they can influence your choices and your behavior. You're more likely to pursue goals and activities that are consistent with what you care about most.

What are your values? For starters, the fact that you're in college means you value education. Perhaps you and your family

What Do You Value Most? When you know what your values are and how each of your courses connects with those values, you'll feel far more motivated to work hard to excel in each course. You'll also seek out experiences that let you express your values. And those experiences can help you gain new skills and knowledge essential for succeeding in your chosen career. Hero Images/Getty Images

make sacrifices so that you can attend school. Maybe you juggle commitments, taking out loans and cutting back on your work hours to free up time and energy for class. You're making these sacrifices because you appreciate what a college education has to offer.

Take a moment to think about what other values you hold dear. All of these values affect the decisions you make. For example, if you want to build a meaningful career after you graduate (and most students do[6]), reflecting on your values can help you pick a major that will help prepare you for such a career. Suppose that taking care of others is one of your values. In this case, a major like nursing or teaching might be the perfect fit for you. If achieving financial independence is among your values, then majors that lay a foundation for lucrative careers—such as finance or business administration—might be good matches. The more you know about yourself, the more meaningful your chosen goals will be—and the more motivated you'll be to keep working toward those goals.

Follow Your Interests

Interests are your preferences for activities, things, people, and places—everything from exercise to animals to cars to music. Why are interests so important? When you define goals that connect with your interests, you're more likely to feel motivated to achieve those goals. For instance, if you're interested in the outdoors, physical activity, and nature, you'll be motivated to complete assignments in courses that incorporate these elements, such as wilderness management and forestry. Finding ways to connect your coursework with your interests—even when the connection isn't obvious—is a great way to stay motivated.

You'll learn more about your interests later in the book, but don't wait until then to start thinking about them. Consider what you like and don't like as you evaluate the courses you're taking, interact with your fellow students, and reflect on your past academic and work experiences. The more you're interested in the work you're doing in school, the more energized you'll feel as you pursue your goals.

More Than Just Hobbies. Your interests matter. If you connect them to your coursework, you'll be more likely to stay motivated even when you encounter challenges. And who knows where your interests could lead you? You might find yourself gravitating toward a career that's not only stimulating but also financially rewarding and personally meaningful. *Left:* Jaromir Chalabala/Shutterstock *Right:* stockphoto mania/Shutterstock

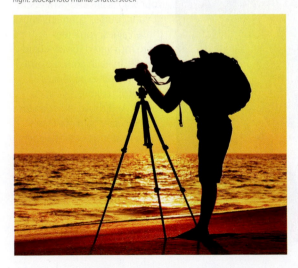

Embrace Your Strengths — and Learn from Your Weaknesses

If someone asked you to describe your strengths, what would you say? Maybe you'd point out that you can negotiate a subway system like a pro, give great advice, or play guitar. What about your weaknesses? Would you find it harder to acknowledge that you have poorly developed writing skills or that you're shy around people you don't know? If so, you're not alone: Many people feel more comfortable talking about where they excel than revealing where they struggle.

But everyone has strengths and weaknesses, and a key to success — and to learning about yourself — is knowing what these are. Armed with this understanding, you can *use* your strengths to set and achieve goals, while also improving areas you find challenging.[7]

As you think about building your strengths, consider basketball. Every team has players with different specialties. For example, the point guard has long-range shooting skills, while the center is typically the tallest player on the court and can secure rebounds. The coach makes sure each player uses his or her best skills while also addressing weak areas.

Coach Yourself to Success. To succeed in college, you have to play to your strengths while working on your weaknesses. Athletes know this, and their coaches help. So think of yourself as your own success coach in school. Where should you start? Be honest with yourself about what you're good at — and where you need to improve. joSon/Getty Images

Getting to Know You: ACES and Other Tools

Before you can use your strengths and address your weaknesses, you need to know what they are. Figuring this out isn't always easy. It requires a healthy dose of self-reflection (and often a reality check) to acknowledge what you do well and where you struggle. It also involves collecting concrete information about yourself, which can come from a number of sources:

- **The Academic and Career Excellence System (ACES).** Did you know that with this book you likely got access to an online self-assessment that will help you understand yourself better? It's called ACES (which stands for Academic and Career Excellence System). ACES helps you identify your strengths and weaknesses and use that information to establish goals. You'll revisit different ACES scores at the beginning of each chapter in the rest of this book and reflect on how you might better use a strength or improve a weak area. By engaging in such reflection, you can read each chapter with a better understanding of what you want to accomplish.

- **Past successes and failures.** Reflecting on your past successes and failures can provide a wealth of useful information. For example, can you recall a time when you were well prepared for an exam and another time when you weren't? How did your grades reflect your preparedness? What lessons can you gain from these contrasting experiences? How can you apply those lessons so that you do better on future exams?

- **Class experiences.** Think about your current classes. Are some more difficult for you than others? What do you think makes them harder for you? Reflecting on where you struggle can help you identify which skills you need to strengthen.

- **End-of-chapter activities.** The activities at the end of each chapter often require you to consider how the chapter material relates to your strengths and weaknesses. You'll also have further opportunities to practice developing your skills and setting goals.

Once you've consulted these sources, then what? Learning about your strengths and weaknesses is great, but this information is useless if you don't use it to create positive change. That's what this book and this class are for: to help you achieve the necessary changes. In each chapter, you'll work on developing a new skill — such as setting goals, managing your time, reading a wide range of course materials, taking notes, and studying for exams. As you build these skills in this class, you can use them to succeed in your other classes, too. Why? Because as we pointed out earlier, all your learning is connected.

Everyone has to practice ball handling, free throws, rebounding, and distance shooting—regardless of whether it comes naturally—because these skills are necessary for the team to succeed.

When it comes to the game of college, you're your own coach. You need to take advantage of your strengths and play to them regularly, but you also need to work on your weak areas. This book, your instructors, and the resources available on campus will help you build winning attitudes and skills. But ultimately, it is your responsibility to put those attitudes and skills into action. By focusing on using your strengths *and* addressing your weaknesses, you'll become as versatile in the classroom as professional athletes are on the court.

FINDING YOUR PURPOSE

Megan Jackson

NAME:	**Russell Jackson**
SCHOOL:	*Iowa State University*
MAJOR:	*Psychology*
CAREER GOALS:	*Professor, Counselor*

I've struggled to find my purpose in life, mainly because I'm terrified of making big decisions. I've been worried that I don't know myself well enough to make the right decision, and I don't want to travel down a road, taking my family with me, if it's not meant for me. I used to go to someone I trusted, listen to *his* suggestion about my future, and run with it.

About a year and a half ago, I ended a career that just didn't fit me. My situation was frustrating and stressful, and I was running out of steam with no idea where to go or what to do. I needed to create some happiness. I realized then that I had never sat down and considered what *I* wanted, what *I* loved, and where *I* wanted to go. I knew I couldn't simply follow everyone else's desires for me anymore. I had to take charge of my destiny and mold it to meet my needs. I had to make changes that would help me prepare for a different career.

For the next year, I worked on finding my purpose in life. I put aside what others thought I should do and focused on my own thoughts, desires, talents, and goals. I thought critically about myself and found my calling. It didn't come all at once, but it did finally develop into a recognizable goal: I want to be a counseling psychologist.

Once my goal was set, everything else fell into place. I enrolled in school, registered for classes, spoke with professors, and found opportunities like volunteering, working in research labs, and helping at the Student Counseling Service. Granted, it's still difficult. Sometimes I have to fight off doubts that I made the right decision. However, I'm able to overcome those fears and doubts by remembering that *I know what I want from my life*. My life is bright and fulfilling, simply because I finally found my purpose.

YOUR TURN: Do you have a sense of what your purpose might be? If so, what is it? Does it influence the goals you define for yourself? If you don't yet know your purpose, how might learning more about your values, interests, and strengths and weaknesses help you find clarity?

> " I thought critically about myself and found my calling."

Feel the Power of Positive Psychology

Have you ever heard the song "Happy" by Pharrell Williams? If so, you may know that it's about deciding to be happy, rather than letting negativity bring you down. The song touches on an important concept: the power of positivity. If you maintain a positive attitude, you're more likely to achieve your goals and lead a fulfilling life.

The idea that positivity can lead to success forms the foundation of **positive psychology**, a branch of psychology that focuses on people's strengths and views weaknesses as growth opportunities.[8] Positive psychology has become a major influence in educational and workplace settings, and it plays an important part in this book. For example, when you reflect on how to build your strengths and learn from your weaknesses, as you did in the previous section, you're using positive psychology.

The positive psychology movement emphasizes four central concepts: self-efficacy, resilience, hope, and personal responsibility (see Figure 1.1). All four will play a large role in your academic and professional success.

FIGURE 1.1
Four Key Concepts in Positive Psychology

Build Self-Efficacy

Self-efficacy is your belief in your ability to do the things required to achieve your goals. Students with a stronger sense of self-efficacy perform better on tasks and persist in those tasks even when things get rough. But not all self-efficacy is created equal. Self-efficacy works best when it's based on a *realistic* assessment of your skills and abilities—and on evidence from your past performance, such as grades and instructor feedback. It's important to neither overestimate nor underestimate your sense of self-efficacy.

Many students arrive at college with a strong sense of self-efficacy, only to have it shaken by poor grades or unexpected setbacks. For instance, Kathleen went to a small high school, where she graduated near the top of her class. She enrolled in a large college and quickly discovered that it was much harder to stand out as an excellent student in such a large population and that the courses were more challenging than in high school. She got some B's and even a C in her first-term classes and started asking herself, "Can I really succeed in college?"

If you have similar experiences, understand that they can present you with valuable learning opportunities. For example, if you do poorly on your first accounting test, don't think of it as a failure; think of it as a starting point for improving your performance. How did you study for the exam? Did you complete all the practice problems at the end of each chapter or find a tutor? If not, would it be worth taking those steps for your next exam? Use learning opportunities like this to develop realistic self-efficacy beliefs and to improve your future performance.

Be Resilient

Have you ever known someone who went through a rough patch in life but came out of the experience stronger and more driven to succeed? Perhaps you have a friend who was devastated when he lost his job but turned things around by getting support from his family, obtaining financial aid, and going back to school to train for a new career. That's **resilience**, the ability to cope with stress and setbacks.[9]

College students often face challenges, and in balancing your academic work with your personal responsibilities, at times you may find yourself stressed out or overwhelmed. During these times, you can demonstrate resilience by getting support and making positive changes. If you receive a D on a biology exam, for example, you can use the experience to improve your study strategies for future exams. Resilience helps you manage challenges, big and small, and stay motivated to achieve your goals.

Keep Hope Alive

Hope is the feeling that you can achieve your goals and that events will turn out for the best. Hope is strong when you have realistic self-confidence and a goal that you're motivated to achieve—one that's personally relevant to you. Charles Snyder, a specialist in positive psychology, offers another definition of hope: "the sum of the mental willpower and waypower that you have for your goals."[10] *Willpower* (sometimes called *agency*) is the mental energy to press forward and achieve a positive outcome. *Waypower* is having resources, plans, and skills (sometimes called *pathways*) to achieve the positive outcome you believe in.

For example, suppose you've always wanted to be a veterinarian. Getting into a school that awards a doctorate of veterinary medicine is tough, so your willpower might help you research colleges that offer a preveterinary curriculum, apply to several schools, and get accepted at one of your top choices. Your waypower, on the other hand, might include critical resources like the time you expend to research colleges, the plans you make to apply for financial support to help pay your tuition, and the resources you use to help you get the grades you need to be accepted when you graduate.

Snyder's own research tells us that hope is an important element of student success. He and his colleagues found that students with high levels of hope had higher GPAs and were dismissed from college far less frequently than students who had lower levels of hope.[11] According to Snyder, though, it's not enough to believe that good fortune awaits us. We also need a plan and the skills to make that good fortune become real. In other words, we have to transform our thoughts and intentions into actions, a process that you'll have many opportunities to practice in this class.

Resilience in Action.
Resilience helps you cope with the stresses you'll experience in your college career and your work and personal life. While the 2013 Boston Marathon bombings were devastating, many spectators and runners who suffered injuries or lost loved ones in the attack developed potent strategies for rebuilding their lives. For some, their resilient response made them stronger than ever.
AP Photo / Michael Dwyer

Take Personal Responsibility for Your Success

Positive psychology is about personal responsibility—taking charge of defining your goals, creating plans for accomplishing them, and seeking out resources that can help you achieve them. Personal responsibility gives you control: *You* have the power to turn negative results into positive ones by treating disappointments as learning opportunities. After all, most of your instructors aren't going to approach you and say, "I see you got a bad grade on the assignment; here's what I think you should do about it." It's up to you to come up with strategies for doing better on the next one. You'll get a chance to think about this topic more fully later, but for now, just remember: When it comes to your success, *you're* the boss.

Recruit Help

There are many ways to build skills on your own, but you don't have to "fly solo" in this effort: You can recruit a team of supporters to help you when you struggle. According to a growing body of research, seeking help can *increase* your level of success.[12] Also, getting help is a form of taking personal responsibility: When you identify what challenges you face, what resources exist, and how to use them, you take charge of your own success.

Help is everywhere, once you know what's available and where to look for it (see Figure 1.2). Off campus, you can find help from family members, friends, and community resources. On campus, you can find help from instructors, classmates, advisers, and support services like the math lab and writing center. To take advantage of the resources around you, follow these steps:

1. **Know what resources exist.** You can choose from countless resources, so find out which ones are available at your school or in the surrounding community.

2. **Know which resources you need.** If you don't know which resources to seek out in a particular situation, ask your instructor or an adviser. They're student-success specialists and will point you in the right direction.

3. **Use available resources.** Once you know which resource is appropriate for a particular need, take action. For example, find out how best to contact the tutoring center (do you need an appointment, or can you just walk in?); then do it. Here are examples of questions you can ask to get help from several key sources:

Advising center

- May I please meet with an adviser? I have some questions about scheduling my classes for next term.

- I want to declare a major in psychology, but my adviser is in the English department. Can she still be my adviser?

Financial aid office

- Are there any opportunities to work on campus?

- I don't want to take on too much debt. Can you help me create a plan for managing my finances?

Instructors

- I'm really struggling in this class. Can you recommend additional reading materials that can help me?

- Do you know of an advanced student who might work with me to understand this material?

FIGURE 1.2
Examples of Supports

College Success Leads to Career Success

In this chapter we've talked a lot about connections—between self-knowledge and your success, between embracing your strengths and weaknesses and growing as a learner, and between having a positive attitude and meeting your goals. But another type of connection is equally important to your future: the connection between college and career. The skills, attitudes, and behaviors you're developing in class will be just as valuable in the working world. It's the ultimate two-for-one deal: When you invest in your education, you also succeed at work.

Take critical thinking. Not only is it important to your academic success and your self-knowledge but it's also something employers look for in potential hires.[13] Critical thinking is known as a **transferable skill** because it's useful in many different settings—not just school. Attitudes and behaviors—including motivation, resilience, personal responsibility, and self-efficacy beliefs—can also be transferable. According to surveys, many of the skills you're building in college and in this class are valued by employers—including communicating, working in teams, making decisions, and staying organized.[14]

We'll discuss transferable skills in more detail throughout this book, and you'll see how the skills you develop in school will serve you well in your chosen profession. To get you started, Table 1.1 shows how specific skills might transfer from one environment to another. Whether you're sure of your career path now or are still considering your options, building skills like these will help you succeed in your career—whatever it turns out to be.

TABLE 1.1   Examples of How College Success Skills Transfer to Work Settings

Skill	Application at school	Application at work
Goal setting	Decide to meet with your instructor during office hours at least once a week	Decide to improve your on-time arrival at weekly staff meetings
Communication	Deliver a well-researched presentation to your history class	Deliver a presentation explaining employee health benefits to your team
Critical thinking	Gather facts supporting the argument in your essay	Review a patient's medical data to determine how a new medication would interact with his current medications
Personal responsibility	Recognize that your low test score may have resulted from not studying enough	Take responsibility for submitting a report too late, and develop strategies to better manage your time
Teamwork	Complete a small-group experiment in your biology lab	Work with representatives from other branch offices to prepare a regional sales report
Listening	Pay attention to your instructor's comments and classmates' questions	Consider the concerns expressed by a high school student's parents about courses you've recommended for her senior year

Chapter 1 Review

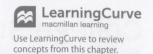

Use LearningCurve to review concepts from this chapter.

CHAPTER SUMMARY

- College is important. By getting your degree or certificate, you'll have more career options, earn more money, and be more likely to get involved in your community.

- Critical thinking involves considering information in a thoughtful way, understanding how to think logically and rationally, and applying those methods of thinking in your classes and your life.

- Personal reflection is a type of critical thinking. By reflecting on your values, interests, and strengths and weaknesses, you can use the resulting self-knowledge to set goals that are personally meaningful, and you can stay motivated to achieve them.

- According to positive psychology, when things don't go your way, you can reframe negative results as opportunities for improvement. Four key ingredients of positive psychology are self-efficacy, resilience, hope, and personal responsibility.

- Many resources are available to help you meet your goals. You can seek help from family, friends, instructors, and support services on campus and in your community.

- There's more to college than learning class material. You'll also develop transferable skills and attitudes that you can apply in whatever career you choose.

CHAPTER ACTIVITIES

Adopting a Success Attitude

COACHING YOURSELF TO MOTIVATION

One aspect of personal responsibility is self-motivation. How can you motivate yourself to keep working toward your goals if you're discouraged or overwhelmed? This chapter has a great suggestion: Be your own success coach. A coach is a source of moral support and inspiration when the going gets tough. To be your own success coach, identify a *mantra*: a quotation, saying, or poem that you find meaningful and that can inspire you when you encounter challenges this year. Why did you select this particular mantra? How will you use it to stay motivated?

Applying Your Skills

ENGAGING PERSONAL SUPPORTS AND RESOURCES

Successful students surround themselves with supports to keep them motivated and to help them improve and succeed. In this exercise you'll learn more about available resources—both in your personal life and on campus.

Personal Supports

1. On a separate sheet of paper, list three people in your life you interact with regularly (for example, friends, roommates, parents, siblings, children, or coworkers).
2. Next to each name, identify three to five ways this person could support you in your quest to be a successful student. For instance, "My roommate could allow me quiet time to study," or "My sister could share the study strategies that she used during college."
3. After you graduate, will any of these people remain personal supports for you as you launch a new or different career? If so, how might they support you in the future? If not, who else could support you, and how?

Campus Resources

1. Visit your college's Web site and identify five available resources that could help you succeed in school or plan your career.
2. Write down the name of each resource. Describe how it could help you and record contact information.

Thinking Critically and Setting Goals

2

Build Your Critical-Thinking Skills

Use Bloom's Taxonomy

Think Critically to Set Goals

Create Your Personal Success Plan

Everyone thinks, but not everyone thinks critically—that is, in a careful, unbiased way. Why does this matter? Because critical thinking helps you make informed decisions based on solid facts and analysis. By seeking out trustworthy information rather than making assumptions or relying on faulty data, your choices will be more well-reasoned and carefully considered. This is important in school—and in life.

In fact, critical thinking is a fundamental element of success in college and the workplace, and that's why we highlight it in this chapter and address it throughout the rest of this book. Critical thinking helps you learn new course content so that you can succeed academically. It also helps you learn about yourself so that you can set meaningful personal goals. In addition, it sets you up for workplace success: Most employers highly value employees with strong critical-thinking skills.

In this chapter you'll explore how critical thinking influences your learning (spoiler alert: it helps you learn more deeply). You'll also see how critical thinking helps you set goals, and you'll get to know the different steps of the goal-setting process. Finally, you'll try out the Personal Success Plan, a tool you can use to map out your goals and build a plan for achieving them.

REFLECTION:
Critical Thinking and Goal Setting

Self-knowledge gives you the power to make positive change. That's why you're using the Academic and Career Excellence System (ACES): to learn more about your strengths and areas where you could improve. By knowing what you're good at, you can use those skills to master course content and build other skills. By acknowledging your weaknesses, you can target areas for improvement.

At the beginning of most chapters in this book, you'll review your score on the related section of ACES. Then you can use that information to focus on chapter content that will help you become a stronger student.

Let's start: Retrieve your Critical Thinking and Goal Setting score and add it to the box on the left. This score measures your beliefs about how well you think critically and set goals. How do you feel about your score? Do you think it accurately reflects your skills? Here's how to *act* on what you've learned about yourself.

- **IF YOU SCORED IN THE HIGH RANGE** on ACES, strengthen your strengths. Take pride in your results, but remember that even if you're good at something, you can always build up that skill even more. A swimmer might win first place at a swim meet, but she'll be back at practice the next morning to refine her stroke. That way, she can work toward competing against more advanced swimmers.

- **IF YOU SCORED IN THE MODERATE OR LOW RANGE** on ACES, target ways to improve. You'll have many opportunities to build your skills in this chapter and throughout the term. With practice, you'll see improvement. This chapter shows you how to get started.

ACES Journal

Do you write your goals down? Do you list steps that you need to take to achieve them? Do you monitor the progress you've made? Spend a few minutes journaling about how *you* set goals. Discuss aspects of your strategy that work well and areas where you could improve.

To find your
Critical Thinking and Goal Setting score,
go to LaunchPad Solo for *Connections Essentials.*

MY ACES SCORE

- ☐ **High**
- ☐ **Moderate**
- ☐ **Low**

LaunchPad Solo
macmillan learning

Build Your Critical-Thinking Skills

Critical thinking can be defined as the ability to consider information in a thoughtful way, understand how to think logically and rationally, and apply those methods of thinking in your classes and your life.[1] You use critical thinking in all kinds of situations: for instance, when you're considering different options for paying for college. You also use it to assess whether information—such as a candidate's political position, an article you've read online, or claims made in a product advertisement—makes sense or is trustworthy.

In this section we'll look at key elements of critical thinking, including the skills involved and tips for mastering those skills.

The Higher-Level Thinking Skills behind Critical Thinking

Critical thinking is made up of a collection of skills that help you assess information, answer questions, and make decisions. These skills are also known as *higher-level thinking skills* because they require you to think in sophisticated ways, such as evaluating and synthesizing information. Yet all higher-level thinking is based on lower-level thinking skills, such as remembering facts, dates, and definitions or describing an object or idea. One way to think of lower- and higher-level thinking is to consider the six questions journalists typically ask: *Who? What? Where?* and *When?* are lower-level questions because they focus on basic facts and information, while *How?* and *Why?* are higher-level questions because they require you to connect and work with those basic facts.

Table 2.1 shows a few examples of higher-level thinking skills. As you read through the rest of this chapter and the book, you'll use these and other critical-thinking skills to make smart decisions about your coursework, life, and career.

How to Use Your Higher-Level Thinking Skills

Now that you have a sense of the types of higher-level thinking skills involved in critical thinking, let's explore how to *use* them. The next time you have a decision to

Truth or Myth? When you think critically, you assess whether information is trustworthy: Does it make sense? Does it come from a credible, unbiased source? Critical thinking helps you avoid the mistake of blindly accepting whatever you see, hear, or read. That means it saves you from reacting to information in a knee-jerk way — like driving for days to see a supposed UFO crash site.
AP Photo / Eric Draper

TABLE 2.1   Examples of Higher-Level Thinking Skills

Skill	Definition	Examples
Comparing and contrasting	Identifying similarities and differences between two or more concepts	• To prepare for a sociology exam, you identify similarities and differences between Marxism and socialism. • You want a new smartphone, so you compare and contrast data plans and other terms offered by several vendors to see which vendor offers the best deal.
Deducing	Arriving at a conclusion using reason and logic	• You notice that all your friends who take time to study for exams get better grades than those who don't study. You deduce that you can improve your grades if you study more. • Someone you've dated several times has stopped responding to your texts and avoids looking at you in class. You conclude that this person has lost interest in spending time with you.
Synthesizing	Combining facts into a larger understanding of a concept	• In your computer programming class, you learn that different techniques for finding and fixing software bugs all have limitations. You figure out a way to combine several techniques to compensate for their various limitations so that you can find and fix more bugs. • As a marketing assistant, you review and synthesize comments from a focus group assembled to examine a new product. Participants' comments suggest that the product name is intriguing but that it doesn't communicate the product's key benefits clearly.
Evaluating	Judging the authenticity or soundness of an argument	• For a journalism class assignment, you read an article arguing against vaccinating children and adults against influenza (the flu) because the vaccine can have side effects and doesn't guarantee immunity. You judge the argument weak because the author doesn't address the fact that vaccination significantly lowers hospitalization rates for the flu.[2] • Your boss says you can't have a raise because the company is having financial troubles. After evaluating the situation, you question this explanation because the company is hiring new employees.
Prioritizing	Determining the order of importance of tasks	• To complete a term paper on the American Revolution, you list all the tasks involved (such as reading source materials, preparing an outline, and writing and revising the paper). You decide that the most important tasks are those that all the others depend on, such as reading sources, and those that will take the most time, such as preparing an outline. • Your manager has just given you several new responsibilities. You prioritize those that directly support an important goal your manager has set for the team: increasing sales.

make, a question to answer, or an argument to consider, follow these guidelines to reach careful conclusions.

Gather and Evaluate Information. To think critically, you need information. The kind of information you need depends on what you're trying to accomplish. If you want to choose a major, you'll need information about your interests, values, strengths, and possible career goals. If you're writing a term paper, you'll need information found in books, your class notes, or readings on reserve in the library.

Having good information can steer you in the right direction and help you avoid mistakes. Imagine you're a doctor treating a sick patient. If you diagnose the person's medical problem using information that isn't accurate, you could end up treating him for, say, an earache when he really has the flu. That's why you have to *evaluate* how reliable your information is. If a source is questionable or hard to assess—maybe you overheard something from a friend's cousin's dog walker—you'll need another source to back up the claims before you can trust the information. Better sources lead to better choices.

Keep an Open Mind. Critical thinking involves keeping an open mind. This means being open to new possibilities presented by information you gather, thinking about old information in new ways, and considering information from different angles. In this way, you'll demonstrate characteristics of creative thinking, not just critical thinking— and that's a good thing! (See "Compare and Contrast: Critical vs. Creative Thinking.")

Apply What You've Learned. To be an expert critical thinker, you need to *do* something with the information you have—either disregard it because it didn't pass your evaluation or apply it in your life and work. For instance, use new knowledge about your strengths to set a goal for yourself, or use information you gained in a class to complete an assignment correctly.

Another way to apply information is to connect something you learned in the past to what you're learning now. What do you already know about mathematics that you can use to learn college algebra? If you've worked on a construction crew, how can you apply knowledge gained from that experience in your architectural design class?

Review Your Outcomes. Reflection is part of critical thinking, so make time to review the outcomes of your decisions and

Critical Components of Success. In college, you'll use the higher-level skills involved in critical thinking to complete assignments for all your classes — whether you're writing a paper or working together on a group project. These students just finished researching how stress affects the body; now they'll apply what they've learned to create a top-notch presentation on stress management for their psychology class. Jacob Lund/Shutterstock

Compare and Contrast: Critical vs. Creative Thinking

It may seem odd that we're talking about creative thinking in a section focused on critical thinking, but bear with us — keep an open mind. Leading experts in the fields of education, psychology, and business don't always agree on the definitions of critical and creative thinking, but they do tend to agree on some of the characteristics of each. For example, critical thinking is often described as **convergent thinking**: It deals with the validity or worth of something that already exists, and it involves a set of agreed-on processes like those described in Table 2.1. In contrast, creative thinking is described as **divergent thinking** (consideration of what is not known), and it involves a very different set of processes — for example, imagination, innovation, playfulness, openness to novelty, and curiosity. There is emerging consensus that *both* types of thinking have value and that, when combined, they can help you achieve greater success than either alone can.

We like to think of critical and creative thinking using an analogy about 3-D glasses: If you put the glasses on but close one eye, you won't see the dimensionality movie producers want you to see — you won't see the full picture. Together, however, the two different lenses permit you to see the film in all the dimensionality intended. Likewise, developing both critical and creative thinking strategies will help you see the full picture of the problem, issue, or opportunity you're facing.

There is increasing emphasis on critical *and* creative thinking in education because future graduates need to be prepared for less structured work environments, where they'll be expected to focus on problem solving, innovation, and social relationships to succeed. By having well-developed critical and creative thinking skills, you too will be better prepared to tackle the academic and workplace challenges you're likely to face.[3]

Practice your creative thinking skills by always being open to new ideas, asking yourself what would happen if you rejected the standard format for problem solving, and taking multiple perspectives on a problem. If you're like most people, you'll be more successful if you step out of your comfort zone and practice "thinking differently" from time to time.

Strange Idea? Or Strangely Brilliant? Critical and creative thinkers see new possibilities in the information they gather. For instance, who'd ever get the strange idea that old shipping containers could serve as student housing? Architects in France did. They created this student-housing complex by stacking one hundred recycled containers, with each one serving as a different student's room. Not so strange after all. Robert Kluba/VISUM/The Image Works

actions. Ask yourself whether your decisions and actions are built on strong critical thinking—or whether you need to improve your thinking process. For example, if your instructors have been skeptical about arguments you've made in several writing assignments, consider whether you need to improve your ability to evaluate your sources' reliability. View such experiences as opportunities for positive change, and get help if you need it to strengthen your critical-thinking skills.

Use Bloom's Taxonomy

Now that you've read about the basics of critical thinking, let's explore how you can apply these skills to learning—which is, after all, your core reason for being in college. Just as there are different levels of *thinking*, there are different levels of *learning*—and some of them require more critical-thinking skills than others.

To get a sense of how the different learning levels work together, think about your experiences in school over the years. When you were in elementary school, you focused mostly on the fundamentals, such as learning how to spell, do simple arithmetic, and remember facts (like names and dates for historical events). But you may not have thought deeply about what you were learning. For example, you probably knew that Christopher Columbus sailed the ocean blue from Europe to the Americas in 1492, but you may not have pondered why he made the trip or what impact his arrival had on the peoples already living in the Americas.

As you've progressed in your education, though, you've used critical-thinking skills more and more. You've likely learned that some questions have more than one right answer and that there can be multiple opinions on a topic. To deal with such ambiguities, you used critical-thinking skills (maybe without even knowing it) to compare, contrast, and evaluate information. Now that you're in college, these sophisticated, higher-level thinking skills are more important than ever.[4]

To better understand how learning moves from a simple to a more complex form, consider the work of educational psychologist Benjamin Bloom.[5] Bloom's taxonomy (Figure 2.1) shows how critical thinking relates to different levels of learning. The lowest level represents learning in its simplest form. At the higher levels, learning becomes more complex—and that's when you really start needing critical-thinking skills. Not everything you learn in college will involve these higher levels of learning,

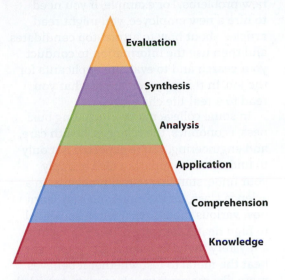

FIGURE 2.1
Bloom's Taxonomy

but much of it will. Let's explore each level in more detail.

- **Knowledge.** Knowledge is the most basic level of learning. When you learn a set of facts and recall them on a test, you demonstrate knowledge. Perhaps you know that the American Revolution ended in 1783 or that the Cuban missile crisis happened in 1962. Think of these facts as forming a foundation you can build on to better understand a topic.

- **Comprehension.** At this level, you can restate facts in your own words, compare them to each other, organize them into meaningful groups, and state main ideas. For example, in your communications class, you may learn two facts: Facebook was launched in 2004, and the current CEO is Mark Zuckerberg. You might categorize Facebook as a type of social media platform, a group that also includes Twitter, LinkedIn, Instagram, and Snapchat. You might further organize these platforms into groups that focus on sharing pictures and those that don't.

- **Application.** At this level, you use knowledge and your comprehension of it to solve new problems. For example, if you need to hire a new employee, you might read articles about how to attract top candidates and then use the information to conduct your search and to evaluate applicants for the job. In this way, you apply what you read to a real-life challenge.

   In some college majors, including business, economics, the sciences, health care, and engineering, you're expected not only to understand a topic but also to apply your understanding to real problems. In a science class, for example, you may learn how various metals react when subjected to high heat. Later, when asked to identify a mystery metal in science lab, you might heat the metal to test whether it behaves more like magnesium, aluminum, or nickel.

- **Analysis.** At this level of learning, you approach a topic by breaking it down into meaningful parts and learning how those parts relate to one another. You may identify stated and unstated assumptions, examine the reliability of information, and distinguish between facts and educated guesses or opinions.

   You'll be expected to use this level of learning frequently in college. For essay exams, group projects, debates, and term papers, you'll formulate arguments based on data. In a modern history course, for example, you may analyze how conflict in the Middle East influenced the foreign and domestic policies of President George W. Bush.

- **Synthesis.** When you synthesize, you make connections between seemingly unrelated or previously unknown facts to understand a topic. As you weave new information into your existing understanding of a topic, you'll understand that topic in new and more sophisticated ways.

Wanted: Fresh Solutions. When you reach the application level of learning, you can draw on prior knowledge to solve new problems. Let's say you wanted to stop global warming in places like the Arctic. What prior knowledge would you seek out? From which disciplines? From which sources? And how would you use that knowledge to solve this important problem?
Yvonne Pijnenburg-Schonewille/Shutterstock

●●● **CHAPTER 2** Thinking Critically and Setting Goals

You can think of synthesis as advanced analysis.

Here's an example of synthesis: To develop a research question for a psychology class, you review research findings on altruism (doing good things for others). You learn that people are less likely to help others when they don't feel a personal sense of responsibility or when there are many other people around who could also help. You use this information to propose a new study on the likelihood that students in the college cafeteria would help a person who slipped and spilled her tray.

- **Evaluation.** At this highest level of learning, you develop arguments and opinions based on a thorough understanding of a topic and a careful review of the available evidence. For instance, an essay question might ask you to establish a position for or against the current U.S. strategy to combat global terrorism. Evaluation is the "expert" level of learning—a level you'll want to achieve in college, especially in your chosen major. After all, would you want to cross a bridge built by an engineer who hadn't reached the expert level of engineering? We wouldn't either.

Those Blooming Test Questions!

Your college instructors want you to remember facts (knowledge) and understand concepts (comprehension). But they will also encourage you to apply, analyze, synthesize, and evaluate information — in other words, to think critically. To test your learning at different levels, instructors will ask you different types of questions. The examples below show the types of questions you might encounter in your college classes and the Bloom's level that each question corresponds to.

- **Knowledge** questions often make use of the following key words: *who, what, where, when, choose, list, label, match.*
  Sample question: In *what* year did the Battle of Gettysburg take place?

- **Comprehension** questions often make use of the following key words: *compare, contrast, rephrase, summarize, classify, describe, show.*
  Sample question: *Classify* the following molecules based on their state (gas, liquid, or solid) at room temperature.

- **Application** questions often make use of the following key words: *apply, organize, plan, develop, model, solve.*
  Sample question: *Apply* your knowledge of chemical compounds to identify the unknown white solid in your tray.

- **Analysis** questions often make use of the following key words: *analyze, categorize, examine, theme, relationships, assumptions, conclusions.*
  Sample question: Drawing on your understanding of *Beowulf* and *King Lear, examine* how the theme of heroism is treated in these two works.

- **Synthesis** questions often make use of the following key words: *synthesize, propose, predict, combine, adapt, test, discuss.*
  Sample question: Using your understanding of motivation theory, *propose* a program that will help high school dropouts return to school.

- **Evaluation** questions often make use of the following key words: *critique, judge, prove, disprove, opinion.*
  Sample question: Based on your review of the evidence presented during the mock trial and your understanding of U.S. law, *critique* the defense's argument.

You can expect different types of questions at different levels of Bloom's taxonomy in different classes. Don't be surprised if you see more multiple-choice questions in introductory-level classes and more questions that rely on higher levels of learning as you move into advanced classes — especially in your academic major.

Think Critically to Set Goals

A **goal** is an outcome you hope to achieve that guides and sustains your effort over time. When you set goals, you think critically about yourself and the information you gather, using many of the skills you've just read about. Thus goal setting represents critical thinking in action. For instance, to set a goal, you *evaluate* your options. And as you work toward a goal, you *analyze* your progress and any obstacles facing you so that you can develop strategies for overcoming the obstacles.

The goals you set provide a roadmap for your success—in college and in your personal and professional life. To achieve your longer-term goal of entering a particular profession, for example, you need to meet another longer-term goal—graduating from college. And to graduate, you need to achieve shorter-term goals like passing required courses. Accomplishing these goals requires you to reach other shorter-term goals, such as completing assignments and class projects. So knowing how to use critical thinking to set and achieve your goals is vital.

Setting any goal involves a five-step process (see Figure 2.2), and each step requires you to apply critical-thinking skills. Let's take a closer look at how the process works.

FIGURE 2.2
The Steps of Goal Setting

Step 1: Gather Information (about *You*)

The first step of goal setting isn't actually *stating* your goal. Rather, it's gathering information about yourself (like what you want to achieve and what your strengths are) so that you can define goals that are realistic and meaningful for you.

You can start by gathering information about your strengths and weaknesses. Review your ACES results and reflect on the classes you find challenging, the grades you've received, and past experiences you've had. Then consider whether you want your goal to focus on addressing a weakness or strengthening something you're already good at. For instance, if you're a chronic procrastinator, you may want to set a goal of improving your

time-management skills. If you're a masterful note-taker, you might want to set a goal of becoming a tutor, since teaching a skill to others often makes you even better at it yourself.

Step 2: Set a SMART Goal

Once you've gathered information about yourself, the next step is to set a goal that expresses what you want to achieve. Express it as a **SMART goal**—one that is *specific, measurable, achievable, relevant* to you personally, and *time-limited*. Avoid stating your goal in vague terms, such as "I'm going to study more" or "I want to get good grades." Such goals are weak because you'll have a hard time knowing whether you've achieved them. (For instance, what does "to study more" actually mean?) By contrast, the SMART approach helps you create strong goals that you can realistically achieve by taking concrete steps to accomplish them (see Table 2.2).

Weak goal	SMART goal
Get good grades in class	Get a B or better in my algebra class this term
Spend more time studying for biology	Study my biology class notes and textbook at least five hours each week this term
Make some new friends	Attend a meeting of at least two on-campus clubs or organizations in the next month
Get some help writing my term paper	Meet with a tutor at the writing center each week for the next three weeks

TABLE 2.2
Weak Goals versus SMART Goals

Specific. When you express a goal in specific terms, you know exactly what you're trying to achieve. Contrast the specific goal "Get a GPA of 3.0 or higher this term" with the vague goal "Get good grades." The vague goal doesn't say what qualifies as a good grade (an A? a B+?), so you don't have a clear idea of what you're working toward.

Measurable. When a goal is measurable, you know when you've reached it. For instance, it's easy to determine if you've earned a GPA of 3.0 or higher by the end of the term. Your school calculates your GPA, so one quick look at your grades for the term tells you whether you've met your goal.

Achievable. Nothing is more frustrating than establishing a goal that's beyond your reach. What is and isn't achievable differs from person to person. For example, if you're working full time and raising two kids while attending college, setting a goal that involves taking five classes and studying four hours a day probably isn't achievable. On the other hand, taking one or two classes and studying one and a half hours a day on weekdays and two hours a day on weekends may be a more reasonable goal.

If you have doubts about whether a goal is achievable, consider revising your goal to increase the chances you'll reach it. Then, once you succeed, you can set the bar higher for yourself. The key is to set goals that are challenging enough to inspire you but not so challenging that you can't reach them.

Relevant to You. When you set goals that matter to you personally, you'll be more

motivated to achieve them. So if you enjoy learning about science and want to become a pharmacist, it will be easier for you to reach a goal of studying chemistry three additional hours a week. And if you plan on a career in the food services industry and believe that hunger is a pressing social problem, volunteering once a week at a food pantry would be relevant to you.

Time-Limited. SMART goals include deadlines by which you aim to achieve the goals (such as earning a GPA of 3.0 or higher by the end of the term). Take care in setting deadlines. If the deadline is too far in the future, you may procrastinate on working toward the goal. But if you set a deadline that's too soon, the goal may start to seem unachievable, and you might feel too overwhelmed and discouraged to tackle it. Setting a time limit for achieving a goal helps you assess whether you've actually accomplished what you intended.

Step 3: Make an Action Plan

To achieve your goals, you need an **action plan**, a list of the steps you'll take to accomplish a goal and the order in which you'll take them. Think of your action plan as a to-do list for achieving your goal.

Write Down Your Actions. The first step in developing a good action plan is to write down the actions you'll take to achieve your goal. You might be tempted to make a mental list of these actions, but writing them down is a *much* better idea. Research suggests that people who write down their goals achieve almost twice as many of those goals as people who don't write them down.[6] Don't worry about making the list perfect or recording the steps in a particular order—just write them down as they pop into your mind. For example, if your SMART goal is to submit your English term paper on the day it's due, you might brainstorm a list of action steps like this:

Action Steps
• Submit final term paper by due date
• Prepare rough draft of term paper
• Submit rough draft to writing tutor
• Buy a dictionary
• Schedule appointment with writing tutor
• Incorporate feedback from writing tutor into final version

Prioritize Your Action Steps. Once you've brainstormed action steps and written them down, determine which steps are critical and which aren't. (Noncritical steps are those that, if ignored, wouldn't jeopardize your goal.) In this example, you might decide that buying a dictionary isn't a top priority—after all, there's one on your computer—so you cross that off the list. The items that remain should be those that are most important.

Put Your Steps in Order and Set Deadlines for Them. Once you've eliminated noncritical steps from your list, arrange the remaining steps in the order in which you'll complete them. For example, if you need feedback from the writing center before editing your paper, put a visit to the writing center higher on your list. Also, add a deadline for each step so you can track your progress.

Here's how your action plan might look now:

Action Plan Steps (in Order)	Deadlines
1. Schedule appointment with writing tutor	This Friday
2. Prepare rough draft of term paper	Three weeks before due date
3. Submit rough draft to writing tutor	Same day as above
4. Incorporate feedback from writing tutor into final version	Within one week of due date
5. Submit final term paper	On due date

Got Goals? They're Your Path to Academic Success

Whether you end up working in business, nursing, law, the military, or another profession, numerous studies have shown that goals will be good for you: People who set goals are more likely to succeed and to report satisfaction with their careers.

Recently, a group of researchers conducted a study to see if goal setting also promotes college success. They recruited undergraduate participants who were having trouble with their studies and divided them into two groups. The first group completed surveys unrelated to goal setting and listed past accomplishments they were proud of. They received no special training on goal setting or achieving goals. The second group of students participated in a Web-based program that introduced them to a process of goal setting and goal achievement. They wrote down seven or eight personal goals, prioritized them, and described how meeting those goals would improve their lives.

The results were impressive. On average, students in group 1 achieved a GPA of 2.25. *On average, those in group 2 achieved a GPA of almost 3.0.* Students in group 2 also completed more academic credits and reported being less anxious about their college success than their classmates in group 1. The bottom line? When you learn how to set goals, you'll likely improve your grades, feel less stressed-out about college, and achieve more of what you consider important.[7]

Step 4: List Barriers and Solutions

Even when you have an action plan for achieving a goal, you can still encounter barriers. A **barrier** is something that prevents you from making progress toward your goal. It might be a personal characteristic (like a tendency to procrastinate) or something in your environment (like too many family commitments). Some barriers (such as poor time management) are under your control. With others (like family or work demands), you might have less control.

As you set your goals, write down the types of barriers you may face. By acknowledging potential barriers, you won't get blindsided if you actually encounter them. Also, you can brainstorm in advance how to overcome them.

And remember that you don't have to face barriers alone. Many helpful resources are available to provide support and encouragement. Faculty members, tutors, and academic and career advisers, for example, can work with you to overcome common barriers. To get help, you just have to ask.

Step 5: Act and Evaluate Outcomes

As you start taking the steps in your goal-setting action plan, regularly evaluate your progress. Are the steps you're taking effective? Are you completing them on time? Are they helping you get closer to meeting your goal? If you're not making the progress you'd hoped for, evaluating your outcomes helps you know this immediately so that you can change your action plan or find resources to get you back on track. Also, evaluation can help you stay motivated to keep working toward your long-term goals. By recording and celebrating your progress on the short-term goals that support your long-term ones, you build up proof that you're getting closer to your long-term goals.

If your evaluation shows that you've experienced a setback, stay positive. The point of evaluating your progress is to identify and deal with setbacks. Each time you do so, you'll get even better at achieving your goals, and you can seek out help if you need it. Remember: Setting and achieving goals takes practice. You didn't learn how to ride a bike on the first try either!

Oops! Even if you've built an action plan for achieving a goal, you can still encounter barriers: You get stuck in a traffic jam, so you're late for a group-project meeting. Your boss needs you to work extra hours, so you have less time to study than you had hoped. By anticipating possible barriers, you can craft strategies for overcoming them if they do arise. Berkomaster/Shutterstock

Kerry Maxime

FOCUSING ON SOLUTIONS

NAME:	**Thamara Jean**
SCHOOL:	*Broward College*
MAJOR:	*Pre-Nursing*
CAREER GOAL:	*Nursing*

> " Making mistakes doesn't mean failure, unless you fail to learn from your mistakes."

Since I was seven years old, I've wanted to be a doctor — I think my goal was influenced by my parents and from watching lots of doctor shows on TV. With that goal in mind, I arrived at college and really struggled with courses like organic chemistry and pre-calculus. It wasn't until I attended a required advising meeting that I realized I wasn't thinking very critically about my goal. I didn't have much information about what was required to get through pre-med and medical school. I realized that semester that choosing medicine was probably a mistake but that making mistakes doesn't mean failure, unless you fail to learn from your mistakes. My adviser and I discussed creating a backup plan that included switching to pre-nursing, getting experience in health care settings, and continuing to gather information about medical school.

That same semester I attended a leadership and goal-setting workshop where I learned about SMART goals and was encouraged to get more involved in campus leadership activities. It was part of a campus initiative called QEP — Questioning Every Possibility. I learned to question, assess, analyze, and even research everything, because my future depends on me!

I immediately set a number of specific goals, like joining Phi Theta Kappa and the campus Honors Committee, passing my classes the next semester, and researching information about how to get into nursing school. To support my goal of passing classes, I set additional goals like getting tutoring in math and science and getting feedback on my papers before submitting them in literature classes. I feel back on track. I recently transferred to Florida Atlantic University, where I'm applying for acceptance into the nursing program, and I'm looking forward to a successful career in nursing.

YOUR TURN: Have you ever set a goal and then discovered significant barriers blocking your way? If so, what did you do to overcome those barriers or adjust your goal to make it more realistic?

Create Your Personal Success Plan

Now that you've explored how to set and achieve goals using critical-thinking skills, put your learning into action with the **Personal Success Plan (PSP).** This tool guides you through the five steps of the goal-setting process. You can use it to establish SMART goals, build action plans, evaluate your outcomes, and revise your plans as needed as you go through this course. You can also use the PSP to set and achieve goals in other courses or in your personal and professional life.

The PSP's major sections mirror the five goal-setting steps you just learned:

1. Gather Information
2. Set a SMART Goal
3. Make an Action Plan
4. List Barriers and Solutions
5. Act and Evaluate Outcomes

An additional section—Connect to Career—helps you consider how a goal you've defined using the PSP can help prepare you for success in your chosen career or a career you're considering.

As you start using the PSP, you'll become a stronger critical thinker and a more independent learner. You'll use critical thinking to gather information, make decisions, and evaluate what you've learned about yourself so that you can get better and better at setting and achieving goals. In short, you'll discover that *you're* in the driver's seat when it comes to defining and meeting your goals—and you'll gain practice taking personal responsibility for your own learning.

The PSP in Action

In this section, you'll get a firsthand look at how the PSP functions. You'll read about the experience of one student, Kayden, as he sets up his PSP, and you'll see the steps he takes to create and accomplish his goal. This is goal setting in action!

Gather Information. Kayden has enrolled in a first-year seminar course, and one of his assignments is to establish a specific goal and action plan. As a first step, Kayden gathers information about himself by reflecting on his strengths and weaknesses. He knows that he's a very motivated student but that he also struggles to manage his time. Therefore he decides that setting a regular study schedule will help him stay on track.

Set a SMART Goal. Kayden decides on his SMART goal: "I'll study for my first-year seminar at least one hour each weekday." This is a *specific* and *measurable* goal. Based on his existing schedule, Kayden believes that this goal is *achievable*. He's motivated to get good grades this term, so it's also personally *relevant* to his success. Finally, the goal has a clearly established *time limit*, which will help him check his progress within a day or two.

Make an Action Plan. To identify the steps he must take to meet his goal, Kayden considers his class and work schedules and upcoming personal commitments. He knows that his brain doesn't kick into gear until noon, so studying after lunch is best. He also knows that he prefers studying in his own apartment, but only when it's quiet. With this information in mind, he makes a plan.

- By Friday, he'll meet with his roommate to plan quiet, afternoon study time in their apartment.
- By Sunday, he'll enter his study schedule into his smartphone calendar.
- By Sunday night, he'll develop a log to record how much he studies.

List Barriers and Solutions. On his PSP, Kayden lists several barriers that might prevent him from achieving his goal and brainstorms solutions for overcoming those barriers. For example, his roommate may need to use the apartment when Kayden wants to study. (Perhaps his roommate is a music major and needs to practice his tuba.) As a backup plan, Kayden decides to look for alternative study areas in the school library. Also, Kayden might not always be able to follow his set schedule or might feel pressure to socialize when he's supposed to be studying. In case these things happen, he develops strategies for staying on track.

Act and Evaluate Outcomes. For the next two weeks, Kayden implements his action plan and records his results in the PSP. He works with his roommate to set aside quiet study time at their apartment (and identifies a backup study location just in case the apartment becomes noisy), enters his study schedule into his smartphone to remind himself when to study, and creates a log to record how much he studies.

He experiences a setback in week 2, when he misses two study periods. But he doesn't give up; instead, he makes up his study time over the weekend and revises his schedule to make it more realistic. And he's so pleased with how useful this study strategy has been

that he decides to build a study schedule for his other courses, too.

Connect to Career. On his PSP, Kayden has identified three skills he is learning as he works toward his goal: managing his time, prioritizing his action steps, and mastering his new smartphone app. These are skills he can use in any current job or any future employment. By recording these skills on his PSP, he can refer to them when he prepares a résumé, writes cover letters, and goes on job interviews.

Create Your First Personal Success Plan

Kayden is off to a great start this term, and now it's time for you to create your first Personal Success Plan. To begin, follow the steps below and sketch out your ideas on the following page. Or visit LaunchPad Solo for *Connections Essentials* to access the PSP online.

1. **Gather information.** What are your strengths and your weaknesses? Review your ACES results to identify a strength (high score) you want to develop further or a low score suggesting an area in which you could improve.

Turn It Down! Building flexibility into your action plan helps you keep barriers from standing between you and your goal. For instance, if your neighbor is an aspiring deejay, take that into account when designing your study plan: Identify a quiet location where you can study in case your neighbor decides to crank up the volume just as you crack open your textbook.
Maxim Blinkov/Shutterstock

my personal success plan

1 my information

Sometimes it's hard for me to manage my time.

I need a regular study schedule to stay on track.

2 my SMART goal

I'll study for my first-year seminar at least one hour each weekday.

☑ **S**PECIFIC ☑ **M**EASURABLE ☑ **A**CHIEVABLE ☑ **R**ELEVANT ☑ **T**IME-LIMITED

3 my action plan

1. I'll discuss apartment quiet time with my roommate (by Friday).
2. I'll enter study times into my smartphone calendar (by Sunday).
3. I'll make a log to record how much I study (by Sunday night).

4 my barriers/solutions

1. If my roommate has a conflicting schedule, I'll find a place to study in the library.
2. If I miss a scheduled study session, I'll find a makeup time.
3. If family and friends want to get together during study time, I'll find a different time for us to meet.

5 my actions/outcomes

1. My roommate and I set quiet hours for the apartment. I also found a good place to study in the library, just in case.
2. I entered my study schedule into my smartphone and created a study log.
3. In week 2, I missed two study periods. I'll make up this study time over the weekend and revise my schedule to be more realistic!

6 my career connection

1. I'm learning to manage my time, which will help me meet deadlines on the job.
2. I'm setting priorities, and I can use this skill to focus on the most important tasks at work.
3. I've mastered my new smartphone app, which I can use to schedule appointments during the workday.

2. **Set a SMART goal.** Define a short-term goal that meets the SMART criteria. You can always revise it later, so don't worry about making it perfect.
3. **Make an action plan.** List steps you'll need to take to achieve this goal, and arrange them in an order that makes sense to you. Give each step a deadline.
4. **List barriers and solutions.** Identify possible barriers to your action steps and brainstorm solutions for overcoming each barrier. If these barriers occur, you'll be ready.
5. **Act and evaluate outcomes.** It's up to you to put your plan into action and to record the completion of each action step and any problems you encounter. Do this to track your progress.
6. **Connect to career.** List the skills you'll develop as you progress toward your goal. Then identify how those skills will help you succeed on the job.

Once you've filled out your Personal Success Plan, you'll have set your first

academic success goal of the term. Congratulations—this is a great first step! Remember, though, that goal setting is an ongoing process that takes practice, and that's why you'll get the chance to set multiple goals over the course of the term. How many goals should you set? Your instructor may provide guidance on the number required for your particular class. Some instructors may ask you to set one goal for each chapter, while others may require only a few goals over the course of the term. Either way, we have included a sample PSP at the end of each chapter to inspire you and to walk you through the goal-setting process. If you aren't setting a goal in a particular chapter, the PSP will still be there to offer suggestions and serve as a model.

You might need some time to get used to the PSP, but as you progress through this course, you'll become an expert goal setter. By the end of the term, you'll have set and achieved a number of goals, and you'll be well on your way to academic and career success.

Employers Value Goal Setting

Supervisors at almost any workplace will expect you to be goal directed, just as your instructors expect you to be goal directed as a student. The good news? You can use the goal-setting strategy you're learning in this course to help you set (and achieve!) career goals. For example, let's say you want to take on more responsibility at work or communicate more effectively with colleagues. You can reframe these general statements as SMART goals and use the PSP to achieve them.

As you develop your own work-related goals, be sure to consider how they support the goals of your whole organization or team. For example, as a licensed practical

nurse, you might decide to increase the number of patient charts you review each hour by 10 percent in the next month. This goal demonstrates enthusiasm and a desire for self-improvement. However, you'll want to consult with your supervisor about which goals would best support both the organization's success and your own professional development. If your employer prefers that you focus on learning how to use a new piece of equipment instead, you might have to modify your original goal to support your employer's top priorities. Developing goals in consultation with your supervisor is a win-win situation and a great way to show your ability to take the initiative.

my personal success plan _____

1 **my information**
_____
_____
_____
_____

2 **my SMART goal**
_____
_____
_____
_____

☐ **S**PECIFIC ☐ **M**EASURABLE ☐ **A**CHIEVABLE ☐ **R**ELEVANT ☐ **T**IME-LIMITED

3 **my action plan**
_____
_____
_____
_____
_____

4 **my barriers/ solutions**
_____
_____
_____
_____
_____

5 **my actions/ outcomes**
_____
_____
_____
_____
_____

6 **my career connection**
_____
_____
_____
_____
_____

Chapter 2 Review

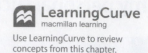

Use LearningCurve to review concepts from this chapter.

CHAPTER SUMMARY

- Critical thinking is the process of approaching information in a thoughtful way, understanding how to think logically and rationally, and applying those methods of thinking in your classes and your life.

- You can use critical thinking to learn in every course you're taking. Bloom's taxonomy helps you identify the level at which you're learning and think about how that learning will be assessed.

- You can use critical thinking to set and achieve goals through a five-step process:

(1) gather information about yourself, (2) set a SMART goal, (3) make an action plan, (4) list possible barriers and solutions, and (5) act and evaluate outcomes.

- The Personal Success Plan can help you set and achieve goals. The steps in the PSP mirror the five goal-setting steps, with one additional step, connecting to career. You can use the PSP to list your goals and action steps, document which steps you've completed, evaluate your progress, and revise your plan if needed.

CHAPTER ACTIVITIES

Adopting a Success Attitude

PERCEIVING SETBACKS AS LEARNING OPPORTUNITIES

Regardless of how realistic your goals are and how many barriers you anticipate, at some point you won't accomplish something you want to. Let's use reflection to turn a goal-setting setback into a learning opportunity.

1. Describe a goal you set but never achieved. Evaluate it using the SMART criteria described in this chapter. Was the goal specific, measurable, achievable, relevant to you, and time-limited? If not, how could you have redefined the goal so that it met all of those criteria?
2. Describe how you felt when you didn't achieve this goal. Did these feelings affect your motivation to continue pursuing your goal?
3. Reflect on what made it difficult to achieve your goal. Try not to place blame, but do consider the ways in which you may have been responsible for the setback.
4. Identify what you could do differently to achieve this goal now and how you could stay positive. Also, list personal or campus resources that could provide support if you experience this setback again.

Applying Your Skills

CONSTRUCTING SMART GOALS

This activity gives you practice turning broad, general goals into specific, measurable, and time-limited goals. We aren't focusing on the A (achievable) and the R (relevant to you) of the SMART acronym because only you can determine if a goal is achievable or relevant.

First, review the Set a SMART Goal section of this chapter. Then rewrite the following goals to make them specific, measurable, and time-limited.

1. Goal: *Look for a job soon.*

   SMarT Goal: _____

2. Goal: *Figure out my major.*

   SMarT Goal: _____

3. Goal: *Make some networking contacts before I graduate.*

   SMarT Goal: _____

4. Goal: *Lead a healthier life.*

   SMarT Goal: _____

5. Goal: *Do well in class.*

   SMarT Goal: _____

Don Mason/Getty Images

3

Motivation, Decision Making, and Personal Responsibility

What Keeps You Motivated?

Make Good Decisions

Take Personal Responsibility for Your Education

MY PERSONAL SUCCESS PLAN

Like many students, you may be surprised at how different college life is from your previous experiences. Most college instructors don't provide a great deal of structure for their students. They expect you to schedule your own time and figure out how — and how much — to study. This freedom and responsibility for managing your life may feel surprising, exciting, and intimidating, sometimes all at once. It's up to you to stay motivated, make good decisions, and take responsibility for achieving your goals.

Yet, also like many students, you may be having difficulty staying motivated, making smart choices, and taking charge of your learning. By understanding more about these important college survival skills, you can truly *own* your college experience. As a result, you'll get the most value from your classes — including new knowledge and skills that will help you excel in your career.

In fact, motivation, decision making, and personal responsibility will be just as critical in your work life as in your college life. Why? Recent college graduates need to develop marketable skills, be flexible, and prepare to find new jobs if necessary. Doing this involves seeking out mentors for guidance and creating action plans to build new skills and strengthen existing ones. In short, to be competitive in today's work world, you need to assume responsibility for your own success.

In this chapter you'll learn how to activate three forces that will keep you motivated in school: believing you can succeed, viewing all your coursework as important to your goals, and cultivating a positive attitude. In addition, you'll learn strategies you can use to make careful decisions and take personal responsibility for your education.

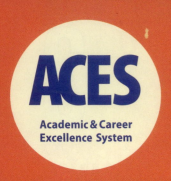

Academic & Career Excellence System

To find your
Motivation, Decision Making, and Personal Responsibility score,
go to LaunchPad Solo for *Connections Essentials*.

MY ACES SCORE

☐ **High**
☐ **Moderate**
☐ **Low**

macmillan learning

REFLECTION:
Motivation, Decision Making, and Personal Responsibility

Take a moment to reflect on your Motivation, Decision Making, and Personal Responsibility score on ACES. Find your score and add it to the box on the left.

This score measures your beliefs about how well you stay motivated, make decisions, and take responsibility for your learning. Do you think it's an accurate snapshot of your current skills in these areas? Why or why not?

- **IF YOU SCORED IN THE HIGH RANGE** and you think this score is accurate, you may be very good at staying motivated, making careful decisions, and taking responsibility for your education. This is great news! Now, though, look for new ways to improve. As you read this chapter, focus on developing even better ways to stay motivated, make decisions, and actively drive your own learning. The more strategies you build up, the better prepared you'll be when you run into those inevitable moments of feeling overwhelmed.

- **IF YOU SCORED IN THE MODERATE OR LOW RANGE**, don't be discouraged. You *can* strengthen your motivation, learn how to make good decisions, and take more responsibility for your learning. This chapter is filled with ideas you can begin using now.

ACES Journal

Your college success depends on taking responsibility for your learning. Think about what that means for this term. Take a minute to write down what you need to take responsibility for in order to succeed in your current classes. Be very specific: For example, what do you need to take responsibility for *this week*? Then write about how you plan to accomplish these tasks. What steps have you taken in the past to keep yourself motivated and focused? Which strategies seemed particularly useful?

_____

_____

_____

_____

What Keeps You Motivated?

Imagine it's Friday night, and you have an investigative story due Monday for your journalism class. You believe you're a good writer, and you think you have a meaningful and important story to tell—plus, you love this class. Given these thoughts and emotions, you'll likely feel motivated to work hard on the story over the weekend. Why? You believe you can do a good job, meaning you have strong *self-efficacy* in your journalism skills. You see this writing task as *relevant* to what matters most to you. And you have a positive *attitude* about the task facing you. These are three key components of motivation (see Figure 3.1).

Let's begin by taking a closer look at each component. Then we'll compare two types of motivation—and explore which is more powerful.

Self-Efficacy

Self-efficacy refers to your belief in your ability to carry out the actions needed to reach a particular goal. In other words, you *believe* you can be effective. The stronger your sense of self-efficacy, the more likely you'll do what's needed to achieve your goals and to keep trying even when you encounter setbacks.

How can you strengthen your sense of self-efficacy? Try the following tactics, suggested by psychologist Albert Bandura.[1]

- **Experience success.** One important component of a SMART goal is that it's achievable. Achieving a goal enhances your self-efficacy beliefs and motivates you to take on your next challenge. In that way, success builds on success. By proving to yourself that you're making progress (as you do on the PSP), you strengthen your sense of self-efficacy and are more likely to succeed in your next goal.

- **Observe others who are successful.** Strengthen your self-efficacy beliefs by watching other people complete a task successfully. Psychologists call this process *modeling*. For

FIGURE 3.1
Three Key Components of Motivation

instance, join a study group and see how students who get the best grades take notes during lectures. Or ask tutors at the math and writing centers to show you the strategies they use to master the subject matter.

- **Seek support and encouragement.** Being supported and encouraged in your pursuits helps you believe more strongly in your ability to achieve goals. So surround yourself with people who want you to succeed. Let them know not only when you're struggling but also when you're making progress toward your goals. Their encouragement will help you feel even more confident in your abilities.

- **Turn stress into a motivator.** Stress is natural—everyone feels it—and it isn't *always* bad. In fact, a little bit of it can energize you to tackle a challenge. Too much stress, however, can sap your motivation. The key is to find a middle ground—just enough stress to inspire you, but not so much that it paralyzes you.

Relevance

If you think that a goal has relevance for you—that achieving it will make a positive difference in some way—you'll feel more motivated to work toward that goal.

(Remember the *R* in SMART?) Relevance can even motivate you to achieve a goal that seems boring or unpleasant in the short term because you know that by meeting this challenge now, you'll get something that's important to you in the long term. For instance, maybe you dread your English composition class. Still, you force yourself to work at the class assignments because you understand that knowing how to write well will help you, no matter what career you choose to pursue.

If a subject or an assignment seems irrelevant to your life at first, connect it to something that is relevant. If your motivation for a particular task starts to wane, try out these strategies.

- **Find something interesting in every class.** Almost all academic topics relate to one another in some way. For example, if you're a psychology major taking a history class, you might be able to write a paper on the history of psychoanalytic thought. Even though the paper is for your history class, the topic connects with something that interests you. If you remind yourself of such connections, seemingly irrelevant projects will become more relevant than you first thought.

- **Connect coursework to your long-term goals.** Doing well in college can give you the knowledge and skills needed to achieve your long-term goals—such as going to graduate school, getting into a highly competitive program like nursing, or effectively managing family or community responsibilities. Always try to keep the big picture in mind.

- **Build transferable skills.** Use general-education courses to develop transferable skills like note taking, writing, time management, and critical thinking.

- **Focus on practical benefits.** Remind yourself of the practical benefits of achieving a goal—for instance, "If I can maintain a 3.5 GPA, I can keep my scholarship" or "If I pass this class, I'll avoid the cost of retaking it."

- **Focus on a love of learning.** The feeling of accomplishment you get from mastering new material—even if that material isn't your favorite—can give a task meaning.

The Power of Relevance. When your goals have relevance to you, you'll stay motivated to achieve them—even in the face of serious setbacks. Take Malala Yousafzai, the Pakistani activist for female education and the youngest person to ever receive the Nobel Peace Prize. After a gunman shot and nearly killed her and the Taliban threatened her life and her father's, her commitment to education only grew stronger. AP Photo / Susan Walsh

Attitude

A positive attitude is a beautiful thing: It makes you more resilient in the face of difficulties, helps you learn from your mistakes, and increases your enjoyment when you succeed. It's also a powerful motivator that can keep you energized and focused on your goals. Use the following strategies to stay positive, even when a project, an assignment, or a class leaves you feeling uninspired.

- **Identify something positive resulting from the work you're doing.** Even little rewards can make difficult tasks more pleasant. Look for those small moments of enjoyment or positivity, and take time to appreciate them. For instance, you might unexpectedly find a photo of a painting that takes your breath away in an art history textbook, or you might realize that you could become good friends with a classmate you're collaborating with on a math assignment.

- **If possible, take at least one course in your intended major each term.** That way, you can spend some time each week focused on the content you most enjoy.

- **Think and speak positively.** Monitor your *self-talk*: what you tell yourself about the courses you're taking, the assignments you're working on, and your goals. Positive self-talk—thinking positive thoughts and making positive statements—protects you from stress, promotes creative thinking, and helps you stay motivated.[2] (See "You're Good Enough *and* You're Smart Enough.")

You're Good Enough *and* You're Smart Enough

Self-talk has been used for decades by athletes and performers to help boost their performance, but it's also gaining in popularity in areas such as academic and workplace success. According to research, there's a good reason for that: Self-talk can be powerful! One recent study showed that academically challenged and stressed undergraduates who engaged in brief positive self-talk improved their problem-solving performance.[3]

How can we best use self-talk to give ourselves a boost? Antonis Hatzigeorgiadis, a famous sports psychologist, suggests that self-talk can be particularly helpful in three circumstances: to instruct, to motivate, and to evaluate.[4] Instructional self-talk is helpful when we're trying to learn a new skill or concept. Motivational self-talk helps us manage or focus on challenging tasks. Finally, evaluative self-talk is important when we reflect on and explain our recent performance.

According to another recent study, *how* you refer to yourself when engaging in self-talk also makes a difference.[5] Interestingly, referring to yourself as "you" rather than "I" tends to be more effective. For example, if you're studying for an upcoming biology exam you might say to yourself, "You can understand the concept of photosynthesis; you just need to focus and spend the time needed to master this topic." The next time you need encouragement, look to yourself: With positive self-talk, you can be your own #1 supporter!

marekuliasz/Shutterstock

Tap into Your Internal Motivation

In your school, work, and personal life, multiple motivations underlie the choices you make. Maybe you decided to go to college not only because you enjoy learning new things but also because you need to build skills that will get you a good job. Perhaps you've joined a study group not only because you'll meet friendly people but also because it will help you get better grades. Each of these decisions reflects the two kinds of motivation identified by psychologists: intrinsic and extrinsic motivation. **Intrinsic motivation** stems from your inner desire to achieve a specific outcome. **Extrinsic motivation** derives from forces external to you, such as an expected reward or a negative outcome that you want to avoid. If you study hard because you enjoy the feeling of success, then you're motivated for intrinsic reasons. If you study hard because you need to maintain a 3.0 GPA to keep your scholarship, then you're motivated for extrinsic reasons.

Both types of motivators can prompt you to meet your goals, but intrinsic motivation has some special benefits over extrinsic motivation. First, intrinsic motivation is usually more reliable because you control it. How? You stay focused on the positive feelings you'll experience when you achieve the goal, and that keeps you motivated. Also, intrinsic motivation is especially helpful in unfamiliar or confusing situations—like your first year in college. Your professors assign course material, but they may not tell you *how* to learn it. You have to figure that out, and intrinsic motivation can spur you on.

The more you know about yourself—your goals, interests, and values—the more you can tap into your intrinsic motivation by seeing how a goal or task is relevant to who you are and what you want. When you understand what makes *you* tick, you can figure out how to keep yourself moving forward.

But how can you find an approach to building intrinsic motivation that works for you? There are many approaches and lots of people giving advice about the best ways. Many techniques are covered in this chapter: using positive self-talk, identifying positive outcomes associated with your effort, and finding something interesting in challenging situations. Leaders of industry, professional athletes, psychologists, salespeople,

Congratulations, Future Self!
One way to build intrinsic motivation is to visualize yourself accomplishing a goal that is important to you — for example, getting your degree or certificate. So paint a positive mental picture to cheer yourself on, and remember: You're working hard for a reason. GILKIS - Damon Hyland/Getty Images

STAYING MOTIVATED IN COLLEGE

Courtesy
J. Altdorfer
Photography

NAME:	**Erin Smith**
SCHOOL:	*Chatham University*
MAJOR:	*Foundations of Higher Education and Student Affairs*
CAREER GOAL:	*Working in a college or university to support student success*

I'm in my sophomore year, and I'm currently feeling unmotivated in some of my classes. I want to pursue a master's degree that will prepare me to work with college students at a university. I'm so happy that I found my passion early in my undergraduate years, but sometimes it makes it hard for me to focus on classes that seem unrelated to my professional goals.

For example, it's sometimes difficult for me to see how my Shakespeare class relates to my interest in higher education institutions and student learning. However, even if I don't immediately recognize a connection between each course and my professional goals, gaining new knowledge intrinsically motivates me. I know that I'm learning important skills in every class, such as how to manage my time, take notes, think critically, and reduce stress. In addition to developing these skills, I'm learning more about complicated issues such as gender, race, class, and identity. I can then apply what I've learned about these issues to my work with college students. In the future I'll appreciate what I learned in these classes and how I've developed as a well-rounded, lifelong learner.

It can be tough to stay disciplined and remain focused in classes that don't strongly capture your interests. But if you connect your passions to each of your courses, it's easier to find something meaningful in every class you take.

YOUR TURN: Do you use particular strategies to connect seemingly irrelevant courses to something you're passionate about? If so, what are those strategies?

> " **If you connect your passions to each of your courses, it's easier to find something meaningful in every class you take."**

Navy SEALs, and others often use another powerful technique—visualization.[6] In visualization you imagine the outcome you'd like to happen and the steps in getting there using all your senses, including sight, sound, smell, and feel. Visualizing a desirable outcome can stir positive emotions and motivate you to work hard. It prompts you to think about your values, the relevance of your goals, and the steps needed to reach them. You'll have a chance to try a visualization activity at the end of the chapter.

Make Good Decisions

In your school, work, and personal life, you might make hundreds of decisions every day. Some choices are straightforward and quick, like selecting tuna over turkey for lunch. Others are more complex, with higher stakes. For example, should you stay in school even if your spouse isn't supportive? Should you buy a car to get to class even though you're already carrying heavy credit card debt? What major will you declare? The outcomes of the choices you make, along with the complexity or difficulty of such choices, can affect your motivation. And your level of motivation can ultimately influence whether you achieve the goals that have personal meaning for you.

With tough choices, you need to weigh your options carefully, but you also have to move forward. If you obsess about making a "perfect decision," you can fall victim to "analysis paralysis," which can sap your motivation and leave you feeling hopeless about selecting a course of action.

How do you make a reasonable decision, especially if you're feeling overwhelmed or frightened by a choice you're facing? Try the following steps, which have a lot in common with the steps in the Personal Success Plan. (See also Figure 3.2 and Table 3.1.)

1. **Identify the decision to be made.** Articulating the decision sets the stage for the rest of the process.
2. **Know yourself.** Identify your strengths, weaknesses, interests, and values. This self-knowledge helps you think broadly about your options.
3. **Identify your options.** With a friend, colleague, or family member, brainstorm options available to you and write them down on a sheet of paper.
4. **Gather information about each option.** Research the details of each option you've listed, such as what actions you'd need to take if you chose that option and who could help you take those actions.

5. **Evaluate your options.** List the pros and cons of each option. Rate each option based on how attractive it is to you and how it will affect the people who are important to you.
6. **Select the best option.** The option with the highest rating is your most reasonable choice. If you feel nervous about committing to this choice, remind yourself that you can always change your mind later if the decision doesn't work out as well as you had hoped.
7. **Develop and implement an action plan.** List the actions you'll take to follow through on your decision. Then take those actions.
8. **Evaluate the outcomes of your decision.** Determine whether your decision has worked out. If not, follow this eight-step process again to arrive at a new decision.

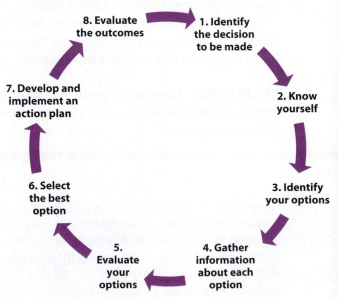

FIGURE 3.2
The Decision-Making Process

1. Identify the decision to be made
2. Know yourself
3. Identify your options
4. Gather information about each option
5. Evaluate your options
6. Select the best option
7. Develop and implement an action plan
8. Evaluate the outcomes

TABLE 3.1 Examples of the Decision-Making Process

Step	Example 1	Example 2
Identify the decision to be made	I need to select a major.	My mom is sick in another country. Should I leave school to take care of her, or should I continue my studies?
Know yourself	I love history, art, music, and literature, but I'm not an artist or a musician. I enjoy interacting with people. I value family, so I don't want to work sixty hours a week. I may want to work in an art museum or possibly in arts management.	I value my family and my education. I'm the oldest of three, so my mom relies on me a lot. I'm also the first in my family to go to college, which is a point of pride for my loved ones. I'm torn between these responsibilities.
Identify your options	I'm considering a major in art history, finance, business, or psychology. Taking various electives is also an option.	I called my brother back home and discussed options: take a year off from school to help Mom; stay in school and my brother will care for Mom; move Mom to a medical facility near home; or hire a visiting nurse to care for Mom twice a day.
Gather information about each option	I'll learn more by meeting with my academic adviser, visiting the career-center library, and interviewing recent graduates who are working in museums and the entertainment industry.	I'll research the answers to some key questions: If I take time off from school, when do I have to come back? Could I keep all my credits? How much would care in a medical facility cost?
Evaluate your options	The information I gathered suggests that art history and business could prepare me for jobs in the arts. But with both majors, I'll have to study aspects of art that don't interest me and take two accounting courses.	Taking a year off from school would make things tough for me. My brother works full-time to support our family, so it will be hard for him to care for Mom. Mom loves her home, so it would be difficult for her to move to a medical facility. Hiring a visiting nurse would let me stay in school and ensure regular care for Mom. It's pricey, though, and two visits a day may not be enough.
Select the best option	I'll major in art history but take electives in business and management.	Balancing all these factors, we'll have a nurse visit Mom twice a day.
Develop and implement an action plan	I'll declare my major and meet with my new art history academic adviser to create a course plan.	My brother lives near Mom, so he'll interview nurse candidates. My brother and I will split the costs. We'll both ask several of Mom's friends to check in on her at least once a day.
Evaluate the outcomes of your decision	I've taken courses in my major for one term and I like them, but my gut tells me that declaring a business major will give me the most options after graduation. I'll need to do more career research before I'm comfortable with my decision.	This arrangement has worked out well. Mom's nurse and friends check in on her during the day, and my brother comes by after work whenever he can. I'm doing well in school, but I really miss Mom—I can't wait to visit her during the next school break.

Take Personal Responsibility for Your Education

Taking personal responsibility for your education is empowering. It puts *you* in control of maintaining your motivation and making smart choices. For instance, if you don't see why a particular assignment is important, *you* can find reasons to care. If you keep missing class, *you* can set two alarms so you'll wake up on time. If friends want you to go out the night before a test, *you* can say no.

By taking responsibility in these ways, you drive your learning and your personal growth. You also prove to yourself that you value your education, and you show respect for your instructors and the classmates who depend on you to complete group projects and assignments. Taking responsibility for our actions isn't always easy, but every college student—and every professional in the workplace—needs to do it. Here are four ways you can get started.

Develop a Growth Mind-set

Stanford University psychologist Carol Dweck proposes that there are two types of students. Those with a **growth mind-set** believe they can improve and further develop their skills.[7] They assume personal responsibility for their success and learn as much as they can from their failures.

By contrast, students with a **fixed mind-set** believe they can't improve their talents, skills, and abilities, and they tend to see themselves as victims of circumstance. Take Maya, who turned in a project late and was penalized one letter grade. She blamed work and family demands for missing the deadline. She didn't reflect on her behaviors or learn how to manage her time more effectively; as a result, she continued to struggle.

When you have a growth mind-set, you take responsibility for setbacks rather than blame others for them. You examine the behaviors that led to the failure, identify what you could have done differently, and apply those lessons to the next situation. For example, if Maya had adopted a growth

Keep a Growth Mind-set. When you have a growth mind-set, you're willing to see setbacks and disappointments from a whole new angle. Instead of coming up with excuses or blaming others for failures, you look for the lessons hidden in these experiences — such as what you can do differently in the future to get a better result. serg_dibrova/Shutterstock

mind-set after losing a letter grade, she might have identified behavior changes to make in the future, such as exchanging work shifts as a deadline approaches or working on assignments when her children are in school.

If you blame others for setbacks, you miss an opportunity to become more competent by learning how you can improve in the future. Adopting a growth mind-set is a win-win situation: When you fail, you take steps to improve, and when you succeed, you get to take credit for your success. Either way, you become a better student and get more value from your education.

Take an Active Approach to Your Learning

If your high school was like many, it had a passive learning environment. Teachers were considered experts who imparted knowledge, and students memorized the information that was presented. By contrast, most colleges encourage *active learning*, in which instructors create a learning environment but students are expected to think critically about course material, engage in classroom discussion and debate, and apply their knowledge and skills to real-world problems and settings. To foster a growth mind-set, embrace active learning. Instead of simply attending class and listening to your instructor, identify and use *learning strategies*—methods for mastering important course material.

As you read this book, you'll find dozens of active learning strategies—from the best ways to schedule your time to tactics for effective note taking and paper writing. Not all strategies work in all situations, but if you experiment, you'll figure out which ones work best for you with each course and assignment. In the meantime, get a head start by giving these suggestions a try.

1. **Get involved.** Asking questions in class can help clarify content you find confusing. Briefly summarize what you do understand about the topic; then ask about the parts that are unclear. For instance: "You said that alternative energy sources, like solar or wind, have influenced the debate about global warming. But can you please describe the scientific research going on in those areas?" Form or join study groups to discuss assignments, brainstorm possible test questions, or debate ideas you're learning about in class.

2. **Look for connections.** What you learn in one class often relates to something you're learning in another or to an experience you've had in the past. Connecting new, unfamiliar material to other material is a powerful active learning strategy. When you make such connections, you're more likely to remember what you've learned,

Active Learning, Personal Responsibility, and Belief Lead to Success!

As you've discovered by now, your instructors expect you to complete assignments outside of class on a regular basis. Homework assignments help you learn course content. They also encourage you to become a more *independent* and *active* learner. And research suggests that being this kind of learner can boost your odds of succeeding in school.

In fact, recent research helps shed light on a key question about homework: Are students who take responsibility for their homework and who believe in their ability to complete assignments more successful than those who don't? Research findings suggest that the answer to that question is yes. One study surveyed more than two hundred university students to see how responsibly the students made plans to complete homework assignments and how strongly they believed in their ability to finish the assignments.[8] Students with high self-efficacy who actively planned how to complete their assignments

earned significantly higher grades than the other students in the study. They took a series of steps—steps that *you* can take—to set themselves up for success:

- Designating a regular place to study
- Estimating the time needed to complete assignments
- Prioritizing tasks
- Completing assignments on time

In addition, the most successful students believed in their ability to

- Take notes
- Find help when they needed it
- Use many different learning strategies

The bottom line: When you take responsibility for completing assignments and believe in your ability to complete them, you're likely to get the best results.

allowing you to use your new knowledge long after the class ends.

3. **Seek applications for your new knowledge.** Look for ways you can apply what you're learning to your personal life, your current job, or your future career. Applying what you've learned is an important critical-thinking skill and makes the concepts you're learning more concrete.

Navigate the Transition to College Life

We're all accustomed to some degree of personal responsibility in our lives, but in college, personal responsibility is a whole new ballgame. For one thing, in college you probably have a lot more independence—and therefore more responsibility—than you had in high school. (See Table 3.2 for common differences between these environments.) Take Theo. In high school his parents woke him up each morning, and his school days were highly structured. In college it's up to him to set his alarm, go to class, and study for tests. Theo—not anyone else—must structure his own time and make choices that keep him on a path to success.

If you entered college a number of years after graduating from high school, you're probably used to personal responsibility. You may have several years of employment under your belt and have a family to help support. Still, you'll likely find yourself accountable for new kinds of decisions when you start college. Vicky is a good example. A first-year

TABLE 3.2 Common Differences between High School and College

In high school	In college
Your time and schedule was structured by others.	You must manage your time and choose how to spend it.
You were told what to learn and often how to learn it. Learning was teacher focused.	You must figure out what to learn and how to learn it. Learning is student focused.
You needed your parents' permission to participate in extracurricular activities.	You must choose whether to participate in co-curricular activities and which fit best with your academic, personal, and other goals.
You could count on parents and teachers to remind you of your responsibilities and to give regular guidance in setting priorities.	You must set your own priorities and take responsibility for achieving them.
You attended class five days a week and proceeded from one class directly to another.	You often have hours between classes and may not attend classes every day. Much of your work will happen outside of class time.
Most of your classes were determined by school counselors.	You must choose which classes to take in consultation with faculty and academic advisers. Your schedule may look easier than it actually is.
Students are not responsible for knowing what is required to graduate or tracking their own progress.	Students are expected to select their own majors and/or minors and are expected to learn the graduation requirements for their programs of study.
Summary: Students are told what to do and corrected if their behavior is not in line with expectations.	**Summary: Students are expected to take responsibility for their path and academic success, as well as the consequences and rewards of their actions.**

"Common Differences between High School and College." Used by permission of the Altshuler Learning Enhancement Center at Southern Methodist University.

student, Vicky has a job and two young children. She's used to caring for her kids and earning a living, but now she has another responsibility: staying focused on her studies. Only she can decide how to balance her various responsibilities as she pursues her degree.

Think about Thinking and Learning

If you're an active learner, you monitor your learning and adjust your strategies based on your results. You're also aware of how you think and learn. Scholars call this awareness **metacognition**, which means "thinking about thinking" or "thinking about learning." For instance, you're engaging in metacognition if you notice that you have an easier time learning biology than learning European history, if you discover that one study strategy works better for you than another, and every time you reflect on your ACES results.

Research shows that metacognition promotes learning.[9] Students who reflect on their approach to coursework remember more information, apply that information to new situations more effectively, and get higher grades. To make use of metacognition to improve your performance in school, try these strategies.

- **Plan and organize.** Set learning goals, and preview assignments so you can decide how best to approach them.

- **Monitor your progress.** Check your progress against time lines you set for yourself. Troubleshoot problems. Ask yourself whether you're doing your best work or whether you could improve your effort.

- **Evaluate your results and make adjustments.** Consider how well your learning strategies helped you achieve a goal. If you weren't as successful as you had hoped, plan how to change your strategy the next time.

These metacognitive strategies may seem familiar because you've seen many of them before. Critical thinking, goal setting, and decision making also call for you to evaluate your learning, apply new knowledge, reflect on your results, and make changes as needed to get better results. Since these skills are all connected, you can use them over and over again, in any setting.

Take a moment now to assess your metacognitive skills. What are you thinking about as you read this section of the chapter? Are you daydreaming, contemplating all the assignments that are due in your other classes, or pondering what to make for dinner? Or are you considering how these concepts can benefit you, be useful in other courses and assignments, and help your future career? If you reflect on both the *content* you're studying and the *processes* you're using to understand and apply material, you're on your way to becoming an active learner who makes good use of metacognition.

Think Your Thoughts. How do you usually think through class assignments? What study strategies work best for you? When you explore these kinds of questions, you're using metacognition — thinking about how you think and learn. And the more you use it, the greater the chance you'll improve your performance in school.
Blend Images/Peathegee Inc/Getty Images

my personal success plan

Are you inspired to set a new goal aimed at improving your motivation, decision-making skills, or ability to take personal responsibility? If so, the Personal Success Plan can walk you through the goal-setting process. Read the advice and examples; then sketch out your ideas in the space provided.

LaunchPad Solo
macmillan learning

To access the Personal Success Plan online, go to LaunchPad Solo for *Connections Essentials*.

1 GATHER INFORMATION

Think about your strengths and weaknesses related to motivation, decision making, and personal responsibility. What strategies have worked for you in the past? What could you do differently? Revisit your Motivation, Decision Making, and Personal Responsibility score on ACES and review the relevant sections of this chapter for ideas.

2 SET A SMART GOAL

Use the information you've gathered to create a SMART goal, making sure to use the SMART goal checklist.

SAMPLE: I'm struggling to stay motivated in my sociology class. By the end of the week, I'll figure out how to make the course content more relevant to my interests and goals.

3 MAKE AN ACTION PLAN

Outline the specific steps you'll take to achieve your SMART goal, and note when you'll complete each step.

SAMPLE: Tomorrow, I'll ask my instructor if I can write my term paper on a topic I'm passionate about: factors that cause economic inequality.

4 LIST BARRIERS AND SOLUTIONS

Think about possible barriers to your action steps; then brainstorm solutions for overcoming them.

SAMPLE: My instructor might reject my term paper idea. If she does, I'll explain my areas of interest to see if there's another topic that I'm just as passionate about that would meet the course requirements.

5 ACT AND EVALUATE OUTCOMES

Now that your plan is in place, take action. Record each action step as you take it. Then evaluate whether you achieved your SMART goal, and make any adjustments needed to get better results in the future.

SAMPLE: My instructor and I were able to identify several alternative topics that interest me and would meet the course requirements.

6 CONNECT TO CAREER

List the skills you're building as you progress toward your SMART goal. How will you use these skills to land a job and succeed at work?

SAMPLE: I'm learning more about my interests and how to incorporate them into my coursework. These skills could help me work with a supervisor to design job responsibilities that appeal to these interests.

1 my information

2 my SMART goal

☐ **S**PECIFIC ☐ **M**EASURABLE ☐ **A**CHIEVABLE ☐ **R**ELEVANT ☐ **T**IME-LIMITED

3 my action plan

4 my barriers/ solutions

5 my actions/ outcomes

6 my career connection

Chapter 3 Review

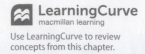

LearningCurve
macmillan learning

Use LearningCurve to review concepts from this chapter.

- Three key components of motivation are *self-efficacy*, or your belief in your ability to carry out the actions needed to reach a particular goal; the *relevance* of a goal to you; and your *attitude* toward the goal. The stronger these components are, the more motivated you'll feel to work toward the goal.

- You can be motivated by either intrinsic rewards or extrinsic rewards, but intrinsic motivators tend to be more powerful.

- The eight-step decision-making process can help you transform your motivation into action by making careful choices.

- To take personal responsibility for your learning, you can develop a growth mindset, take an active approach to learning, successfully navigate the transition to college, and use metacognition.

CHAPTER ACTIVITIES

Adopting a Success Attitude

VISUALIZING SUCCESS

Try this short activity to help you reflect on your motivation for being in college.

1. Find a quiet, peaceful place where you can be alone. Close your eyes and breathe in deeply through your nose. Hold for a count of three, and then breathe out through your mouth. Repeat this process until your mind clears.

2. Imagine yourself in a graduation gown walking across the stage to receive your diploma. As you walk off the stage, a reporter asks if she can interview you for a "graduation success story." You agree. Think about how you would respond to her questions: "What does this accomplishment mean to you? How did you stay motivated when the going got tough? How will your life change now that you have this degree?"

3. Translate your thoughts and feelings about getting your degree into action steps. What three actions could you take this week to help make this graduation scenario come true?

Applying Your Skills

MONITORING, EVALUATING, AND ADJUSTING FOR COLLEGE SUCCESS

When you monitor your progress, evaluate the results of your strategies, and adjust your strategies as needed, you take responsibility for your learning. Let's practice these skills.

Monitoring Progress Pretend that you're the instructor of this course and that you have to assign yourself a letter grade as a student. Give yourself a grade that honestly reflects three criteria: your attitude, effort, and results up to this point in the term.

Evaluating Results Explain why you gave yourself this grade by responding to the following questions:

1. How would you describe your attitude toward this class? How might you consciously or unconsciously convey this attitude toward your actual instructor?

2. What kind of effort have you put into this course so far?

3. What results have you achieved in this class up to this point? Results can include quiz grades, class attendance, participation, and assignments turned in on time.

Making Adjustments Give yourself both positive and constructive feedback on your attitude, effort, and results. What are you doing well? What adjustments will you make this week to improve your performance?

4

Understanding Learning

Learning That Works: What the Research Tells Us

Make Learning Personal

Succeed in Different Learning Environments

MY PERSONAL SUCCESS PLAN

As a student, you're learning all the time, about all kinds of things. You're learning about yourself as you progress from your first term to graduation. And you're learning material in different subject areas as you work toward your certificate or degree.

It's difficult to succeed in college without understanding how to learn, and that's why this chapter is all about learning: what science tells us about learning, what we know about our own preferences for learning, and how we can use what we know to succeed in many different environments. As you read, you'll have the chance to think *metacognitively* about yourself as a learner, as well as target different strategies you can use

to succeed. Both of these activities will help you become more self-aware and self-directed in college, and they'll also serve you well in your career, where you'll constantly be working with new information.

We begin this chapter by looking at what research tells us about learning — including which strategies are useful for everyone. We'll then look at two ways to classify your own personal learning preferences: the Myers-Briggs Type Indicator (MBTI) and the VARK (Visual, Aural, Read-Write, and Kinesthetic) model. Finally, we'll consider best practices for succeeding in a variety of learning environments — including those that go outside your comfort zone.

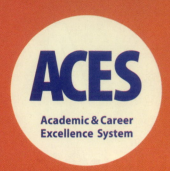

ACES
**Academic & Career
Excellence System**

To find your
**Learning Preferences
score,** go to LaunchPad
Solo for *Connections
Essentials.*

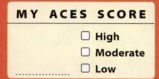

MY ACES SCORE

☐ **High**
☐ **Moderate**
☐ **Low**

REFLECTION:
Your Learning Preferences

Take a moment to reflect on your Learning Preferences score on ACES. Find your score and add it to the box on the left.

This score measures your beliefs about how well you understand your learning preferences. Do you think it's an accurate snapshot of your understanding? Why or why not?

- **IF YOU SCORED IN THE HIGH RANGE** and you feel that this score is accurate, you may have a solid understanding of how you learn. Put that information to good use in your classes and when you study. As you read this chapter, be on the lookout for new techniques you can use to learn information. Seize the opportunity to hone your existing learning strategies *and* develop new strategies.

- **IF YOU SCORED IN THE MODERATE OR LOW RANGE**, now is the perfect time to discover more about your learning preferences. Let's say you took up juggling as a way to relieve stress. Though you probably couldn't keep all the balls in the air the first time, chances are that the more you practiced, the better you got. Most people don't fully understand their learning preferences right away, but with time and practice they become more self-aware. Use this chapter to learn more about yourself and which strategies can work for you.

ACES Journal

Think about the learning strategies you use now in the classes you're taking. Do some of those strategies work better than others? Do different strategies work in different classes? Take a minute to write down which strategies are working, which courses they are working in, and why you think they're so successful.

_____

_____

_____

_____

_____

_____

Learning That Works: What the Research Tells Us

Scientists have been studying how we learn for over one hundred years, and they've discovered that not all learning strategies are created equal. For example, which of the following strategies do you think is more effective in helping you learn new material: recopying your notes in the evening after you get home from class or creating your own practice tests that cover the material you're expected to learn? As it turns out, creating your own practice tests is more effective, and we know this because of recent research on learning.[1]

In this section, we'll review *learning science*—the study of how we learn, including which learning strategies are most effective—and we'll focus on top strategies that research shows are useful for many people in many settings. These techniques will empower you to learn and remember material—both in the classroom and beyond.

Test Yourself

As a student, you have a considerable amount of experience taking tests—primarily, tests that are written by instructors to evaluate how much class material you've learned. But there's also another type of testing that every student should use on a regular basis: self-testing. Self-testing is the process of creating practice tests for yourself, outside class, as a means of studying, and research shows that you can use this method to create longer-lasting learning in a wide variety of subject areas.

If creating your own tests sounds complicated, fear not: It doesn't have to be. One method of self-testing that's both easy and effective is creating flash cards (see Figure 4.1). If you're studying a foreign language and trying to learn vocabulary, for example, create a set of flash cards with the foreign word on the

FIGURE 4.1
Flash Cards for Self-Testing

front and the English translation on the back. Prompt yourself to provide either the English translation or the foreign word, and get immediate feedback by flipping the card over to see if you're correct. Then be sure to review the cards periodically to make sure the learning sticks.

Self-tests can be used in other classes as well, and you can use different methods to create them. If you're trying to learn anatomy, for example, make a photocopy of a picture in your book and white out the correct labels to create an effective self-test. You can also try your hand at creating your own multiple-choice, short-answer, or essay tests to assess your learning in other subjects. And don't hesitate to make this a team effort: If you pair up with another student, you can each create your own tests and then exchange them with one another to assess your knowledge of the concepts.

What is it about self-testing that makes it so effective? For one thing, this method helps you learn the correct answers to test items — that's clearly a good thing! In addition, it forces you to think more deeply about the material — deeply enough to create items for your test. It also prompts you to consider what information your instructor has identified as most important (that is, which concepts should be tested in the first place) and how to understand similarities and differences between closely related content, like competing theories or perspectives.

Space Out Your Studying

You've probably heard the term *all-nighter*, which usually refers to a frantic, last-ditch effort to cram for an exam or prepare a paper the night before it's due. By definition, all-nighters deprive you of sleep at a time when your brain needs to rest and process the learning that occurred that day. Further, any illusion that you've found your second

Room to Breathe. "Cramming" right before a test is like trying to pack a lot of luggage into a very small space: Chances are, not everything you need is going to fit. Instead, give yourself some breathing room: Space your studying out over multiple days and weeks and you'll find that you're a lot less anxious — and a lot better at remembering what you've learned. Laurence Dutton/Getty Images

wind when the sun comes up is just that—an illusion. You're exhausted and probably very anxious. Needless to say, this isn't the best way to approach learning, and it won't get you the best results.

Research strongly supports the idea that *distributed studying* is the best method to promote long-term learning. Distributed studying involves spacing your studying out over multiple days or weeks. For example, you'd be better off studying for your American history midterm 2 hours a week for six weeks (a total of 12 hours) than you would be staying up all night studying the evening before your exam (approximately 10–12 hours).

When researchers investigated why distributed studying works, they came up with a couple of possible explanations. According to one theory, when you study over multiple days or weeks, each study session occurs in a different context—in a different place or during a different time of the day—and this is beneficial because the more you vary the contexts in which you learn, the more likely it is that the learning will stick. A second compelling theory suggests that when you study on multiple occasions, you're able to retrieve what you learned in previous sessions and use it to facilitate and provide structure for the learning in your current study session. To put this simply, the learning sessions are interdependent (they inform one another) and thus they're more effective.[2]

Change Up Your Material

Research shows that if you mix up what you're learning on a regular basis, switching between different topics rather than focusing on only one topic, you may learn more effectively.[3] For example, if you're studying for an accounting exam that will cover principles of expense, revenue, and gross and net profit, don't wait till you've mastered the principles of expenses before you move on to studying revenues and profits. Instead, create a study plan in which you move regularly from one of these concepts to the others and back again. The official name for this technique is *interleaved practice*, since the most common definition of the term *interleave* is "to insert alternatively and regularly between the parts of something else."[4]

Interleaved practice appears to be particularly helpful when you're learning concepts that will eventually be connected (such as calculation of gross and net profit). Why? Because when you constantly move from one topic to another related topic, you're better able to see the similarities and differences between them. This method of studying can also be powerful if you're taking multiple classes on different topics and you intermix your studying for these classes. For example, if you're taking accounting and literature, consider studying accounting for an hour and then taking a break to read one of your literature assignments. You might find that you understand accounting principles better when they're interspersed with some *Macbeth*.

Make Connections So Learning Lasts

You can make lasting memories of new information by linking what you're studying to your own life, to memories you already have, or to information you already know. Making connections helps strengthen your understanding of new material and may even enhance your understanding of the information you're already familiar with. Further, brain science suggests that when you connect information mentally, you're actually causing new connections to form between brain cells—and those connections are what cause learning.[5]

According to research, there are a number of learning techniques that appear to help you connect current learning with prior learning. We'll explore two of them below.

Ask "Why?" *Elaborative interrogation* is a learning strategy that involves asking yourself an important question: "Why?"[6] This method of self-questioning appears to be particularly useful for learning factual information, and it's more effective when you already have a basic familiarity with the content you're trying to learn (as opposed to when you're learning brand-new facts) because it helps you make connections between old and new information.

For example, let's say that you're in a physiology class and you need to remember a key fact: Arteries are thicker and more elastic than veins. Let's also suppose that you already know a little bit about circulation—for instance, that arteries carry recently oxygenated blood from the heart to the organs of the body and the heart pumps in spurts. If you ask yourself a "why" question ("Why are arteries thicker and more elastic than veins?"), your basic knowledge about arteries might prompt you to reach the following well-reasoned conclusion: "We need larger and more elastic arteries to accommodate the varying rhythms of our heart—for example, how our heart beats at rest versus during a 5k running race." In this example, you've connected new facts with other facts that you're already familiar with, which makes you more likely to remember what you're learning.

Engage in Self-Explanation. *Self-explanation* involves asking yourself questions or generating examples related to what you're learning.[7] Self-explanation prompts you to consider your own thinking and learning, which makes it a *metacognitive* activity. To use self-explanation, you might find yourself asking questions like "Do I have all the information I need to compare and contrast these two competing perspectives? If not, where can I find that information?" Or you might ask, "How does this new information relate to what I already know about the concepts being learned?"

The use of examples is another way to engage in self-explanation. Have you ever noticed that your textbooks and instructors use examples to help you learn new concepts? That's because examples help you put learning in context and promote the generalization of what you are learning to different situations. Creating your *own* examples can be a powerful method for learning new material.

The simple act of engaging in self-explanation can be helpful because, as with asking why, it encourages you to connect new material to your existing knowledge. It also causes you to slow down your learning process, thus prompting you to become more intentional (metacognitive) about your learning. And it encourages you to think critically about what you're learning and ask questions about what can be learned next.

Use Verbal *and* Visual Information

Later in this chapter, we'll describe how some people prefer processing information using language (for example, verbally or through reading and writing), while others prefer learning visually (by looking at diagrams or creating mental images of what they're learning). As it turns out, no matter what your preferences are, doing both might help you learn even better.[8] Verbal information and visual information are processed differently by the brain—to some extent, they're even processed in different parts of the brain. According to one theory, called *dual coding*, learning is strengthened by making connections between the visual and the language portions of our brains.

Consider the example from the last section—learning about the elasticity of arteries. When you read that example, did you create a mental image of a rapidly beating heart and envision how the arteries coming from the heart could expand and contract to accommodate blood flow? If you did, you were using both language and visual imagery to learn simultaneously, and as a result, you'll probably remember this fact better. In a later section we'll provide other examples of how it's beneficial to develop *multimodal*, or flexible, learning strategies like this.

Your Brain Is Required for Learning!

The statement above may seem self-evident: Of course your brain is required for learning! But let's dig a bit deeper into this very important relationship. Specifically, let's take a closer look at what decades of cognitive neuroscience research have revealed about the brain, how it works, and how it helps you learn.

- **Your brain cells are organized in interconnected systems and pathways.** Learning occurs when new connections between cells and across systems are established.[9] That happens when you sit in a class lecture, engage other students in dialogue, take notes, read your text, and use the learning strategies described in this section of the book.

- **More information isn't necessarily better.** Research suggests that having more information doesn't necessarily result in more learning.[10] The term *cognitive overload* describes the point at which more information is detrimental to learning — when your brain just can't divide its attention between all the different elements presented to it. Minimize distractions while you learn and practice recognizing the point at which "a lot" becomes "too much" — and if you reach that point, take a break and come back later.

- **Learning is a lifelong endeavor.** Recent research also suggests that the brain is a dynamic organ.[11] People used to believe that the number of brain cells you had in your life was fixed by the time you were a teenager.

Scientists now know that the brain can grow new cells and that new connections between cells (learning) can happen across your entire life span. Take a lifelong approach to learning because you *can*.

- **Your emotions influence your ability to learn.**[12] If you're too stressed-out, your brain will inhibit your ability to learn new material. Interestingly, though, a small to moderate amount of stress may facilitate learning new information. The key is to keep an eye on how stressed you are and look for ways to alleviate stress that is too severe.

- **Mistakes lead to learning.** Have you ever heard that you can learn from your mistakes? Well, science supports this age-old idea,[13] which is captured in a famous quote by educational philosopher John Dewey: "Failure is instructive. The person who really thinks learns quite as much from his failures as from his successes." Neuroscience research, however, suggests it's not helpful to dwell on your mistakes, because doing so further reinforces incorrect brain pathways; rather, you should focus on how to complete the task at hand correctly.

- **Bored? Try something new.** Research tells us that boredom is not conducive to learning.[14] To promote learning you'll need motivation and novelty — for example, think about new ways of approaching your learning or new applications of things you already know.

Make Learning Personal

Now that you're familiar with what science says about effective learning, it's time to think more deeply about your own preferences for learning and the preferences of others around you—including your classmates, your colleagues at work, and even your instructors. Most students can identify ways that they prefer to learn, if given the choice. For example, you might love attending lectures and taking notes but feel less enthusiastic about a group discussion or group project. Alternatively, you might prefer focusing on "big picture" concepts before tackling the details—or vice versa.

While these preferences exist, however, it's important to note that our ability to learn isn't *limited* by these preferences. In fact, there is little evidence for the idea that you actually learn better using your preferred styles of learning—or even that you learn better when someone teaches according to your preferences.[15] Preferences aren't a specific prescription for learning, and we shouldn't treat them as such; rather, they're important because of what they teach us about ourselves, about people we interact with, and about the learning environments in which we find ourselves. Different classes will require different types of learning, different teachers will structure their classes different ways, and different classmates and group members will bring different preferences to the table. When you understand what preferences involve, and how they work, you're prepared to learn as effectively as possible in many different kinds of environments. In other words, understanding your own (and others') preferences for learning helps you stay flexible, self-aware, and responsive in different learning situations.

In the section that follows, we'll look at two different models you can use to better understand how you prefer to learn: the Myers-Briggs Type Indicator (MBTI) and the VARK (Visual, Aural, Read-Write, and Kinesthetic) model. You can use each of these instruments, or both in combination, to identify your learning preferences. In fact,

evaluating your results from both can give you valuable insights that can, in turn, help you develop effective learning strategies.

Use the Myers-Briggs Model

Katharine Briggs and her daughter Isabel Myers created the MBTI based on the work of psychologist Carl Jung. In Jung's theory, four dimensions of our personalities guide our behavior, influencing where we focus our energy, the kinds of information we prefer working with, how we make decisions, and how we organize our time and activities. Each of the four dimensions—Extravert/Introvert, Sensing/Intuitive, Thinking/Feeling, and Judging/Perceiving—can be thought of as a continuum.[16]

Extravert/Introvert. The Extravert/Introvert dimension describes where you tend to focus your energy. Extraverts are action oriented and like spending time with others. Being with people energizes them, and they often learn best by interacting and discussing their learning with others or by applying their learning to real-life problems.

By contrast, Introverts are more thought oriented and are energized by spending time alone. Introverts often prefer to learn through reflection and feel most comfortable discussing ideas once they've had a chance to think about them. They can still work effectively in groups, but they may want time to process new information before they feel prepared to discuss it with others.

Sensing/Intuitive. The Sensing/Intuitive dimension relates to the kind of information you prefer working with: the details and facts or the big picture. Sensing learners prefer working with information as it comes to them through their senses. They love details and facts and have an easy time remembering and organizing such information. They choose to focus on "what is" rather than on "what might be," and they enjoy making connections

What's Your Sense of Snow? Suppose you've never seen snow before. If you're a Sensing learner, you'd probably look at the snowflakes (the details) first as a way to understand the concept of a snowstorm (the big picture). If you're an Intuitive learner, you'd pay attention to the snowstorm and then use your understanding of it to grasp the concept of individual snowflakes. *Left:* Kichigin/Shutterstock *Right:* Creative Travel Projects/Shutterstock

between seemingly unrelated pieces of information. Sensing learners use the facts to build an understanding of the big picture.

By contrast, Intuitive learners prefer to pay attention to facts and details only long enough to understand the big picture—the theory behind the concept or how the concept connects to other material. They focus on the possibilities ("what might be") rather than on just the facts. They like to get an overview of a topic before digging into the specifics and want to know answers to broad questions, such as "How does this topic relate to the last topic presented in class?"

Thinking/Feeling. The Thinking/Feeling dimension relates to how you make decisions. Thinking decision makers prefer to use analysis and logic to arrive at a decision. By contrast, Feeling decision makers tend to make choices that maintain harmony or that demonstrate concern about human values and needs.

Being a Thinking learner or a Feeling learner can influence how you react during the various steps in the decision-making process (see the chapter on motivation, decision making, and personal responsibility). When evaluating the available options and weighing the pros and cons of each alternative,

Thinkers may focus on the option that has more pros, whereas Feelers may concentrate on how the decision will affect the important people in their lives.

Judging/Perceiving. The Judging/Perceiving dimension describes how you organize your time and activities. Judging learners plan the details of their actions before proceeding, focus on actions that directly contribute to achievement of a goal or task, and generally have structured routines. They prefer making decisions and sticking with them and like to complete one project before starting another.

Perceiving learners are more comfortable taking action without first developing a plan. They multitask and juggle different projects at once and prefer keeping their options open rather than committing to a decision.

Your Preferences. Now that you're familiar with the four dimensions of the MBTI, take a moment to record where you think you fall on each dimension. Using Figure 4.2, place an X on each line to designate your preference and how strong you think it is. For example, an X far to the right on the Extravert/Introvert line would indicate that you have a strong

	Strong Preference	Moderate Preference	Neutral	Moderate Preference	Strong Preference	
Spend time with people Learn through discussion Share ideas in the moment	**Extravert**				**Introvert**	Prefer time alone Learn through reflection Think about ideas before sharing
Focus on details Prefer facts Focus on "what is"	**Sensing**				**Intuitive**	Focus on big picture Prefer concepts Focus on "what might be"
Consider facts when making decisions Make decisions based on logic Decide with my head	**Thinking**				**Feeling**	Consider people when making decisions Make decisions based on values Decide with my heart
Like coming to decisions Like structure Like to plan	**Judging**				**Perceiving**	Avoid decisions in favor of exploring options Go with the flow Comfortable without a plan

FIGURE 4.2   Myers-Briggs Self-Rating Chart

Introvert preference, whereas an X far to the left would show a strong Extravert preference. An X somewhere in the middle would suggest a more moderate or a neutral preference.

Once you've recorded your self-rating, ask yourself: How can I use this information to become a better learner in all my classes? If you're an Extravert, for example, you might try joining a study group that lets you share ideas with others. If you're a Feeling learner, you might find ways to make course material more relevant to your life, so you feel more personally connected. And if you're a Judging learner who likes to keep your materials organized, you might find it helpful to create binders for each of your classes. Knowing more about your preferences isn't meant to define how you *must* learn, but it can help you try out strategies that you may not have considered previously.

Use the VARK Model

The VARK is another model that can help you understand how you prefer to learn.

Proposed by Neil Fleming, a high school and university teacher, VARK describes what types of information people prefer to work with while learning[17]—**V**isual, **A**ural (auditory), **R**ead-Write, and **K**inesthetic (hands on, action based). Many people feel comfortable working with more than one of these types of information. As you read the descriptions of each preference, consider which one(s) fits you best.

Visual (V). Visual learners prefer working with information that comes in such forms as charts, diagrams, maps, and graphs. They may translate material presented in class into concept maps, flowcharts, or other graphic forms to better understand course concepts and see how they relate to each other.

Aural (A). Aural learners prefer working with information that comes in auditory forms, such as lectures, podcasts, and discussions with others. In class, for example, Aural learners might ask to record their instructors' lectures, so they have the opportunity to listen again later.

Learning by Doing. The people hanging from these poles are taking a climbing course offered by a utility company. They're students at a workforce institute affiliated with a nearby community college. The three-week course supports kinesthetic learning — learning by doing. Students master skills that will prepare them to compete for jobs in the utility industry, such as pre-apprentice lineworker. Justin Sullivan/Getty Images

Read-Write (R). Read-Write learners prefer learning from the written word. They may read a lot, use text-heavy slide presentations, and seek out books and journal articles using popular online sources such as Google Scholar. They may prefer to study by reading through important material, revising and reorganizing class notes, or preparing brief written responses to anticipated essay questions.

Kinesthetic (K). Kinesthetic learners prefer experience and practice as a means of learning. They learn by doing or by watching others, and they enjoy watching demonstrations, trying their hand at simulations, analyzing case studies, and conducting lab experiments.

The VARK Questionnaire. Now that you understand the VARK model, you can assess your preferences using the VARK dimensions. Take a few minutes to respond to the items on the following pages and score your

assessment. Place a check mark next to all the answers that apply to you; you can choose more than one response per question, or you can leave the question blank if none of the responses apply to you.

Keep in mind that your score in each learning preference category (V, A, R, and K) represents the strength of your preference for that type of information. Some students have clear preferences (for example, **V = 11**, A= 3, R = 1, K = 1), while other students' preferences are more evenly distributed (for instance, V = 2, A = 1, **R = 6, K = 7**).

Once you have your results, reflect on them. What is your highest score? Does that learning preference make sense to you based on your understanding of yourself? Do you have two or three scores that are relatively close together? If so, what are they? How might this new understanding of yourself help you learn and study for different types of classes?

VARK Questionnaire

1. You are helping someone who wants to go to your airport, the center of town, or a railway station. You would:
   - ☐ **A.** go with her.
   - ☐ **B.** tell her the directions.
   - ☐ **C.** write down the directions.
   - ☐ **D.** draw, or show her a map, or give her a map.

2. A Web site has a video showing how to make a special graph. There is a person speaking, some lists and words describing what to do, and some diagrams. You would learn most from:
   - ☐ **A.** seeing the diagrams.
   - ☐ **B.** listening.
   - ☐ **C.** reading the words.
   - ☐ **D.** watching the actions.

3. You are planning a vacation for a group. You want some feedback from them about the plan. You would:
   - ☐ **A.** describe some of the highlights they will experience.
   - ☐ **B.** use a map to show them the places.
   - ☐ **C.** give them a copy of the printed itinerary.
   - ☐ **D.** phone, text, or e-mail them.

4. You are going to cook something as a special treat. You would:
   - ☐ **A.** cook something you know without the need for instructions.
   - ☐ **B.** ask friends for suggestions.
   - ☐ **C.** look on the Internet or in some cookbooks for ideas from the pictures.
   - ☐ **D.** use a cookbook where you know there is a good recipe.

5. A group of tourists wants to learn about the parks or wildlife reserves in your area. You would:
   - ☐ **A.** talk about, or arrange a talk for them about, parks or wildlife reserves.
   - ☐ **B.** show them maps and Internet pictures.
   - ☐ **C.** take them to a park or wildlife reserve and walk with them.
   - ☐ **D.** give them a book or pamphlets about the parks or wildlife reserves.

6. You are about to purchase a digital camera or mobile phone. Other than price, what would most influence your decision?
   - ☐ **A.** Trying or testing it.
   - ☐ **B.** Reading the details or checking its features online.
   - ☐ **C.** It is a modern design and looks good.
   - ☐ **D.** The salesperson telling me about its features.

7. Remember a time when you learned how to do something new. Avoid choosing a physical skill, e.g., riding a bike. You learned best by:
   - ☐ **A.** watching a demonstration.
   - ☐ **B.** listening to somebody explaining it and asking questions.
   - ☐ **C.** diagrams, maps, and charts — visual clues.
   - ☐ **D.** written instructions — e.g., a manual or book.

8. You have a problem with your heart. You would prefer that the doctor:
   - ☐ **A.** gave you something to read to explain what was wrong.
   - ☐ **B.** used a plastic model to show what was wrong.
   - ☐ **C.** described what was wrong.
   - ☐ **D.** showed you a diagram of what was wrong.

9. You want to learn a new program, skill, or game on a computer. You would:
   - ☐ **A.** read the written instructions that came with the program.
   - ☐ **B.** talk with people who know about the program.
   - ☐ **C.** use the controls or keyboard.
   - ☐ **D.** follow the diagrams in the book that came with it.

10. I like Web sites that have:
    - ☐ **A.** things I can click on, shift, or try.
    - ☐ **B.** interesting design and visual features.
    - ☐ **C.** interesting written descriptions, lists, and explanations.
    - ☐ **D.** audio channels where I can hear music, radio programs, or interviews.

11. Other than price, what would most influence your decision to buy a new non-fiction book?
    - ☐ **A.** The way it looks is appealing.
    - ☐ **B.** Quickly reading parts of it.
    - ☐ **C.** A friend talks about it and recommends it.
    - ☐ **D.** It has real-life stories, experiences, and examples.

12. You are using a book, CD, or Web site to learn how to take photos with your new digital camera. You would like to have:
    - ☐ **A.** a chance to ask questions and talk about the camera and its features.
    - ☐ **B.** clear written instructions with lists and bullet points about what to do.
    - ☐ **C.** diagrams showing the camera and what each part does.
    - ☐ **D.** many examples of good and poor photos and how to improve them.

(continued)

13. Do you prefer a teacher or a presenter who uses:
    - ☐ **A.** demonstrations, models, or practical sessions.
    - ☐ **B.** question and answer, talk, group discussion, or guest speakers.
    - ☐ **C.** handouts, books, or readings.
    - ☐ **D.** diagrams, charts, or graphs.

14. You have finished a competition or test and would like some feedback. You would like to have feedback:
    - ☐ **A.** using examples from what you have done.
    - ☐ **B.** using a written description of your results.
    - ☐ **C.** from somebody who talks it through with you.
    - ☐ **D.** using graphs showing what you had achieved.

15. You are going to choose food at a restaurant or cafe. You would:
    - ☐ **A.** choose something that you have had there before.
    - ☐ **B.** listen to the waiter or ask friends to recommend choices.
    - ☐ **C.** choose from the descriptions in the menu.
    - ☐ **D.** look at what others are eating or look at pictures of each dish.

16. You have to make an important speech at a conference or special occasion. You would:
    - ☐ **A.** make diagrams or get graphs to help explain things.
    - ☐ **B.** write a few key words and practice saying your speech over and over.
    - ☐ **C.** write out your speech and learn from reading it over several times.
    - ☐ **D.** gather many examples and stories to make the talk real and practical.

The VARK Questionnaire™, Version 7.8. Copyright © 2017 held by VARK LEARN Limited, Christchurch, New Zealand. Reprinted with permission.

Your VARK Score

Use the following scoring chart to find the VARK category that each of your answers corresponds to. Circle the letters that correspond to your answers. For example, if you answered B and C for question 3, circle V and R in the question 3 row.

Responses to Question 3:	A	B	C	D
VARK letter	K	(V)	(R)	A

Question	A category	B category	C category	D category
1.	K	A	R	V
2.	V	A	R	K
3.	K	V	R	A
4.	K	A	V	R
5.	A	V	K	R
6.	K	R	V	A
7.	K	A	V	R
8.	R	K	A	V
9.	R	A	K	V
10.	K	V	R	A
11.	V	R	A	K
12.	A	R	V	K
13.	K	A	R	V
14.	K	R	A	V
15.	K	A	R	V
16.	V	A	R	K

MY HIGHEST SCORES

Total number of Vs circled =

Total number of As circled =

Total number of Rs circled =

Total number of Ks circled =

USING LEARNING STRATEGIES IN COLLEGE

Courtesy of Terri Baskin Photography

NAME: **Brittnee Nicole Baskin**

SCHOOL: *Western Carolina University*

MAJOR: *Motion Picture and Television Production*

CAREER GOALS: *Director or Cinematographer*

"Sometimes you have to use more than one resource to make it through a class successfully."

I learn best from classes with lots of group discussions and visual aids. I like group discussions because they give me a chance to hear other people's opinions and understand where they're coming from. It can be difficult for me to stay focused in large lecture classes, so I sit close to the front and try to get to know the other people that I'm sitting around. That way, when there's time, we can have group discussions about the class material.

It doesn't matter what subject it is, ever since elementary school I've needed pictures or diagrams to help me understand concepts. When I'm writing a paper, I like to start by drawing a diagram. I use arrows to help me understand what is going on and what direction I want to go in.

In classes where teachers don't use lots of visuals, I've had to supplement with other material. Sometimes you have to use more than one resource to make it through a class successfully. I often use YouTube videos or find other visual information on the Internet. I've also found tutors who can help explain things using visuals.

One day I'd like to be a director or cinematographer. When I read books or hear things, I always visualize them in my head just like a movie. I hope my career will give me the opportunity to use my learning preference to help other visual learners see things in a way that they will appreciate and understand.

YOUR TURN: Brittnee's strongest VARK preference is Visual. Have you ever used any of the learning strategies that Brittnee describes? If so, which ones? If not, do you plan to try any of these in your classes this term? Why or why not?

Succeed in Different Learning Environments

Regardless of your academic major, you'll need to learn in a number of different environments in college. Professors will expect you to work independently, in groups, in classrooms or labs, and possibly in simulated or real work environments. In addition to the learning strategies and preferences described earlier in this chapter, then, it's important to consider some of the challenges you might face as you learn in these different settings and come up with strategies you can use to stay successful. Here we'll consider the challenges of working in a group and becoming a multimodal learner, and we'll look at how to seek help if you're challenged by a learning disability.

Work in a Group

Many instructors are big fans of group projects and with good reason: Research has shown that group work contributes to learning and success in college,[18] and many jobs require you to work effectively in groups. As beneficial as it can be, though, group work can also be challenging—you'll be collaborating with other students, and many of them will have learning preferences that differ from your own. The good news? The more you understand your own learning preferences and those of other group members, the more you'll all be able to leverage each person's strengths. For instance, suppose your group includes Fadi, who's a Visual, Intuitive, and Judging learner. Fadi gladly takes responsibility for creating a project plan during the kickoff meeting. This "big picture" takes the form of a chart outlining which tasks have to be done when, and by whom, so that the group can submit a high-quality project on time. Fadi would likely do a great job with this responsibility.

Team Effort. In every group project you're involved in during your college and professional career, group members will have different learning preferences. When group members understand their own and other members' preferences, they can take advantage of diverse strategies and work more effectively as a team. Roy Mehta / Getty Images

When the inevitable difficulties arise, group members can also use their understanding of one another's learning preferences to resolve issues. For example, suppose you notice that Anatole, a Read-Write and Perceiving learner, has missed deadlines on some tasks he's responsible for. To make it easier for him to fulfill his responsibilities, you translate the project plan chart into a written list of tasks for him to complete each day until the project is done. As a Perceiving learner, he's comfortable without a plan, but you believe that the written list will appeal enough to his Read-Write preference that he'll then complete the parts of the project he's responsible for.

Diversity in learning preferences and strategies can greatly benefit group work—especially when all group members understand their own and other members' preferences.

Make Sure You're Multimodal

Regardless of your preferred mode(s) of learning, chances are good that as a student you'll be expected to excel in a variety of learning environments: After all, most students have to attend lectures, participate in hands-on learning activities in labs, read lots of books, and write lots of papers—whether they're Read-Write learners, Introverts or Extraverts, or big-picture thinkers or detail people. As a college student, it's your job to get comfortable using the learning strategies that are called for in the different classes you take. You'll need to become a **multimodal learner**,

Flex Your Learning Muscles. Not every course you take will be a perfect fit—perhaps your instructor loves to lecture, while you prefer hands-on projects. But succeeding in a variety of environments means having different learning strategies at your fingertips and making sure you're multimodal. This takes practice—but it also makes you a flexible learner who gets the most from your courses. Klaus Vedfelt/Getty Images

Seek Help for Learning Challenges

As you realize by now, people have different ways they prefer to learn. Beyond differences related to learning preferences, however, some people experience differences in how their brain receives or processes information — differences that can cause significant difficulty in listening, speaking, reading, writing, spelling, and interacting socially. In such cases, these people may be diagnosed with what's called a *learning disability*. Don't let this term fool you: People with learning disabilities still learn — just not in the same way as someone without one. A learning disability is really a learning difference.

Because learning disabilities can affect how people work with course material, students with diagnosed learning disabilities may be eligible to have their learning environment adapted (or *accommodated*) to suit their learning needs. For example, a student might be able to record lectures or receive extended time in which to complete an exam. The purpose of these adaptations is not to provide an advantage but rather to level the playing field. That way, all students have an equal chance to learn the material and demonstrate their new knowledge and skills.

If you have a learning disability and need academic accommodations, visit your school's disability services office. The staff will review documentation of your disability and determine your eligibility for services. You can also visit the disability services office if you suspect you have an undiagnosed learning disability. The staff will help you seek appropriate testing, which will determine if you meet specific criteria to be diagnosed with a learning disability. The disability services office is a valuable resource you can use to better understand learning disabilities — and to get any help you might need.

or someone who can use different learning strategies based on the situation at hand.

By developing the ability to use different learning strategies, you boost your chances of doing well in all your classes—not just the ones you like best. You also demonstrate personal responsibility: Instead of passively expecting instructors to change their approaches to suit your preferences (which they won't do!), you take charge of your own education.

To increase your range of learning strategies, try the following tactics.

- **Talk with students in your classes** who have learning preferences that match how your instructor teaches the class. Use these students as models. Ask them to share what works for them; then try the strategies they recommend.

- **Visit a tutor** associated with a course you find difficult. Ask for advice on how to develop learning strategies that work for that course.

- **Talk to your instructors.** Visit them during office hours and have a conversation. They may be able to suggest specific ways to master the course content, even if that content challenges you to go outside your comfort zone.

my personal success plan

Are you inspired to set a new goal related to understanding learning? If so, the Personal Success Plan can walk you through the goal-setting process. Read the advice and examples; then sketch out your ideas in the space provided.

LaunchPad Solo
macmillan learning

To access the Personal Success Plan online, go to LaunchPad Solo for *Connections Essentials*.

1 GATHER INFORMATION

Think about how you learn, the learning strategies you use, and your Learning Preferences score on ACES. Would you like to learn more about how you learn? Would you like to try a new learning strategy — even if it challenges you to go outside your comfort zone?

2 SET A SMART GOAL

Use the information you've gathered to create a SMART goal, making sure to use the SMART goal checklist.

SAMPLE: In my history course, I'll try distributed studying. I'll study every day for the next two weeks.

3 MAKE AN ACTION PLAN

Outline the specific steps you'll take to achieve your SMART goal, and note when you'll complete each step.

SAMPLE: Tomorrow I'll create a schedule showing which content I'll study each day.

4 LIST BARRIERS AND SOLUTIONS

Think about possible barriers to your action steps; then brainstorm solutions for overcoming them.

SAMPLE: If my friends want to get together at a time that interferes with my study schedule, I'll join them once I've completed the work I've scheduled for that day.

5 ACT AND EVALUATE OUTCOMES

Now that your plan is in place, take action. Record each action step as you take it. Then evaluate whether you achieved your SMART goal, and make any adjustments needed to get better results in the future.

SAMPLE: I created a distributed studying schedule and I've kept to my schedule for the last three days. The weekend is approaching and my schedule accommodates both my studying and my social plans.

6 CONNECT TO CAREER

List the skills you're building as you progress toward your SMART goal. How will you use these skills to land a job and succeed at work?

SAMPLE: By establishing a distributed study schedule I've practiced my time-management skills, and I'm learning valuable strategies I can use to tackle long-term work projects in the future.

my personal success plan

1

my information

_____
_____
_____
_____
_____

2

my SMART goal

_____
_____
_____
_____

☐ **S**PECIFIC ☐ **M**EASURABLE ☐ **A**CHIEVABLE ☐ **R**ELEVANT ☐ **T**IME-LIMITED

3

my action plan

_____
_____
_____
_____
_____

4

my barriers/ solutions

_____
_____
_____
_____
_____
_____

5

my actions/ outcomes

_____
_____
_____
_____
_____
_____

6

my career connection

_____
_____
_____
_____
_____
_____

Chapter 4 Review

LearningCurve
macmillan learning
Use LearningCurve to review
concepts from this chapter.

CHAPTER SUMMARY

- Learning-science research can help you understand and apply proven strategies to promote learning. These strategies include self-testing, spacing out and alternating studying, making connections between new information and prior learning, and using dual processing.

- A learning preference is the way a person prefers to acquire and work with information. The Myers-Briggs and the VARK models represent two ways of thinking about learning preferences.

- Using your preferences doesn't guarantee success, but learning about your preferences will help you better understand your learning challenges or successes when combined with research-based learning strategies.

- To succeed in the diverse learning environments of college, you'll need to learn to work in a group successfully and become a multimodal learner.

- If you're challenged by a learning disability, reach out to someone at your school's disability services office.

CHAPTER ACTIVITIES

Adopting a Success Attitude

ENSURING A POSITIVE GROUP WORK EXPERIENCE

You can use your knowledge of the MBTI to make your future group-work experiences positive and productive. Imagine you've been assigned to work in a group, and your task is to determine whether college athletes should be paid for playing their sport. The group has to research each position in the debate and put together a presentation that argues for one side or the other. Respond to the following scenarios:

1. The group has four Extraverts and four Introverts. How could you ensure that everyone has a voice in the group process?
2. The group has four Sensing and four Intuitive people. How could you best use everyone's strengths in doing the research and writing the presentation?
3. The four Thinkers in the group disagree with the four Feelers as to whether college athletes should be paid. The group needs to choose one position. How do you make a decision that will make the greatest number of people happy?
4. The four Judgers want the group to create a plan for meeting, distributing tasks, and setting deadlines. Three of

the Perceivers aren't comfortable with so much structure. Although you're a Perceiver, you see the benefits of creating a plan. What can you say to the other Perceivers to help them understand these benefits?
5. The group creates a plan for managing the tasks involved in this assignment. At the next meeting, two students arrive without having completed their assigned tasks. Those who completed their tasks are angry. How do you bring the group together to achieve your goal?

Applying Your Skills

TESTING YOURSELF

In this chapter you learned that self-testing is an effective way to learn. Create a brief seven-item quiz based on important material in this chapter. How do you know what's important? Revisit the introduction, headings, and summary and make note of key ideas.

Then, to test yourself further, create a set of flash cards with a word or concept on one side and the definition or explanation on the other side. Use these flash cards to review key concepts on a regular basis.

Organization and Time Management

5

Get Organized

Take Control of Your Time

Overcome Procrastination and Minimize Distractions

MY PERSONAL SUCCESS PLAN

Do you know people who are *very* organized—people who label every drawer in their house, arrange their socks by color, or schedule each week down to the minute? If so, you may be tempted to dismiss those behaviors as excessive or over the top. After all, taken to extremes, any behavior can be unhealthy. But to a degree, the skills of being organized and managing your time are not only healthy; they're also essential for succeeding in college. These skills help you take control of your environment by clarifying what tasks you have to do, when you have to do them, and what resources you'll need. When you're in control, it's easier to stay focused on your goals and minimize distractions that threaten to derail your plans.

By staying organized and managing your time, you'll keep your academic life on track. And you'll make an attractive job candidate because managers want employees who arrive at work on time, show up for meetings, and keep track of important documents.

With these realities in mind, this chapter examines how you can take control of your environment and manage your life effectively. We start with organization—how you can get a handle on your course materials. Then we explore strategies for improving your time management, including reflecting on how you spend your time, setting priorities, and using a scheduling system. Finally, we discuss how to deal with procrastination and distractions.

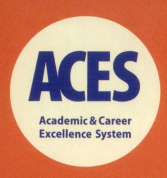

Academic & Career Excellence System

To find your **Organization and Time Management score,** go to LaunchPad Solo for *Connections Essentials.*

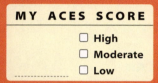

MY ACES SCORE

☐ High
☐ Moderate
☐ Low

REFLECTION: Organization and Time Management

Take a moment to reflect on your Organization and Time Management score on ACES. Find your score and add it to the box on the left.

This score measures your beliefs about how organized you are and how well you manage your time. Do you think it's an accurate snapshot of your current skills in this area? Why or why not?

- **IF YOU SCORED IN THE HIGH RANGE** and you feel this score accurately reflects your skills, you're probably quite organized and manage your time well. That's great news! As with all skills, however, you can improve on your strengths. For instance, if you already use a weekly schedule to organize your time, you might add a to-do list for each day so that you can track your progress and stay on target. Trying new organization and time-management strategies will keep you at the top of your game.

- **IF YOU SCORED IN THE MODERATE OR LOW RANGE**, don't be discouraged. You *can* get more organized and manage your time more effectively. This chapter is filled with ideas for getting a better handle on your class materials and your commitments.

ACES Journal

You've probably tried a number of different organization and time-management strategies throughout your life. Which of these have worked well? Which haven't been as successful? What are you doing right now to keep organized or stay on top of your schedule? Describe two or three specific things that you'll do over the next week to stay organized and manage your time efficiently.

_____

_____

_____

_____

_____

_____

Get Organized

Getting organized can be challenging, particularly if you're juggling competing demands of school, work, and family. But with practice and commitment, you can learn to manage your many priorities. And once you do, you'll feel calmer—and you'll be more productive.

Create a Clean Study Space

The first step in getting organized is to find a clean space where you can study. When your study space is clutter free, you can concentrate better on what you're doing and quickly find documents and other items that you need. There's no one "right" way to create a clean work area—pick what works best for you.

Whether you've got an office space at home or a quiet room in a residence hall, fix it up to make it inviting. Find a place to stash your books and papers, and give yourself plenty of room for your computer. Set aside a drawer or some cups for pens and pencils, and pick an area to spread out books and notes. Does your study space serve as the kitchen table during the day and then become your desk when the kids go to bed? If so, consider using totes or a rolling cabinet to organize everything you need to study. When the dishes are done and the kitchen table is clear, you can pull out your materials and get to work.

Do you study in the break room at work? In the library because things are too chaotic at home? If so, organize your backpack so you can easily find your pens, highlighters, notebooks, and other tools and still have room for your laptop, books, and class assignments.

Organize Your Documents

To keep your study space clean, you'll need to keep track of all the documents you collect and generate for your classes. If you set up a system for organizing and storing your documents, you can easily find what you need. Pick a storage system that's easy to use and that works with your

Choices, Choices. You're ready to sit down and read a textbook chapter, and you have two choices: the room on the top or the room on the bottom. Which room will you pick? Better go for the neat one. A clean, organized space helps you stay focused when you're studying. Richard Morrell / Corbis

personal preferences. Many people use some combination of electronic and paper storage systems.

Electronic Systems. You'll create most of your school papers and projects electronically, and you'll need a way to organize them. You can save these documents in folders on your computer, or you can use a **cloud**-based system. Available on the Internet, cloud systems let you store files online and access them from your laptop, tablet, or smartphone or even from an on-campus computer lab.

You can also save documents and other materials in an *electronic portfolio*. Many colleges use portfolio systems as a way for students to store and showcase documents and projects they create for their courses, including papers, blogs, and videos of classroom presentations. Keep your next job interview in mind if you develop an e-portfolio of your coursework; showing an electronic version of a stellar project could help you stand out in a field of applicants for the job of your dreams.[1]

Paper Systems. You might also want a system for organizing documents in paper form. Many instructors hand out syllabi on the first day of class, and a paper-based system helps you store these syllabi so you can find them easily. Also, people often feel secure using a paper-based system because they don't have to worry about computer problems. (Paper files can't get viruses.) To store paper documents, use an alphabetized filing cabinet or tote, or binders and folders that you can carry with you. Pick something that works with how mobile your materials need to be.

File Backup. If you've ever spilled coffee on a document or crashed your computer, you know how crucial it is to back up your files. To keep paper files safe, scan your documents and save them in an electronic format you can access if the originals get lost or destroyed. For electronic files, use an external hard drive or a thumb drive to store backup files separately from your computer or cloud system.

Whatever system you create to get organized, take time each day to keep it working smoothly. For instance, spend just five minutes every night putting papers into folders or organizing your electronic files. Keep clutter and confusion from creeping back into your life!

What's in a Name? How to Label Your Files and Folders

Whether your organizational system is electronic, paper, or a combination of the two, labeling your documents can help you keep things in order and greatly increase your productivity. Here are some ideas.

- **Use color.** Differentiate materials for different courses by using colors — for instance, green folders, highlighters, and notebooks for biology; yellow for sociology; blue for English; and so on. You can also use colors to signify priority: for example, a red font or pen color for your highest-priority to-dos; yellow for moderate priority; and green for low priority.

- **Create meaningful file and folder names.** Use file and folder names that are consistent and easy to decode. For example, for each class, create folders with the names "Exams," "Projects," "Papers," "Notes," and "Syllabus," and then name your files based on the folder in which they belong: "Notes from Sept 5," "Project — Voting Rights," and so on. This way, you can easily track down documents when you need them.

- **Create "In Progress" and "Complete" folders.** In the "In Progress" folder, store documents for projects you're actively working on. As you finish an exam or a paper, move it to the "Complete" folder so you can focus on documents that need your active attention.

Take Control of Your Time

Organizing your class materials is a great first step, but to really set the stage for success in college and work, you also have to take control of your time. Master the art of time management using the four-step process shown in Figure 5.1: First, track your time, by documenting how you spend your time during the course of a week. Second, identify your priorities—the activities that matter most to you—based on your values and goals. Third, build a schedule that focuses on your priorities. And fourth, use tools to track your progress on all your assignments.

Let's explore each of these steps in detail.

Step 1: Track Your Time

If you're like most college students, you sometimes (maybe even often) feel as though you have too much to do and not enough time to do it. That's not surprising: You're probably juggling lots of different demands, such as going to class, caring for kids or elderly parents, or holding down a job. If you're just out of high school, you might also be setting your own schedule for the first time, a responsibility that can feel overwhelming. Whatever your situation, before you can take control of your time, you have to figure out where your time is currently going. What do you actually do as the hours tick by every day?

To get a complete picture of how you're spending your time, you need to record—in writing—what you do every day and how long each activity takes. Why bother writing all this down? Your perceptions about how much time you spend on daily activities could be quite different from reality. By recording specifics, you'll build a more accurate picture of where your time goes.

To begin, on a calendar or piece of paper write down exactly what you do each day and how long each activity takes (see Figure 5.2). Do this for an entire week. As you collect this information, ask yourself:

FIGURE 5.1
Four Steps to Effective Time Management

- What activities are taking up most of my time?
- Am I spending too much time on unproductive or distracting activities? If so, what are they?
- When am I most productive? Least productive?

Then give your critical-thinking skills a workout: Examine the patterns you see in your time tracker, and analyze your responses to the questions. Use all this information to draw conclusions about how you're spending your time and how you might manage it more effectively. For example, let's say that before you started this exercise, you believed that your many obligations left you little time to study. As you evaluate the information you've gathered, you realize that you spent twenty-five hours gaming. Because you're studying English literature, not video-game design, you conclude that you could free up time to study by cutting back on your gaming. You've uncovered a wealth of time that you didn't realize was available.

FIGURE 5.2 Sample Time Tracker

Look at this excerpt from one student's time tracker. On Monday, the student had some downtime—just the right amount. But on Tuesday, she streamed a long TV show, had a leisurely lunch, and texted *a lot*, even while she was reading. When it finally came time to study that night, she fell asleep. Had she made different choices earlier in the day, she could have finished studying and still made it to bed at a reasonable hour. Now she has the information she needs to make a change.

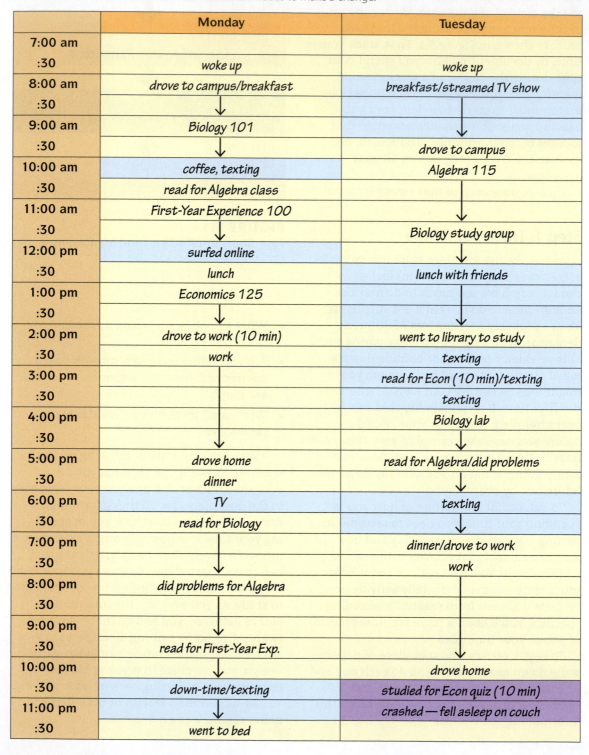

	Monday	Tuesday
7:00 am		
:30	woke up	woke up
8:00 am	drove to campus/breakfast	breakfast/streamed TV show
:30	↓	↓
9:00 am	Biology 101	↓
:30	↓	drove to campus
10:00 am	coffee, texting	Algebra 115
:30	read for Algebra class	↓
11:00 am	First-Year Experience 100	↓
:30	↓	Biology study group
12:00 pm	surfed online	↓
:30	lunch	lunch with friends
1:00 pm	Economics 125	↓
:30	↓	↓
2:00 pm	drove to work (10 min)	went to library to study
:30	work	texting
3:00 pm	↓	read for Econ (10 min)/texting
:30	↓	texting
4:00 pm	↓	Biology lab
:30	↓	↓
5:00 pm	drove home	read for Algebra/did problems
:30	dinner	↓
6:00 pm	TV	texting
:30	read for Biology	↓
7:00 pm	↓	dinner/drove to work
:30	↓	work
8:00 pm	did problems for Algebra	↓
:30	↓	↓
9:00 pm	↓	↓
:30	read for First-Year Exp.	↓
10:00 pm	↓	drove home
:30	down-time/texting	studied for Econ quiz (10 min)
11:00 pm	↓	crashed—fell asleep on couch
:30	went to bed	

Step 2: Identify Your Priorities

Once you've tracked your time for a week and analyzed the results, consider whether you're allocating enough time to the things that matter to you most. Are trivial tasks eating up too many hours each week? Does your current use of time reflect how important your education is to you? With numerous obligations and activities competing for your attention, you have to make choices about where to focus your energies. In other words, you have to **prioritize** your commitments and use these priorities to decide how much of your time an activity deserves.

Prioritizing commitments is a deeply personal process that depends on your values and goals. For one person, earning a degree while also spending time with family may be top priorities. For another person, completing college and getting a promotion at work may be most important. When you're clear about your priorities, you make smarter choices about how to use your time. For instance, if doing well in your classes is a top priority, you'll choose to study for an exam the night before, instead of going out with friends who don't have a test the next day.

To practice prioritizing, review your one-week time tracker, and write down the activities that currently take up most of your time. Describe these activities in broad terms, such as "attending class," "studying," and "working." Determine how important each activity is to you personally, and indicate that importance using the following four-point scale:

- 4 = critically important
- 3 = highly important
- 2 = moderately important
- 1 = of little or no importance

Critically important activities (those you've rated 4) are those that you've decided you must do because they relate directly to your values and responsibilities. For instance, each week you may need to go to work, attend all your classes, and be home by 3:00 p.m. when your children get off the bus. Highly important activities (rank = 3) will also have an impact on your success—such as doing five extra problems for math each evening. Activities you've rated 4 and 3 may not always be fun or exciting, but you consider them crucial for achieving your goals or living your values. Activities you view as moderately important (rank = 2) or of little or no importance (rank = 1) are less essential to your values or goals.

To define your priorities, you need to think critically about what's most important to you. And to honor your priorities, you sometimes have to make tough decisions, such as giving up activities that you enjoy or disappointing someone who wants some of your time. For example, what if your boss needs you to work Tuesday night, but you're supposed to meet with classmates to start a group project? These kinds of choices are never easy, but we all face them and have to learn how to manage them. If you know what your priorities are, you can make the tough calls and be at peace with your decisions.

Step 3: Build Your Schedule

Once you've tracked your time and clarified your priorities, you can build a schedule that reflects the most important commitments in your life. Find a scheduling method and tools that work for you—whether it's a paper planner, an app on your phone, a calendar tied to your e-mail system, or a mix of these. You can also create schedules that cover different time frames—terms, months, weeks, and days. (For an example of a five-day schedule, see Figure 5.3.)

The activities you put on your schedule will depend on your priorities, but because you're in college, we assume that one of your top priorities is graduating. So you'll need to think about and plan for the following responsibilities:

- **Classes.** Include class time in your schedule. If your class is on campus rather than online, plan to arrive a few minutes early so that you can get settled and prepare to learn.

- **Study time.** Set aside two hours of study time for each hour of class time. The most common college class format is about

FIGURE 5.3 Sample Schedule

Building a complete schedule — including time for classes and studying, as well for exercise, work, and relaxation — helps you take control of your time. Hold yourself accountable for sticking to your schedule, and celebrate when you accomplish everything you planned each day.

	Monday	Tuesday	Wednesday	Thursday	Friday
7:00 am	BREAKFAST	DRIVE TO CAMPUS	BREAKFAST	DRIVE TO CAMPUS	BREAKFAST
:30	DRIVE TO CAMPUS	YOGA	DRIVE TO CAMPUS	YOGA	DRIVE TO CAMPUS
8:00 am	CHEMISTRY 101		CHEMISTRY 101		CHEM LAB
:30		COFFEE/BREAKFAST		COFFEE/BREAKFAST	
9:00 am	STUDY: CHEM 1 HR. ENGLISH 1 HR.	ALGEBRA II (QUIZ!)	STUDY: CHEM 1 HR. FYE 1 HR.	ALGEBRA II	
:30					
10:00 am					DRIVE TO WORK
:30		FREE TIME		STUDY: ALGEBRA 1 HR. 15 MIN. SOCIOLOGY 45 MIN.	
11:00 am	ENGLISH 124		ENGLISH 124		WORK
:30					
12:00 pm					
:30	LUNCH	LUNCH	LUNCH	LUNCH	
1:00 pm	FIRST-YEAR EXPERIENCE (FYE) 102	SOCIOLOGY CLUB MEETING	FIRST-YEAR EXPERIENCE (FYE) 102	STUDY: CHEM, ENGLISH, FYE 1 HR. EACH	
:30					
2:00 pm		STUDY: FYE 1 HR. 30 MIN. SOCIOLOGY 1 HR. 30 MIN.			
:30	CHEM STUDY GROUP		STUDY: ALGEBRA 1 HR. 30 MIN. SOCIOLOGY 1 HR.		
3:00 pm					
:30					
4:00 pm	DRIVE HOME			FREE TIME	
:30					
5:00 pm	FREE TIME	DRIVE HOME	DRIVE TO WORK		
:30		DINNER		DINNER	
6:00 pm	DINNER WITH COUSINS	STUDY: ALGEBRA 1 HR. CHEM 30 MIN.	WORK		DINNER
:30				SOCIOLOGY 105	
7:00 pm	STUDY: ALGEBRA 1 HR. CHEM 30 MIN.				
:30		EDIT ENGLISH PAPER			
8:00 pm					TIME WITH FRIENDS
:30	FREE TIME		DRIVE HOME		
9:00 pm		FREE TIME	DINNER	DRIVE HOME	
:30			FREE TIME		
10:00 pm				FREE TIME	
:30		BED	BED		
11:00 pm	BED			BED	DRIVE HOME
:30					BED

three hours of class time a week, which involves six hours of studying outside of class. If you're taking four three-hour classes this term, you should budget twelve hours of class time and twenty-four hours of study time each week. Research shows that full-time students spend an average of a little less than fifteen hours per week studying.[2] That's not nearly enough time. If you can find two hours to study for each hour of class time and if you use that study time wisely, you'll likely get much better grades than students who invest less time in studying. Also, arrange your study time in a way that maximizes your learning. Spacing out your study time across multiple days and studying in small blocks of time is the most productive way to learn new material.[3]

- **Exams and assignments.** In your schedule, include the time needed to take exams, to complete regular assignments and major projects, and to develop presentations for class.

- **Work.** Add your work hours to your schedule. If you commute between home, work, and school, factor in travel time.

- **Family.** Include high-priority family time in your schedule, such as having dinner together each evening or blocking off an afternoon to celebrate a loved one's birthday. These relationships can be a source of support as you manage the many demands of being a college student.

- **School events.** Schedule time for high-priority events at school, such as attending tutoring sessions and study groups for difficult classes, going to important cultural events, or participating in student organizations. While it can be difficult for busy students to make time for these activities, it's worth it: Active involvement on campus can strengthen your commitment

Manage Time When You Learn Online

If your schedule includes online classes, keep in mind that they sometimes present unique time-management challenges. Your traditional courses are scheduled on particular days and times, and you can block off this class time in your schedule. With many online classes, though, the time you spend participating in class is less structured. Most online courses don't require you to attend at any specific time, so deciding when you'll create and respond to online posts and complete other course requirements is up to you. In addition, while some students expect online classes to be easier or less intensive than face-to-face courses, most online classes take as much time as do in-person classes (and sometimes even *more* time). Try these tips for staying on top of your online coursework.

- **Get comfortable with this class format.** If you're new to online classes, block out time in your schedule to learn how to navigate the online class system. Your instructor and institution can help.

- **Devote time *each week* to work on your assignments.** Be sure that your weekly schedule includes time for studying, reading, and posting work online for your class.

- **Log in to your online class each day.** Even if it's just for five minutes, log in to check for updates from your instructor or posts from other students. That way, you can make sure you're keeping up with assignments and monitoring class discussions.

- **Know your deadlines.** If your instructor gives specific due dates for class assignments, enter them into your schedule for each week of the term.

- **Schedule time for live meetings hosted by your instructor.** Hosted via tools like Skype or a text chat, live meetings give you opportunities to interact with classmates and instructors in real time.

to college and help you develop teamwork and communication skills.

- **Exercise and leisure.** To do well in college, you have to be healthy—both physically and mentally. So be sure to schedule time for regular exercise and leisure activities to balance out the great amount of time and effort you'll be devoting to your coursework.

- **Rewards.** Schedule time to reward yourself for your successes in college. For instance, schedule a movie with friends or family members the night after an exam. These rewards don't have to consume a lot of time, but they can help recharge your batteries so you can stay motivated for another round of hard work at school.

As you create your schedule, try to build some flexibility into it, in case something goes wrong. For instance, suppose you commute to school, and one of your classes starts at 8:30 a.m. on Tuesdays and Thursdays. You know traffic can be heavy at that time, so when you schedule time for commuting on those days, you add a "cushion" in case you get stuck in traffic. When you build flexibility into your schedule, you can shift gears more easily if surprises come up.

Step 4: Use Tools to Track Progress on Your Projects

Tracking your progress helps you evaluate how effectively you're managing the time allocated to your priorities. By doing this, you hold yourself **accountable**, or responsible, for completing the tasks and meeting the obligations that are connected to your priorities. Here are some tools that can help you keep your projects on track and help you meet your goals.

To-Do List. A to-do list helps you manage time and activities on a daily basis by reminding you of key tasks (see Figure 5.4). Try creating a to-do list for the next day each night before you go to bed or for the current day when you get up in the morning. It takes only a couple of minutes. You can make your list using an e-mail program, the calendar on your smartphone, apps on your tablet, or a piece of paper. Experiment with color coding or numbering the tasks on your to-do list by priority. Try different methods to discover which strategies work best for you.

FIGURE 5.4 Sample To-Do List

To-Dos
Date: Wednesday
1. ~~Read for history class.~~
2. ~~Complete biology lab write up.~~
3. Read book on reserve in the library for literature class.
4. Go running.
5. Go to dinner with the kids.
6. Make dentist appointment.

Project Plan. Your schedule will include time to work on major school projects, and when you create project plans to accompany them, you can track your progress on each of these projects. A project plan helps you break down an assignment into smaller, more manageable steps and budget time to complete each step. This tool builds on key concepts in the chapter on thinking critically and setting goals, such as identifying action steps, prioritizing them, and giving each step a deadline. To create a project plan, you estimate how much time will be required to complete each step in the project. That way, you can build enough time into your schedule to complete all the steps by the assignment's due date.

Consider Mia, who has six weeks to write a major paper on Greek architecture. Figure 5.5 shows how Mia has broken down the tasks involved in completing this paper. She starts with the due date and adds a goal statement for this assignment. She lists the steps needed to complete her paper. Since Mia is a new college student, she isn't sure how much time each task will take, but she wrote papers in high school and often pulls together documents for her boss. She draws on these experiences to estimate how much time she'll need for each task.

One advantage of creating a project plan is that you can use the deadlines to hold yourself accountable. Also, crossing off tasks as you complete them gives you a feeling of accomplishment, which can be crucial for maintaining momentum throughout the project.

FIGURE 5.5 Project Plan

Project:	Greek architecture paper		
Due date:	October 31		
Goal:	Demonstrate new knowledge of Greek architecture through written work		
Action steps	**Estimated time**	**Deadline**	**Done**
Read assigned textbook chapters	5 hours	September 20	**X**
Find and read three additional resources	18 hours	October 3	**X**
Find six images of architecture	4 hours	October 5	
Write an outline for the paper	3 hours	October 10	
Write first draft	12 hours	October 20	
Revise to create second draft	6 hours	October 24	
Revise to create third draft and polish the paper	4 hours	October 28	
Hand in the paper and celebrate!		October 31	

TOOLS FOR TIME MANAGEMENT

Photograph by
Isheeta Rahman

NAME: **Amni Al-Kachak**

SCHOOL: *University of California, Irvine*

MAJOR: *Biological Sciences*

CAREER GOAL: *Ph.D. in Biological Sciences*

" I can't live without schedules and lists."

When I started college, I knew I'd have to work even harder than I did in high school. To be proactive, I started a scheduling system; now I can't live without schedules and lists. I make special timelines that include goals and when I want them done by. I make a list for the year, a list each week, and a daily list and keep them all on paper. Seeing it written down makes it feel more achievable for me, and I love the feeling I get when I can cross something off my list!

I've always believed that academics come first, then work, then fun. Whenever I schedule things, I put them in that order. For example, if I have a homework assignment due, I get it done first. After that, if I have any work for my job that needs to get done, I'll do that. Then, if I'm done with my immediate academic and work priorities, I squeeze in study time. I like to make a habit of studying every day, just so the information stays fresh in my head without having to stressfully cram it in during test time. After I've completed all of the tasks on my list, I can reward myself by having fun with my friends. I always do things according to deadline and importance.

It can be hard to stick to my schedule. One day I was reading my biology textbook, but then my friend texted me. We started a conversation that lasted for about an hour. Because I'm so aware of my time, I felt really guilty because I could have spent that hour doing a million things. From then on, I decided to put my phone away while I was studying. Although the work I'm doing may be difficult or boring, I'm much happier with myself if I focus and get it done instead of procrastinating.

YOUR TURN: **Do you have strategies you use to stay focused on your top priorities? If so, what's an example of a strategy you've found helpful? If not, which of the strategies that Amni describes might be useful to you going forward?**

Overcome Procrastination and Minimize Distractions

If you're like most people, you sometimes put off getting down to work. You check Twitter one more time, send a text—do anything except what you're supposed to be doing. In short, you **procrastinate**. When you procrastinate, you open yourself up to distractions—events or objects in your environment that take your attention away from the task you need to complete.

Procrastination and distractions can undo all the effort you've put into getting organized and taking control of your time. So the next time you find yourself procrastinating or getting distracted, use your critical-thinking skills. Ask yourself: "Why am I putting off this task?" or "Why am I not focusing on what I should focus on?" The more you know about what's causing you to fall victim to procrastination or distractions, the more you can work to change your behavior so that you can accomplish your goals.

Beat Procrastination

People procrastinate for various reasons. By understanding the most common root causes, which we'll explore in the section that follows, you can identify when you're falling victim to these causes—and apply the right antidotes.

Low Motivation. If you don't feel motivated to complete a task, you might be tempted to procrastinate. Fight low motivation with these tactics.

- **Engage in self-reflection.** You may feel unmotivated because you lack a sense of self-efficacy regarding the task at hand, you don't see it as relevant to you, or you have a negative attitude about your studies in general. Try to identify which of these three key ingredients of motivation you're missing. Sometimes simply understanding why you're unmotivated can spur you to take action.

- **Just get started.** If you have reading to do, pick up your textbook and begin. If you have to do research for a paper, log on to the library's Web site, and start searching for articles. In some cases, just telling yourself it's time to work will revive your motivation.

- **Move.** Grab your materials, go somewhere new, and clear your head. Physical motion may be enough to motivate you to focus on the work you need to do.

Not-So-Good Housekeeping. Aaron has a test tomorrow, but instead of studying, he has suddenly decided it's time to do laundry. Guess what: He's procrastinating — and he'll have less time to prepare for the test. The lesson? If a task isn't crucial, do it after finishing your *real* priorities.
Robyn Breen Shinn/Getty Images

Perfectionism. Some people avoid starting projects because they want to achieve a perfect result and worry that they won't be able to. If this happens to you, try these strategies to combat perfectionism.

- **Reframe your expectations.** Give yourself permission to let go of perfectionistic thinking. Instead of telling yourself that everything you work on must be perfect, tell yourself that you'll put your best effort into each project or task.

- **Start small.** Complete some small tasks related to the work you're procrastinating on; then use your success to gain momentum for finishing another set of tasks. Eventually, you'll complete the whole project.

Feeling Overwhelmed. If you feel overwhelmed by the amount of work facing you, it may be daunting just to get started. Try these tactics to keep moving forward.

- **Be realistic.** Remind yourself that you can't do everything at once and that every journey—however long or short—starts with a single step. Then pick a place to start.

- **Trick yourself.** Tell yourself that you're going to read or write for only ten minutes or that you'll read or write only three pages. Once you get involved in the work, you may look up forty-five minutes later and discover that you're almost finished—and that's a good reason to keep going.

Minimize Distractions

Distractions can be a big challenge for some students, causing them to veer off track. If you intend to study chemistry for two hours but then spend forty-five minutes playing on the Web, you'll lose time you can't get back. To minimize distractions, consider these tips.

- **Find strength in numbers.** With your roommates or family members, agree on a time when everyone focuses on coursework (or schoolwork for your kids) or other quiet tasks. This creates an environment of support and accountability: When everyone around you is studying or working, you'll find it easier to stay focused.

- **Use the "off" switch.** Turn off the television, your phone, and any other devices that create visual or auditory distractions. Log out of Facebook, Twitter, and other social networking sites. Click the setting that turns off that annoying little chime that lets you know you've just received an e-mail. As you plan your study time, allow five minutes each hour to check these devices and respond to messages. That way, you won't feel tempted to do so while you work.

- **Block out other sources of distraction.** For example, close the curtains or pull down the shades in your room so you can't see what's happening outside. If your neighbor is playing loud music, invest in a set of earplugs to block out the noise.

....

Be a Productivity Pro. To avoid watching your productivity plummet, resist any urge to give into distractions. Stick to the schedule you've created. And remind yourself: Cute cat videos will still be there when your work is done. *Chris Wildt/www.CartoonStock.com*

"...and this was that really cute kitty cat video on YouTube."

Find Your Flow

Have you ever had the experience of being "in the zone," or fully present while completing a task? If so, you were probably in a mental state of *flow*. You have this experience when you're completely immersed in a task that you consider enjoyable, such as studying, playing sports, praying, or playing video games. Flow involves concentration and reduced self-consciousness. People in a state of flow feel as though they're in control, and they often lose track of time. When you eliminate distractions around you, you can help create the optimal conditions for flow.[4]

A recent study examined college students' experience of flow and the impact on their emotions.

- Half of the fifty-seven student participants were asked to identify a positive, focused activity they enjoyed (a flow activity) and to engage in that task once during a two-week period.

- The other half of the students were asked to identify an everyday activity (a nonflow activity) to participate in.

- All the students recorded their experience of flow and their emotions before and after the activity.

Interestingly, the two flow activities chosen by the greatest number of students in this research were exercising and going to class / studying. The students who engaged in a flow activity experienced more positive emotions than did students who engaged in everyday activities. The more intense the flow experience, the greater the positive feelings.[5]

The bottom line? You *can* get into a state of flow when you study. To do so, find something in your coursework that interests you, minimize distractions, and completely immerse yourself in that material. Not only will you learn, but you'll also feel good.

my personal success plan

ORGANIZATION AND TIME MANAGEMENT

Are you inspired to set a new goal aimed at improving your organization and time-management skills? If so, the Personal Success Plan can walk you through the goal-setting process. Read the advice and examples; then sketch out your ideas in the space provided.

1 GATHER INFORMATION

Think about your strengths and weakness related to organization and time management. What strategies have worked for you in the past? What could you do differently? Revisit your Organization and Time Management score on ACES and review the relevant sections of this chapter for additional ideas.

2 SET A SMART GOAL

Use the information you've gathered to create a SMART goal, making sure to use the SMART goal checklist.

SAMPLE: I'll use my Outlook calendar to plan my time over the next two weeks.

3 MAKE AN ACTION PLAN

Outline the specific steps you'll take to achieve your SMART goal, and note when you'll complete each step.

SAMPLE: Tomorrow night, I'll type my class, study, work, and activity schedules for the next two weeks into my calendar.

4 LIST BARRIERS AND SOLUTIONS

Think about possible barriers to your action steps; then brainstorm solutions for overcoming them.

SAMPLE: Sometimes I forget to check my calendar. To remind me, I'll set the alarm on my phone for 9:00 a.m. and 3:00 p.m. every day. When the alarm goes off, I'll look at the calendar to see if I'm on track.

5 ACT AND EVALUATE OUTCOMES

Now that your plan is in place, take action. Record each action step as you take it. Then evaluate whether you achieved your SMART goal, and make any adjustments needed to get better results in the future.

SAMPLE: I typed my schedules into my calendar as planned. I'm staying on top of my commitments.

6 CONNECT TO CAREER

List the skills you're building as you progress toward your SMART goal. How will you use these skills to land a job and succeed at work?

SAMPLE: I work part-time as a Web designer, and using a calendar will help me meet deadlines and remember client meetings.

1 my information

_____

2 my SMART goal

_____

☐ **S**PECIFIC   ☐ **M**EASURABLE   ☐ **A**CHIEVABLE   ☐ **R**ELEVANT   ☐ **T**IME-LIMITED

3 my action plan

_____

4 my barriers/ solutions

_____

5 my actions/ outcomes

_____

6 my career connection

_____

Chapter 5 Review

CHAPTER SUMMARY

- To get organized, you need a clean, quiet study space and a system (electronic, paper, or both) for managing and backing up course documents.

- Applying a four-step process can help you manage your time: (1) Track how you're using your time now, (2) identify your priorities, (3) build a schedule that allocates enough time to your top priorities, and (4) use tools to track your progress on your projects.

- Procrastinating can prevent you from reaching your goals and make you vulnerable to distractions. When you figure out why you're procrastinating, you can address the cause, which may range from low motivation to perfectionism.

- Eliminating distractions (for example, by turning off electronic devices) can help you focus on the work at hand and use your time wisely.

CHAPTER ACTIVITIES

Adopting a Success Attitude

STANDING UP FOR YOUR PRIORITIES

As you work to clarify your priorities, you'll face some tough choices about how to spend your time, especially when people you care about make requests for (or demands on) your time. In some cases, you'll have to assert yourself and say "no" or offer ideas for arriving at a compromise.

Describe a recent incident in which you should have said "no" to someone who made a request for (or demand on) your time but you said "yes" instead. Which of the following beliefs led you to say "yes"? Check all that apply.

_____ **1.** Saying "no" will hurt and upset them.

_____ **2.** Saying "no" will make them feel rejected.

_____ **3.** If I say "no," they won't like me anymore.

_____ **4.** Others' needs are more important than mine.

_____ **5.** I should always try to please others.

_____ **6.** Saying "no" is rude.

_____ **7.** Saying "no" is unkind and selfish.

To feel better about saying "no," think critically about each belief that you checked off.

For each belief, provide a more helpful way of viewing the situation. For example, instead of "Saying 'no' will hurt and upset them," tell yourself, "They might be hurt if I say 'no,' but if they care about me, they'll understand," or "I may hurt someone by turning down their initial request, but maybe I can fulfill the request another time."

Applying Your Skills

PLANNING FOR LARGE CLASS ASSIGNMENTS

If you break down large, complex class assignments into smaller chunks and distribute the workload over time, they'll seem much more manageable. Review Figure 5.5 and create your own project plan for a big, complicated assignment you'll need to complete this term.

Be sure to record the name of the project, the date that it is due, and a goal statement for the assignment. Then list your action steps, the estimated time required for each, and the deadlines that you have set for yourself.

Once you've started using the project plan, respond to the following questions: How is this tool working for you? Has it helped you track your progress and complete your assignment on time? Why or why not?

olaser / Getty Images

Reading for College Success

Embrace Reading!

Prepare to Read

Read with Focus

Review What You've Read

Read Different Types of Materials

MY PERSONAL SUCCESS PLAN

What you're doing this very second — reading — is one of the most powerful learning activities you'll do in college. And you'll be doing a lot of it. In fact, reading is the second most frequently used form of communication among college students, after listening.[1]

Do you wonder why your instructors assign so much reading? Consider this: A central reason you're in college is to acquire knowledge. In most of your face-to-face classes, you're in the classroom only a few hours each week, listening to lectures. In online, blended, practical, and discussion-based classes, you spend even less time listening to lectures. By adding reading assignments to the mix,

your instructors can cover more material — and that benefits *you* in the long run.

Reading will play a critical role in your work life, too. After all, can you think of a job that requires no reading at all — none? It's not easy to do. Almost every job requires some kind of reading, whether it's e-mails or invoices, medical charts or memos, recipes or research reports.

In this chapter we examine why reading is so important. We present a three-step process for getting the most from reading: preparing to read, reading with focus, and reviewing what you've read. And finally, we describe strategies for reading effectively in math, science, and online classes, as well as strategies for reading journal articles.

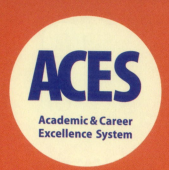
To find your
Reading score, go to
LaunchPad Solo for
Connections Essentials.

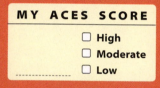

MY ACES SCORE

☐ High
☐ Moderate
-------------- ☐ Low

REFLECTION:
Reading

Take a moment to reflect on your Reading score on ACES. Find your
score and add it to the box on the left.

This score measures your beliefs about how well you read. Do you think it's
an accurate snapshot of your current skills in this area? Why or why not?

- **IF YOU SCORED IN THE HIGH RANGE** and you're confident that
  this score is accurate, then you can likely count reading among
  your strengths. This is excellent news. As you know, however, even
  strengths can be improved. For instance, let's say you've developed
  some great strategies for reading your history and psychology
  textbooks, but you find it more challenging to read your biology
  book. Using the information in this chapter, you can develop new
  strategies to increase your confidence in reading different types of
  materials, including your science texts.

- **IF YOU SCORED IN THE MODERATE OR LOW RANGE,** take steps
  to improve your reading skills. Explore the ideas and practices in this
  chapter, and apply them to your course material. When you do, you'll
  find that you *can* become a more efficient and effective reader. Just
  give it a try!

ACES Journal

Reflect on your current reading habits and respond in writing to
these questions: How do you feel about your reading assignments?
Are they manageable, overwhelming, boring, or interesting? Are you
building enough time to read into your schedule? Do you know where
to get help when you run into reading challenges? Then write a brief
paragraph in which you discuss which of your reading strategies have
been effective, as well as ways you might improve your reading habits.

_____

_____

_____

_____

_____

Embrace Reading!

In our connected world, most of us spend a great deal of time watching and interacting with screens. We can learn a lot from them, but they're not the only way to learn. Reading is a powerful and necessary skill that you'll be required to master in college, and it will be one of your strongest assets in the workplace. You may even find that you enjoy it! Even better, reading offers unique advantages: It grows your vocabulary, exposes you to new ideas, and may even help you develop a deeper understanding of others.

As you read, you'll uncover theories, discover how things work, gain insights into the past, get immersed in a variety of cultures—and even have fun. Reading is also the gateway to helping you master new skills, such as how to design an experiment, craft a marketing campaign, or write computer code. Depending on your course load, your instructors may ask you to read everything from textbook chapters and novels to scientific articles and transcripts of great speeches.

Read Actively in College

How you read in college will probably differ from how you've read up to now. College work requires **active reading**, which involves interacting with the content you read, not just gazing at words on the page. You pay close attention. You think about the content carefully. You ask questions about what makes sense and why. These actions help you stay focused, which in turn saves time: You learn and remember more of the material the first time around so you don't have to relearn it later. Active reading has three main steps: preparing to read, reading with focus, and reviewing what you've read (see Figure 6.1). We will explore each of these steps in the sections that follow.

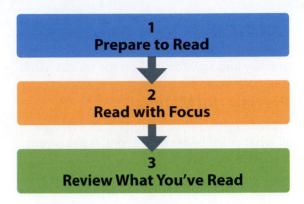

FIGURE 6.1
Three Steps to Active Reading

Connect Reading with Other Study Skills

Before we move on, however, it's important to emphasize the strong connection between reading and your success. Reading is a central life skill: With rare exceptions, successful people use reading skills to gain information and extend their learning. Reading is also a central study skill that sets the stage for the other study skills discussed in this book. Reading and attending class kick off your learning experience: When you read and go to class, you take in (or *input*) new information into your brain. You then put *effort* into taking notes and studying, which help you absorb and remember the information. Finally, you demonstrate (or *output*) what you've learned through tests, papers, and classroom presentations.

All of these academic skills work together. In fact, many of the strategies that help you read successfully—like maintaining a positive attitude, eliminating distractions, and thinking critically about information—can also help you excel at note taking, studying, and writing. When you weave all of these skills together, you maximize your learning—in every course.

Prepare to Read

With reading, as with many things in life, it pays to make sure you're prepared. Try the following tips so that you're ready to read actively and stay focused on the task at hand.

Preview the Material

Previewing gives you a big-picture overview of what you'll be reading about. It helps your mind predict the subject matter and think about how information you already know relates to what you're about to read.[2] The next time you open up your textbook, take these steps to preview what's coming.

- **Read the preface or introduction.** Review the preface or introduction at the beginning of the book. Authors use these sections to describe the book's chapter structure and goals and to offer tips about how to use the material in each chapter. In the preface of this book, for example, we explain why we've included features such as Student Voices of Experience and the Personal Success Plan.

- **Read the table of contents.** At the beginning of any textbook is a table of contents listing the main and supporting headings for each chapter, and often the major features in each chapter. Before you begin an assignment, glance at the contents for the chapter you're about to read.

- **Read the chapter summary.** Many textbooks (including this one) provide chapter summaries, which give an overview of the contents of each chapter and highlight the main ideas. Scan the summary before you read.

- **Look for headings and key terms.** Skim through the chapter, looking at section headings, bold or italicized words, and definitions of key terms. All of these indicate the important concepts you'll be learning in the chapter.

Make a Plan for Your Reading

Do you ever run out of time to complete the reading for your classes? Are you surprised when an assignment takes you longer to complete than you thought it would? If so, prepare yourself by making a plan: Before you read, assess how much material you have to get through and estimate how long that reading will take.

It can be tricky to estimate time frames at first, but with experience you'll get better at this activity. Start by timing how long it takes you to read and understand five pages of material in each of your classes. Keep in mind that not every reading assignment will take the same amount of time and that each person reads at a different pace. For example, you might read novels in your English literature course relatively quickly, whereas reading chapters in your algebra book might take you longer — or vice versa.

You can make a simple table like this one to figure out how much time you need for each class each week. Use this method to get control over your reading and make sure you're budgeting enough time to get things done. You may even find that some of your reading goes more quickly than you anticipated!

Class	Time to read 5 pages	Number of pages in average week	Reading time for the week
English			
First-Year Experience			
Biology			
Economics			

Identify Purposeful Reading Questions

After you preview the material, think of questions you expect to be able to answer once you've finished reading. These are called **purposeful reading questions** because your goal (purpose) in reading the material will be to answer them. Identifying these questions helps you focus your reading on what's most important. Purposeful reading questions vary in complexity; for example, you might want to know the definition of a term (low level of complexity) or the causes of an event (higher level of complexity).

How, precisely, do you go about identifying purposeful reading questions? Sometimes, the material itself provides questions you can use. For example, many textbooks include focus questions at the beginning of each chapter or review questions at the end of each chapter that spotlight key concepts (see Figure 6.2).

You can also create your own purposeful reading questions. Keep it simple at first by drafting questions drawn from the chapter's headings and key terms. For instance, if a heading in your calculus book is "Polynomials," you could create the question "What are polynomials?" and then work up to more complex questions, such as, "How are polynomial equations solved?" and "How are polynomials used in mathematics and science?" Here are some additional examples of purposeful reading questions you might create in a variety of classes.

- "What were three causes of the War of 1812?" (American history class)

- "What's the difference between the unconditioned and the conditioned stimulus in classical conditioning?" (Introduction to Psychology class)

- "How do I diagram the components of a nerve cell and describe the major function of each component?" (Introduction to Biology class)

- "How can I apply the three steps in the active reading strategy?" (this class)

FIGURE 6.2 Creating Purposeful Reading Questions

Purposeful reading questions can come from questions in your reading, such as the outcomes in this textbook excerpt. Or create your own. Here, *leadership* is a key term, so you can ask "How do you define *leadership*?" Text excerpt from *Real Communication: An Introduction, 3rd ed.*, p. 274, by Dan O'Hair et al. Copyright © 2015 by Bedford / St. Martin's. Used by permission.

chapter outcomes

After you have finished reading this chapter, you will be able to

- Describe the types of power that effective leaders employ

- Describe how leadership styles should be adapted to the group situation

- Identify the qualities that make leaders effective at enacting change

- Identify how culture affects appropriate leadership behavior

- List the forces that shape a group's decisions

- Explain the six-step group decision process

What makes a leader? Power? Experience? Decisiveness? In this chapter, we continue our discussion of group communication by examining two additional processes that often emerge in groups: leadership and decision making. These two processes are tightly interrelated: a group's leader affects how the group makes decisions, and the decisions a group makes affect how the leader operates. When leadership and decision making work together in a constructive way, a group stands the best possible chance of achieving its goals. To understand how these processes influence a group's effectiveness, let's begin by taking a closer look at group leadership.

Understanding Group Leadership

It's a word that's constantly tossed about in political campaigns, highlighted on résumés, and used in book titles and biographies. But just what is *leadership*? Scholars have grappled with the task of defining leadership for many years.

Two key terms that show up in many definitions over the years have been *direction* and *influence*. That's because in its most essential form, **leadership** is the ability to direct or influence others' behaviors and thoughts toward a productive end (Nierenberg, 2009). This capacity for influence may stem from a person's power or simply from group members' admiration or respect for the individual.

Read with Focus

Once you're prepped and ready to go, take the next step: Complete your reading. Keep in mind that you won't be able to remember every word in your reading assignments—no one can. So you need to read with focus: Figure out what information is *most* important, and concentrate on that. To do this, use your critical-thinking skills to identify key information and to evaluate the quality of that information. And use your active learning and metacognition skills to select reading strategies that work best for you, depending on your learning preferences and the subjects you're studying.

Mark Up Your Reading Material

Marking up a text helps you interact with the material you're learning, which in turn helps you understand and remember it. You can mark up reading material in several ways (see Figure 6.3), including annotating the margins of your text, highlighting and underlining key words and phrases, and taking notes.

Annotate. You can *annotate* your reading material by jotting down quick notes, inserting your own examples, drawing symbols ("DEF" might indicate a definition; "EX" might call out an example), and writing quick summaries in your own words—all in the margins of the book or article. Making notes and restating information in your own words requires you to process information more carefully than if you just highlight or underline (see the next section). Annotating takes some time, but it's worth it—you'll remember the material better later on, and you'll have notes that you can use to study.

Are you reading online? You can still use this approach, but instead of a pen or pencil, use digital tools to mark up the content (see the Read Online Course Materials section later in this chapter).

Highlight and Underline. Highlighting and underlining help you identify main ideas and call out key content such as math formulas, diagrams, and definitions. These popular techniques offer a quick and easy way to spotlight important points and then locate that information later when you're studying. But research shows that when using these techniques, you should proceed with caution: If you highlight or underline mindlessly, then you're not processing the information carefully.[3]

To take a more focused approach to using these tools, read each section of the material before you make any marks. Ask yourself: What are this section's main ideas? Then go back to the material and highlight or underline *only* the content that's most important.

Take Notes. You can take notes while you read using a laptop or notebook, and you can return to these notes when it's time to study. If your goal is to read the material just once, take thorough notes (see the note-taking chapter for specific methods). Later, as you prepare for a test, you'll study directly from these notes. If you plan to reread the material, try taking broad notes as you read. For example, jot down key words with definitions, record where to find diagrams or charts in the chapter, or write a short summary of the material.

As you read and take notes, look for the answers to your purposeful reading questions, and write them down as you find them. For example, if one of your questions is "What are polynomials?" and you come across the definition of *polynomials* in the chapter, add it to your notes or mark it in your book so that later you can go back and study the definition.

Think Critically about What You Read

College would be simpler if everything you read was trustworthy, but that's not always the case. In fact, one of the best skills you'll develop in college is the ability to *evaluate* the quality, accuracy, and usefulness of

FIGURE 6.3 Marking Your Textbook: A Sample Page

As you can see from this sample textbook page, you can use a number of techniques to mark your book: making annotations in the margins, highlighting main ideas, and underlining key points. You can also jot down purposeful reading questions and answer them on the page itself (if there's space) or in your notes. Text excerpt, p. 147, from *Psychology*, 6th ed., by Dan and Sandra Hockenbury. Copyright © 2013 by Worth Publishers. Used by permission.

Purposeful Reading Question (PRQ): What's the difference between dreams and sleep thinking?

Ex: Being chased through woods

☆ Key Theme!

Dreams and Mental Activity During Sleep

▰ KEY THEME

> A dream is an unfolding sequence of perceptions, thoughts, and emotions that is experienced as a series of actual events during sleep.

▰ KEY QUESTIONS

more great purposeful reading questions!

> How does brain activity change during dreaming sleep, and how are those changes related to dream content?

> What roles do the different stages of sleep play in forming new memories?

> What do people dream about, and why don't we remember many of our dreams?

Dreams have fascinated people since the beginning of time. By adulthood, about 25 percent of a night's sleep, or almost two hours every night, is spent dreaming. So, assuming you live to a ripe old age, you'll devote more than 50,000 hours, or about six years of your life, to dreaming.

Wow. I will spend a ton of time dreaming.

SLEEP THINKING = SLEEP MENTATION

Although dreams may be the most interesting brain productions during sleep, they are not the most common. More prevalent is **sleep thinking,** also called *sleep mentation.* Sleep thinking usually occurs during NREM slow-wave sleep and consists of vague, bland, thoughtlike ruminations about real-life events (McCarley, 2007). Sleep thinking probably contributes to those times when you wake up with a solution to some vexing problem. But at other times, the ruminating thoughts of sleep thinking can interfere with your sleep. For example, on the night before an important exam, anxious students will sometimes toss and turn their way through the night as they mentally review terms and concepts during NREM sleep thinking.

DEF: SLEEP THINKING

WHEN I HAVE SLEEP THINKING:
– Wake up w/great idea
– Negative: toss and turn w/worry

In contrast to sleep thinking, a **dream** is an unfolding sequence of perceptions, thoughts, and emotions during sleep that is experienced as a series of real-life events (Domhoff, 2005). Granted, the storyline and details of those dream events may be illogical, even bizarre. But in the unique mental landscapes of our own internally generated reality, the bizarre and illogical are readily accepted as disbelief is suspended.

DEF: DREAM

Most dreams happen during REM sleep, although dreams also occur during NREM (Domhoff, 2011). When awakened during active REM sleep, people report a dream about 90 percent of the time, even people who claim that they never dream. The dreamer is usually the main participant in these events, and at least one other person is involved in the dream story. But sometimes the dreamer is simply the observer of the unfolding dream story.

So most people do dream.

PRQ:	*Dream*	*Sleep Thinking*
Answer:	• *Sequence of ideas, thoughts, emotions*	• *About actual events*
	• *Seems like real life*	• *General, unclear thoughts*
	• *May be bizarre*	• *Worry or great ideas*
	• *Mostly during REM*	• *Normally during NREM*

Student Voices of Experience

GAINING CONFIDENCE IN READING

Courtesy of Jennifer Torres

NAME: **Robert E. Moreno III**

SCHOOLS: *Glendale Community College; Northern Arizona University*

MAJOR: *Communication Studies*

CAREER GOAL: *Education field*

> "One thing I find helpful is to write in the margins of my book and make side notes."

Reading is something I've improved on greatly over the years, especially during my time at Glendale Community College (GCC). As a kid, I loved to read — it was fun. However, when I got to school, it became much more difficult. There was a lot to read! And in class they would make you read out loud. I always worried that my speech impediment would show. It wasn't until I attended GCC that I gained confidence in my reading, found my voice, and started to speak out more.

When I first got to college, I realized two things about reading. First, I'd have to do a lot more reading than I ever did as a kid. And second, I wasn't able to read things as quickly as the other students. However, I've implemented a few techniques to increase my reading speed and my retention of the material. One thing I find helpful is to write in the margins of my book and make side notes. If I don't know a particular word, I look it up so I'll understand what I'm reading. To increase my speed, I learned to first preview the chapter — to quickly look through the layout of the chapter, the headings, the pictures, and get an overall sense of what I'm going to read. Then I go back and fully read the chapter. This might take a little more time initially, but I found it's a great way to understand what I'm reading.

Now when I read out loud, I take my time and control my breathing. This helps me control my stuttering and speak fluently. I've found that reading has helped me become not only a better speaker but also a better writer. And as someone with a speech impediment, I enjoy expressing my thoughts, ideas, and passion in writing for others to read.

YOUR TURN: Have you used any of the reading strategies Robert has used? If so, which ones? What benefits have these strategies provided for you? What challenges?

information — that is, to think critically about what you're reading. As a critical thinker you can evaluate the soundness of the arguments presented in each reading, as well as the authors' credentials, and then formulate your own thoughts about what the material is saying and whether it's trustworthy.

In addition to evaluation, another important component of critical thinking is application. *Applying* what you read to your own life or to everyday situations can help you learn and remember the material. Imagine you're reading about the power of eye contact in your communications textbook. To connect the material to your own life, you think about how disconnected you felt on a recent first date when your date wouldn't look you in the eye, and how welcoming it feels when the barista at the coffee shop looks right at you and smiles. By making this connection, you're processing the material more deeply, a strategy that will help you remember what you learned later in the term.

Clarify Confusing Material

As you read, you'll inevitably run into content—a word, a concept, an example—that you don't understand. Try these techniques to clarify confusing content.

- **Carefully reread the material.** You might understand it on the second or third try.
- **Expand your vocabulary.** Look up definitions of unfamiliar words, and use the words in sentences to grasp their meaning.
- **Move on.** Something you read later in the material might clarify things. Or simply giving yourself a few minutes away from the confusing content might help you see something you missed the first time.
- **Ask a classmate** or a knowledgeable friend to explain the material.
- **Find help online.** Reading another author's interpretation of confusing content might help. However, remember that not all Internet sources are trustworthy, so use your critical-thinking skills to evaluate what your search engine throws at you.
- **Ask your instructor.** His or her job is to help you learn, so don't be afraid to ask for clarification when you have questions.

Boost Your Reading Efficiency

Reading efficiently can help you stay focused on the most important material so that you don't waste time and effort on less relevant content. You can supercharge your reading efficiency by mastering the art of concentration and by increasing your reading speed.

Sharpening your powers of concentration can help you avoid an all-too-common problem: realizing that your mind has wandered

Reading: It's Good for You!

Did you know that motivation to read is connected to reading improvement? According to a three-year study of 1,500 middle school students, those who are internally motivated to read have better outcomes than those who are externally motivated.[4] Students told the researchers about their motivation to read and then completed an assessment of their reading ability once a year during the study. Some students read for enjoyment, meaning they found reading to be a pleasant activity and read in their free time. Other students read because they found the subject matter interesting. Still other students read for competitive reasons—to become better readers than their peers.

The researchers then compared the students' motivation for reading to their reading performance. Students who read for enjoyment and because they were interested in the material displayed the most improvement in reading performance over the three years of the study. Students who read for competitive reasons, on the other hand, displayed no improvement in reading performance.

There are two important takeaways from this research. First, you'll definitely have a lot of required reading in college, but if you also find time to read for fun, you might see your overall reading skills improve. Second, try looking for interesting topics in all class readings, even if the class isn't your favorite. This, too, may help improve your reading performance!

and that you have no idea what you just read. Try the following tactics for enhancing your concentration.

- **Set brief reading goals.** Create very short-term, focused reading goals if you're unfocused. Instead of trying to read for ninety minutes, for example, set a goal of reading four pages from your religious studies book and reading your marketing text for fifteen minutes. Dividing your reading into small chunks and switching between topics can help you cover all your reading assignments without feeling overwhelmed and losing focus.

- **Move around.** If you're bored with your reading and can't concentrate, get up and move. Take a one-minute walk around the stacks in the library, grab thirty seconds of fresh air outside, or throw your book into your bag and head for a different study carrel. Then get back to reading.

- **Remove distractions.** If distractions—noises, people passing by, text message or e-mail pings—are preventing you from concentrating, remove them. For instance, turn off your phone, or close the curtains or blinds so you can't see what's happening outside. See the chapter on organization and time management for more ideas on creating a distraction-free zone.

In addition to sharpening your powers of concentration, increasing the speed at which you read can help you make better, more focused use of your reading time. Reading faster is a skill that you can build with practice. Before you spend any of your money on a speed-reading class, try the following techniques.

- **Read in chunks.** Instead of reading one word at a time, try reading groups of words. (Here's how you could "chunk" the preceding sentence: "Instead of reading—one word at a time—try reading—groups of words.") As you focus on groups of words, your speed will increase. There's no one "right" way to do this; when you read, try different groupings to see what works for you.

- **Use a cue.** Place your fingertip at the middle of the first line of a paragraph.

Slowly drag this "cue" down the middle of the paragraph, reading each line as you go. When you use a cue, your eyes follow your finger instead of moving left to right across each line. This forces your mind to read each line in chunks rather than each word individually. This technique may take some practice, but the more you do it, the easier it gets.

- **Skim.** If you have a lot of reading to do and not much time, skim the material. Move your glance quickly across each line or read the first and last sentence of each paragraph. Skimming isn't the most effective strategy for deep understanding of material—you'll likely trade some comprehension for speed—but it's better than not reading at all. Just try not to use this approach unless you're pressed for time.

A Rocket-Assist for Your Reading. Boosting your reading speed lets you get maximum value from your reading time. But you don't necessarily have to take a speed-reading class to master this skill. Instead, you can try some simple but effective tactics.
Tony Zuvela/www.CartoonStock.com

Review What You've Read

After you complete a reading assignment, you might be tempted to say, "Okay, check that off the list!" and continue on with your day. Do your best to resist that impulse: There's still work to be done. By revisiting what you've read, you'll improve your comprehension and recall of the information, and you won't have to relearn the material from scratch as you prepare for exams and assignments. Reciting, summarizing, and reviewing and studying are three potent techniques you can use.

Recite

After you read, take a few minutes to recite the main ideas, key words, and new information you've gained from the reading. When you *recite*, you state the information you've learned out loud (if you're by yourself) or in your head (if you're in the library). Reciting new knowledge helps you remember the information you've learned.

Summarize

Gather the central ideas from a reading, and write them down in your own words, either in your notes or at the end of each section of your textbook. Summaries can take different formats, including bulleted lists and short paragraphs. For example, you might write the following summary for this section of the chapter.

Reading Follow-Up
- *State the main ideas out loud.*
- *Write a summary of the key concepts.*
- *Schedule time to review and study reading notes each week.*

Like reciting, summarizing requires you to think carefully about the material you've read, which boosts your comprehension of new concepts.

Review and Study

There are many different ways to review and study the material you've read. If you wrote

A Rave Review. Mira knows that reviewing what she has read can help her remember the key concepts in the material. Here she's flipping through a textbook chapter, reciting to herself the main ideas she just learned. You can use this and other reviewing strategies — just pick the ones that work best for you.
Rei and Motion Studio/Shutterstock

summaries, study them while you eat breakfast. Here are some additional ideas.

- After you read a chapter, take ten minutes to discuss the main ideas in it with a study partner.
- Recall the answers to your purposeful reading questions while you drive to school each morning.
- Make up your own test items for each chapter, and share them with members of your study group.
- Share your reading notes with a friend, ask for feedback, and fill in any information missing from your notes.
- Check out the memory, studying, and test taking chapter of this book where you'll find a number of additional tips you can use to review.

Read Different Types of Materials

The tips you've learned so far in this chapter can help you with any reading assignment in college. However, there are also more specific tips you can use for particular types of reading materials, such as math and science books, original research articles, and readings for online courses. Give these a try.

Read for Math and Science Classes

Math and science courses aren't identical, but they share enough in common that you can use similar strategies for both types of reading assignments.

- **Budget your time wisely.** Math and science reading tends to be dense, so schedule enough time to complete it by the due date.

- **Keep up with your work.** Many math and science classes are *linear*: To solve problems in week 2, you have to use what you learned in week 1, and so on. As you read, if you encounter a topic you don't understand, spend enough time on it to grasp it. If you're still struggling with it, get help before your instructor moves too far ahead.

- **Follow the rules.** Math and science have rules that must be followed, so be sure you understand each step of the formula or theorem you're reading about. If you miss a step or break a rule when trying to solve an equation or prove a theorem, you'll be more likely to come up with incorrect answers.

- **Understand symbols and formulas.** If you feel as though you're learning a new language in your math and science classes, that's because in some ways you are. In mathematics and in sciences such as chemistry, engineering, and physics, key information is often expressed in symbols and formulas rather than in words (see Figure 6.4). To understand the material in these classes, pay special attention to these elements—don't skip over them as you read.

- **Study diagrams and models.** While some sciences rely heavily on symbols and formulas, reading material in others—such as biology, anatomy, and geology—includes more text-based descriptions and diagrams and models. Closely examine these visual elements; the information they contain is often just as valuable as the accompanying text.

- **Practice.** Do the exercises in the book, even if your instructor doesn't assign them. Practice helps deepen your understanding of the material.

- **Use flash cards to memorize terms.** You'll encounter many terms in your science courses—for example, the names of organisms in a biology course or the parts of the human body in an anatomy class. Creating flash cards can help you learn and remember these terms.

Read Journal Articles

Have you heard of the *New England Journal of Medicine, Science,* or *Nature?* These are examples of well-known *journals*—scholarly magazines that publish academic and scientific papers, many of which are written by college professors. In journal articles, professors describe research they're conducting, share new ideas or theories, summarize findings from a broad area of research, or present original works such as poetry or short stories.

Journal articles are packed with useful information, but they can be more complex than other sources. To read and understand them, you have to know which parts of the article to focus on. Many articles, particularly research articles, have the following sections:

- *Abstract*: a paragraph summarizing the article

- *Introduction*: a review of previous research that supports the study and a description of the research questions, often called *hypotheses*

- *Methods*: a description of what the authors studied and how they studied it

Dosage Calculations

For some medicines prescribed for patients, the dosage must be adjusted according to the patient's weight. This is especially true when administering medicine to children. For example, a dosage of "8.0 mg of tetracycline per kilogram body weight daily" is a dosage based on the weight of the patient. A patient's weight is often given in pounds, yet many drug handbooks give the dosage per kilogram body weight of the patient. Therefore, to calculate the correct amount of medicine to give the patient, you must first convert the patient's weight from pounds into kilograms with an English-metric conversion, using Table 1-3.

It is important to recognize that the dosage is itself a conversion factor between the mass or volume of the medicine and the weight of the patient. Whenever you see the word *per*, it means *in every* and can be expressed as a ratio or fraction where *per* represents a division operation (divided by). For example, 60 miles *per* hour can be written as the ratio 60 mi/1 hr. Similarly, a dosage of 8.0 mg *per* kg body weight can be expressed as the fraction 8.0 mg/1 kg. Hence, dosage *is* a conversion factor:

$$\frac{8\text{ mg}}{1\text{ kg}} \quad \text{or} \quad \frac{1\text{ kg}}{8\text{ mg}}$$

Dimensional analysis is used to solve dosage calculations by multiplying the patient's weight by the appropriate English-metric conversion factor and then multiplying by the dosage conversion factor, as shown in the following worked exercise.

> Some common abbreviations indicating the frequency with which a medication should be administered include *q.d.* and *b.i.d.*, derived from the Latin meaning administered "daily" and "twice daily," respectively. If the medicine is prescribed for two times daily or four times daily, divide your final answer by two or four to determine how much to give the patient at each administration.

WORKED EXERCISE | Dosage Calculations

1-19 Tetracycline elixir, an antibiotic, is ordered at a dosage of 8.0 mg per kilogram of body weight q.d. for a child weighing 52 lb. How many milligrams of tetracycline elixir should be given to this child daily?

Solution

Step 1: Identify the conversions. Since the dosage is given based on a patient's weight in kilograms, an English-to-metric conversion must be performed. From Table 1-3 this is 1.000 kg = 2.205 lb. The dosage itself is already a conversion factor.

Step 2: Express each conversion as two possible conversion factors. The English-to-metric conversion factors for the patient's weight are

$$\frac{1\text{ kg}}{2.205\text{ lb}} \quad \text{or} \quad \frac{2.205\text{ lb}}{1\text{ kg}}$$

The dosage *is* a conversion factor between the mass of medicine in milligrams and the weight of the patient in kilograms:

$$\frac{8.0\text{ mg}}{1\text{ kg}} \quad \text{or} \quad \frac{1\text{ kg}}{8.0\text{ mg}}$$

FIGURE 6.4 Reading Science Textbooks

This page from an allied-health-themed chemistry textbook shows several types of information you might encounter while reading math and science material: abbreviations for dosages, a practice exercise, and a formula for getting the right medicine dosage for people of different weights. Text excerpt, p. 23, from *Essentials of General, Organic, and Biochemistry*, 2nd ed., by Denise Guinn. Copyright © 2014 by W. H. Freeman. Used by permission.

- *Results*: a description of the statistical analysis used to answer the research questions

- *Discussion*: a written summary of the findings or answers to the research questions

You can follow these steps to understand the material in a research article.

1. Read the *abstract* and state the article's main idea in your own words. Once you

can do this, you're ready to read the article itself.

2. Read the *introduction*, focusing on the hypotheses at the end of this section. Make sure you know what questions the authors are trying to answer.

3. Read the *discussion*, focusing on the first few paragraphs. The authors will likely state the answers to the research questions in prose form (as opposed to statistical form, which often appears in the results section).

4. Once you understand the research results from the discussion, read the *methods* and *results* sections to see more clearly how the authors came to their conclusions.

Journal articles are written primarily for other college professors, researchers, and experts in the field, so don't worry if you feel confused or overwhelmed at first: You're probably not the only one. Ask for help when you need it. Being able to read and understand even the basic ideas in a journal article is a useful skill, so it's worth investing time now in learning how to do it.

Read Online Course Materials

If you're taking an online class for the first time this term, you may be a bit worried. Does the class have more required reading than your face-to-face classes? Is it a hassle to access the readings online? These are legitimate concerns, but here's good news: You can use a few powerful strategies to handle your online course reading.

- **Be prepared to do more reading.** It's true that online classes require more reading because you don't spend as much time in class listening to lectures. Now that you know, you can plan in advance how to complete all your reading on time.

- **Create your own schedule.** If your online class doesn't have regular reading assignments or quizzes to help you stay on track, build your own reading schedule—then stick to it.

- **Make sure you can access online materials.** If you have to access reading materials online, make sure you can do so when the class begins. If you run into any difficulties, ask the instructor for help right away. That way, you'll be confident you can

Ask for Help with Reading Challenges

Many students find reading to be challenging but are uncomfortable asking for help. Is this true for you? If so, try thinking about your situation this way: Just as athletes, musicians, and business executives work with coaches to improve their performance, you can work with people on campus to improve your reading performance. Knowing when and how to ask for help is a valuable skill that will benefit you now and in the future. So take a moment to consider the following helpful resources.

- **Staff at the Learning Assistance Center.** Most campuses have a tutoring or learning support center that focuses on helping students with reading, studying, and many other skills essential for college success. To find the office on your campus, browse your school Web site or type keywords such as "tutoring" or "academic support" into the site's search function.

- **Advisers.** Advisers are used to working with students who need assistance, and they have likely helped others in your position. Talk with your adviser or someone in the advising office about how to approach reading.

- **Staff at the Disability Services Office.** If you have a diagnosed learning disability or think you might have a reading disability, visit your school's disability services office to find out how the staff there can help.

access what you need to complete your assignments.

- **Learn how to mark up text online.** If you're reading online, learn how to mark up text using the tools available with your program or device. Documents in PDF format, for instance, often allow you to highlight text and make notes in the margins. E-books frequently have the same features (see Figure 6.5). In addition, when you read electronically, you often have access to a search function, which allows you to find something you wrote in a note or to search for a specific term.

- **Consider printing out materials.** If your reading materials are provided electronically but you prefer to annotate them in paper form, investigate whether you can print them out.

- **Read and respond to online posts.** You'll often be required to read and respond to other students' online posts in discussion boards for the course. Take time to read and reflect on the posts. You can learn a lot from what others have to say.

FIGURE 6.5   Marking an E-book

When you're reading online, you can use tools to mark up the material. In this excerpt from a biology textbook, the student has used yellow highlighting to emphasize a key point. She has also included a note reminding herself to add a key term to flash cards she's creating for the chapter.

FIGURE 5-11 presents an overview of the processes of transcription and translation. In transcription, which in eukaryotes occurs in the nucleus, the gene's base sequence, or code, is copied into a middleman molecule called **messenger RNA (mRNA).** (Because prokaryotes don't have a nucleus, transcription occurs in the cytoplasm.) This is like copying the information for the chocolate chip cookie recipe out of the cookbook and onto an index card. The mRNA then moves out of the nucleus into the cytoplasm, where translation allows the messages encoded in the mRNA to be used to build proteins.

c lembo   5/29/2017 5:03 PM
Key term! Add messenger RNA (mRNA) to flash cards.

Reply

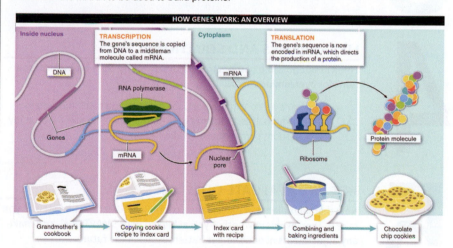

FIGURE 5-11   Overview of the steps from gene to protein.

my personal success plan

READING

Are you inspired to set a new goal aimed at improving your reading skills? If so, the Personal Success Plan can walk you through the goal-setting process. Read the advice and examples; then sketch out your ideas in the space provided.

LaunchPad Solo
macmillan learning

To access the Personal Success Plan online, go to LaunchPad Solo for *Connections Essentials*.

1 GATHER INFORMATION

Think about your strengths and weaknesses related to reading. What reading strategies have worked for you in the past? What could you do differently? Revisit your Reading score on ACES and review the relevant sections of this chapter for additional ideas.

2 SET A SMART GOAL

Use the information you've gathered to create a SMART goal, making sure to use the SMART goal checklist.

SAMPLE: I'll create purposeful reading questions before I read the next chapter in my economics book.

3 MAKE AN ACTION PLAN

Outline the specific steps you'll take to achieve your SMART goal, and note when you'll complete each step.

SAMPLE: Tomorrow night, I'll turn each bullet point from the chapter summary into a purposeful reading question.

4 LIST BARRIERS AND SOLUTIONS

Think about possible barriers to your action steps; then brainstorm solutions for overcoming them.

SAMPLE: I've never done this before, so I might have a hard time writing questions. If so, I'll ask my study partner Ethan to take a look at my questions before class on Friday.

5 ACT AND EVALUATE OUTCOMES

Now that your plan is in place, take action. Record each action step as you take it. Then evaluate whether you achieved your SMART goal, and make any adjustments needed to get better results in the future.

SAMPLE: My purposeful reading questions were mainly about definitions, which limited how much I learned from the chapter. Next time, I'll try writing more analytical questions.

6 CONNECT TO CAREER

List the skills you're building as you progress toward your SMART goal. How will you use these skills to land a job and succeed at work?

SAMPLE: Using purposeful reading questions helped me read with focus. I'd like to become a financial analyst, and I'll need that type of focus while I read annual reports and profit-and-loss statements.

1 my information

_____

2 my SMART goal

_____

☐ **S**PECIFIC ☐ **M**EASURABLE ☐ **A**CHIEVABLE ☐ **R**ELEVANT ☐ **T**IME-LIMITED

3 my action plan

_____

4 my barriers/ solutions

_____

5 my actions/ outcomes

_____

6 my career connection

_____

Chapter 6 Review

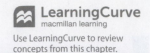
LearningCurve
macmillan learning
Use LearningCurve to review
concepts from this chapter.

- Along with attending class, note taking, studying, test taking, and writing and presenting, reading is a critical academic skill. Reading and attending class set the stage for excelling at other study skills, so reading is foundational to your success.

- To understand, remember, and apply what you learn from reading, you need to take a three-step active reading approach: (1) prepare to read, (2) read with focus, and (3) review what you've read.

- Strategies for preparing to read include evaluating how long your reading will take; previewing your textbook preface, table of contents, and key terms; and developing purposeful reading questions.

- Strategies for reading with focus include marking up your reading materials, thinking critically about what you're reading, clarifying material you don't understand, and boosting your reading efficiency by sharpening your concentration and increasing your reading speed.

- Strategies for reviewing what you've read include reciting key concepts in your own words, summarizing them in a bulleted list or paragraph, and reviewing and studying your notes.

- In addition to using the other strategies mentioned in the chapter, you'll want to master strategies for reading specific types of materials, such as math and science textbooks, journal articles, and readings assigned in your online classes.

CHAPTER ACTIVITIES

Adopting a Success Attitude

DISCOVERING ENJOYMENT IN READING

Reading for pleasure has numerous benefits: It can build your knowledge, improve your vocabulary, boost your reading speed, enhance your creativity and imagination, relieve stress, and promote positive emotions.

Choose four literary genres from the following list. For each genre you choose, identify a book that you might like to read. (Search online or go to a bookstore to get ideas.) Provide the book's title, the author's name, a brief description of the book, and the reason it interests you. Now set a goal for your reading. When will you read the titles you've listed?

classic literature	science fiction	biography
fantasy/adventure	mystery	autobiography
historical fiction	romance	nonfiction
crime/detective	humor	poetry

Applying Your Skills

LEARNING TO READ WITH A PURPOSE

Preparing to read is a critical step in the active reading process, and previewing your reading is one method you can use to prepare.

Preview one of the chapters in this textbook that you haven't read yet. Read the title, the chapter outline, and the first few paragraphs of the chapter (the introduction). Then look for the main headings and any boldfaced terms and read the chapter summary. Finally, write down five purposeful reading questions—ones you would like to answer after you've read the full chapter. If you have trouble, look back at the examples in this chapter or try crafting *Who? What? When? Where? How?* and *Why?* questions.

When you read the chapter later in the term, see if you can answer the purposeful reading questions you've developed.

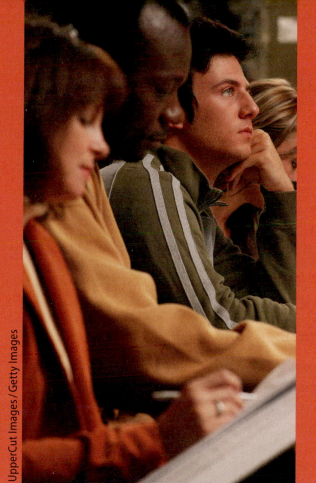

UpperCut Images / Getty Images

7

Taking Effective Notes

Supercharge Your Note Taking with a Four-Step Strategy

Experiment with Note-Taking Methods

Note-Taking Tips for Math, Science, and Online Classes

MY PERSONAL SUCCESS PLAN

Let's be honest: Note taking isn't the most exciting topic to study. In fact, you probably groaned at the thought of reading a whole chapter about taking notes. Now that we've got this out in the open, how can you approach this chapter with a positive attitude? Try to change your thinking about note taking.

At its heart, note taking is much more than writing or typing words: It's a way to record, organize, and manage information so that you can *learn* from and *use* it. To be a good note-taker, you need to recognize which information is most important, figure out how to record the information so it's clear, and use your notes to study. When you build these skills — as you'll do by using the strategies in this chapter — you'll better understand what you're learning and, as a result,

perform better on exams and homework assignments. In short, note taking is a survival skill for college.

Note taking can also help you learn and manage information at work. For example, you might record ideas when brainstorming with colleagues or write down important information from clients so you're sure to meet their needs.

In this chapter we present a four-step strategy for taking notes: (1) prepare to take notes; (2) actively listen, watch, read, and participate when you read or attend a lecture; (3) record information; and (4) review your notes. We then examine four note-taking methods: outlining, charting, the Cornell system, and mapping. Finally, we explore specific strategies for taking notes in math, science, and online courses.

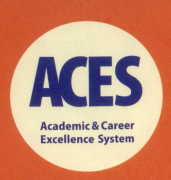

ACES

Academic & Career Excellence System

To find your **Note Taking score,** go to LaunchPad Solo for *Connections Essentials.*

REFLECTION:
Note Taking

Take a moment to reflect on your Note Taking score on ACES. Find your score and add it to the box on the left.

This score measures your beliefs about how well you take notes. Do you think it's an accurate snapshot of your current skills in this area? Why or why not?

- **IF YOU SCORED IN THE HIGH RANGE** and you have a strong track record of effective note taking, then this is likely one of your strengths. Excellent! Now think about how you can enhance this strength. For instance, you might learn a new strategy in this chapter that helps you maintain focus during lectures. Or you might find a way to restructure your notes so they're easier to follow when you study for exams. The more strategies you have, the better you'll get at taking notes.

- **IF YOU SCORED IN THE MODERATE OR LOW RANGE,** you've got the perfect opportunity: Use the strategies in this chapter to strengthen your note-taking skills. Sample some of the different techniques presented, and figure out which ones help you most effectively record the information you need. Take control of your learning!

ACES Journal

Think about how you developed your note-taking methods. Did you learn in a class? From a friend or sibling? Did you teach yourself? Some study skills like note taking aren't formally taught in school. Write a brief paragraph about how you developed your note-taking skills. Then write a few sentences about the effectiveness of your notes: How well do they work for you? Finally, conclude your reflection by describing two ways you'd like to improve your note-taking skills this term.

_____

_____

_____

_____

_____

Supercharge Your Note Taking with a Four-Step Strategy

Note taking plays a key role in academic success.[1] When you combine it with other important study skills and activities—reading, going to class, studying, taking exams, and writing and speaking—note taking helps you absorb, think about, remember, and use new information you're learning in your courses.

There is no "right" format for taking notes; you can choose from a variety of methods, depending on what works best for you. But no matter which method (or methods) you choose, you'll get the most learning power from your notes if you approach note taking strategically. We recommend a four-step strategy: Get prepared; actively listen, watch, read, and participate; record the information you're learning; and review your notes (see Figure 7.1).

Let's take a closer look at each step.

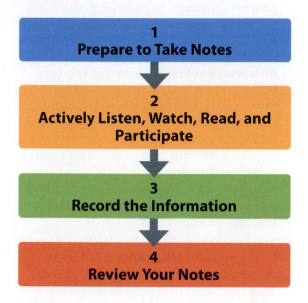

FIGURE 7.1
Four Steps to Effective Note Taking

Step 1: Prepare to Take Notes

When you *prepare* to take notes, you'll find it much easier to focus on the most important information once you actually *take* notes—for instance, when you're listening to a lecture, reading an assignment, or watching a video. Because preparation helps you focus, it boosts the quality and usefulness of your notes. Use these tactics to prepare successfully.

- **Gather the materials you'll need to take notes.** For example, find your textbook and the previous notes you took for that class or project. Decide ahead of time whether to handwrite your notes or type them on a laptop or tablet (see "Taking Notes? Grab a Pen and Paper" later in this chapter). If you choose to write by hand, make sure to have a notebook, pens, and a highlighter handy. If you're trying out a new note-taking app, get comfortable with it before using it in class.

- **Create a system to label, organize, and store your notes.** That way, you can easily find

and review your notes later when you want to use them to study for an upcoming exam or to complete a homework assignment. The chapter on organization and time management contains ideas for creating a system for labeling, organizing, and storing your notes.

- **Preview key concepts.** If you're preparing to take notes during a lecture, review the course syllabus and complete any required reading before class. If you're preparing to take notes while reading, use the previewing strategies described in the reading chapter, such as reviewing textbook chapter summaries, headings, and definitions to get a sense of the major ideas in the reading material.

- **Follow your schedule.** If you're attending a lecture, arrive a few minutes early to review your notes from the previous class. If you're taking notes on a reading, follow your study schedule and begin work at the time you had planned.

- **Review your instructor's PowerPoint slides and bring them to class.** If an instructor provides slides in advance, you can start to familiarize yourself with the key concepts that will be covered in class. That way, you won't have to write or type what's already on the slides during the lecture. Instead, you can focus on the instructor's verbal explanation and take notes that expand on the information in the slides, either on the slide printout itself or in a separate document. In fact, taking your own notes instead of relying solely on your instructor's slides has huge benefits: You think more about the information you're learning, so you stand a better chance of understanding, remembering, and applying it.

- **Bring unanswered questions to class.** If you have unresolved questions about your reading assignments, bring them to class. Your instructor may provide the information you're looking for—or you can ask the questions in class to get the answers you need.

Step 2: Actively Listen, Watch, Read, and Participate

To take good notes, you'll need to focus on the information you're receiving, whether it comes to you during a lecture, from something you're reading or discussing, or even from a video you watch for class. Focusing helps you identify the most important information in what you're hearing or seeing so that you can capture it accurately for later review and use.

To sharpen your focus on the key information, *engage* with that information by actively listening, watching, reading, and participating (depending on the note-taking situation). These techniques can help.

- **Eliminate distractions.** Even when you're trying hard to pay attention, it can be tempting to grab your phone and text friends or check out social media. When you give in to distractions, though, you

miss chunks of information you're supposed to absorb and record. So, take steps to eliminate distractions—for example, turn off your phone when you need to focus. The organization and time management chapter offers additional ideas for creating a distraction-free zone.

- **Empower yourself to concentrate.** If you're taking notes in class, sit in the front; you'll find it easier to hear your instructor and participate in class discussion. Plus, when your instructor is looking you in the eye, you'll be less likely to daydream or doze off. If you're taking notes while reading, find a quiet location in which to work.

- **Look for written cues to important concepts in your reading.** When you take notes while reading, look for section headings as well

Attention, Please! To get the most out of class, your best bet is to stay focused on the information you're receiving. With that in mind, show courtesy to your instructors when you attend lectures. For instance, listen attentively and resist any urge to fiddle with your phone. These behaviors lead to better learning—and better notes. Aaron Bacall/www.CartoonStock.com

"Before I begin today's lesson, please close Facebook, close Twitter, close Instagram, close your phones, and open your minds."

as boldfaced terms. These signal important concepts in the material. (See the reading chapter for more information.)

- **Listen for verbal cues from your instructors about what's important.** In class, instructors' speech patterns can signal that certain information is especially crucial—for example, raising or lowering their voice when emphasizing points or slowing down and repeating key concepts. Instructors might also use certain words and phrases alerting you to important material: "The main advantage . . . ," "Some of the challenges . . . ," "What we can conclude from this . . . ," and (a student favorite) "People, this will be on the test."

- **Watch for nonverbal cues.** Pay attention to your instructors' gestures and movements during class. Some instructors step out from behind the lectern, stop moving, point to a PowerPoint slide, or make direct eye contact when emphasizing an important point. We know of one instructor who rang a cowbell each time he introduced an important concept. (Most instructors are probably subtler than this!)

- **Participate in class.** Get involved in what you're learning in class. If your instructor encourages discussion, become an active participant: Contribute your thoughts about the topic of the day; ask questions about topics you're curious about; and volunteer responses to your instructor's questions. Participating in class can be intimidating—particularly if you're uncomfortable speaking in front of others, the class is large, or you find the topic of discussion confusing—but give it your best shot. By participating actively, you can clarify confusing concepts, gain additional insights into what you're learning, and stay focused on the material. And all of this helps you take better notes.

Step 3: Record Information

When it's time to record information you hear or read, do it quickly, accurately, and in a way

Make Your Voice Heard. Become an active participant in your classes by raising your hand, asking questions, and offering observations. You'll feel engaged and empowered when you play an active role in your education — and you'll learn a lot, too.
© DisabilityImages.com

that makes sense to you. Later in the chapter, you'll learn specific methods for recording information, but these general strategies can also help.

- **Label your notes.** At the top of the page, include a label with the course title, date, and a page number. If you handwrite your notes, use only one side of the page, and start notes for each lecture or reading assignment on a new piece of paper. If you type your notes, create a new document or move to a new page for each lecture or reading assignment.

- **Resist the urge to write down *everything*.** Your instructors will talk faster than you can write, and not everything said in class or printed in a book is critical information. Instead, record only the main points and the most important details, using the active learning techniques you just read about.

- **Learn to paraphrase.** Recording information *verbatim* (word for word) is important with chemical or mathematical formulas, definitions, dates, names, and diagrams because later you might need to reproduce these exactly on tests, in lab reports, or in papers. Often, though, it's best to **paraphrase** information by restating it in your own words.[2] For example, when you take notes as you read, if you just copy the words on the page into a notebook, you're not interacting with the material. When you paraphrase, however, you have to think about what you're reading and then translate your understanding into your own words. Because you're interacting with the information, you're more likely to understand and remember it. Paraphrasing is also useful in class when you need to summarize the main points of a lecture or record key ideas from a PowerPoint slide. Table 7.1 shows an example of paraphrasing.

- **Use symbols and abbreviations to save time.** You can create your own shorthand using symbols and abbreviations that work for you. For example, you might use an asterisk (*) to flag important information and the approximately symbol (≈) to indicate approximate numbers. (See Figure 7.4 and Figure 7.5 for more examples of useful symbols and abbreviations.)

- **Use metacognition to recognize when you don't understand information.** If you realize you have no idea what your instructor is saying or notice that you don't understand a sentence you just read, you're using metacognition. When you recognize that you're confused, you have information you can act on: Write down your questions and get clarification as soon as you can. You might use a star, an exclamation point, or a question mark to indicate the confusing material or leave space to later jot down notes when you get answers to your questions. Taking action to clarify concepts will get you the answers you need—*before* you see the material on a test.

- **Ask questions.** If your instructor allows questions during class (and most do!), raise your hand when you don't understand material. Asking questions shows your instructor that you care about what you're learning. If the instructor prefers to answer questions after class or during office hours, speak with him or her at the designated time and place.

- **If you have a disability, make use of accommodations.** Depending on the type of disability you have, you may be able to audio- or video-record lectures or have another person take notes for you.

TABLE 7.1 Example of Paraphrased Content

Original content	Paraphrased content
"The first human beings to arrive in the Western Hemisphere emigrated from Asia. They brought with them hunting skills, weapon- and tool-making techniques, and other forms of human knowledge developed millennia earlier in Africa, Europe, and Asia. These first Americans hunted large mammals, such as the mammoths they had learned in Europe and Asia to kill, butcher, and process for food, clothing, and building materials. Most likely, these first Americans wandered into the Western Hemisphere more or less accidentally in pursuit of prey."	• First people in Western Hemisphere came from Asia • Thousands of years of knowledge and expertise: hunting, tools, weapons • Hunted mammoths—source of food, clothing, shelter • Probably accidental migration, searching for food

Information from: James L. Roark et al., *The American Promise: A History of the United States*, 7th ed. (Boston: Bedford/St. Martin's, 2017), p. 4.

Taking Notes? Grab a Pen and Paper

With the popularity of laptops and tablets, more and more college students are coming to class with a computer. Typing notes is convenient, after all, and it's often neater and faster than writing. But a question arises: When it comes to learning information for tests, is one method more effective than the other? According to research, the answer may be "yes."

In one study, students watched brief recorded lectures and took notes using either a laptop or pen and paper.[3] Students used their regular note-taking procedure from class — either typing or writing. After the note-taking activity, they spent about thirty minutes doing other things and then were tested using two types of questions: fill-in-the-blank questions that required them to recall facts from the lecture and essay questions that required them to apply the ideas from the lecture.

Both groups performed equally well on the recall test (fill-in-the-blank questions), but students who handwrote their notes did much better on the application test (essay questions). As it turns out, students who typed their notes recorded more information from the lecture — normally a good thing — but much of it was word for word. As you just saw in this chapter, paraphrasing is often the best way to learn and remember.

The bottom line? If possible, try writing your notes by hand. If you do, you're more likely to paraphrase information, which can lead to higher-quality notes and enhanced comprehension, than to record it word for word.

Step 4: Review Your Notes

After you take notes, review them. Are they accurate? Complete? Do you have unanswered questions? If the information in your notes looks wrong or you don't understand it, your notes won't help you learn the material and use it to answer test questions or do class projects. Use these tips for reviewing your notes.

- **Review your notes when ideas are fresh in your mind.** After you've taken notes, spend a few minutes skimming them to check that the information still makes sense. If you find things that are questionable, mark them so you know to come back and get clarification. Try to review your notes within a day to fill in missing information; otherwise, you might come back to the material a few days later and have no idea what your notes mean.

- **Compare your notes with other students' notes.** See whether you're recording the same information and capturing the same level of detail as your classmates, and take the opportunity to clarify any concepts you found confusing.

- **Talk with your instructor.** Visit your instructor during office hours, and ask for feedback on the quality of your notes. If you have questions or don't fully grasp the material, ask for help.

- **Practice paraphrasing.** If you wrote something down word for word in your notes, try paraphrasing this content to understand the ideas more fully.

- **Compare your notes to the study guide.** If your instructor provides a study guide, compare your notes to the material it contains. Are the main ideas from your notes similar to those of the study guide? If not, add any missing content to your notes.

- **Clarify and reorganize your notes.** If your handwritten notes are hard to read, type them out. If your typewritten notes are confusing, retype them in a clearer form in a new document. Reorganize the content of your notes to clarify the connections between ideas. If your notes are incomplete, fill in the gaps. According to research, meaningful time spent reviewing and rewriting your notes more clearly may help you get higher scores on exams.[4]

Experiment with Note-Taking Methods

There is no single "best" note-taking method: Different methods work well for different people in different courses. In this section we describe four popular methods. As you read about each one, think about the note-taking methods you've used in the past. Which ones worked well for you? Which ones didn't? Keep in mind that note taking is a survival skill. As you gain experience and score more successes, your note-taking skill will improve, and your sense of self-efficacy will grow stronger.

Outlining

Creating an outline is a common, formalized way of taking notes (see Figure 7.2). Outlining helps you organize the material as you record your notes, making it easier to search for and review key information when you study. It works particularly well when instructors use a similar approach in their PowerPoint slides, but outlining can be used in any note-taking situation—inside and outside class. You've probably used outlines to write papers; you can use the same format when taking notes.

- **First level.** Use uppercase Roman numerals (such as I, II, III) to represent the main ideas from a lecture or reading. You may be able to identify these before you read by previewing the chapter or before class by reviewing lecture slides posted by your instructor.

- **Second level.** Use uppercase letters (such as A, B, C) to record the key points that support the first-level headings.

- **Third level.** Use Arabic numerals (such as 1, 2, 3) to record facts, details, or examples that support and illustrate the ideas in the second-level headings.

- **Additional levels.** You can add additional levels by indenting further and using alternating numbers and letters at each level.

- **Bullet points.** If you find letters and numerals too formal, use different levels of bullet points instead.

Find Your Personal Style. Your personal note-taking style, that is. When you experiment with different methods of recording information, including outlining, you're sure to find one or more methods that are just the right fit. ESB Professional/Shutterstock

FIGURE 7.2 Taking Notes in Outline Format

First-Year Experience 101—September 23—Page 1

I.   Motivation
    A. Affects how much homework I get done
    B. 3 key components influence my motivation
II. Self-efficacy
    A. Definition: Belief that I can perform the actions needed to reach a goal
    B. Can I be effective?
    C. Stronger self-efficacy means more likely to manage setbacks
    D. 4 factors strengthen self-efficacy—from Albert Bandura
        1. Having success
        2. Observing successful others (modeling)
        3. Getting support/encouragement from others
        4. Using a little bit of stress as a motivator
III. Relevance
    A. Relevance: Achieving a goal will make a positive difference
    B. More relevance means increased motivation
    C. 5 strategies to make things more relevant
        1. Pick out a topic of interest in every class
        2. Connect course content to long-term goals
        3. Focus on transferable skills I can get from each class
        4. Keep it practical: Keep GPA up to keep scholarships
        5. Remember that I love to learn—each class is an opportunity
IV. Attitude
    A. Good attitude makes me resilient, allows me to enjoy success and
        learn from mistakes
    B. Positive attitude will help me be more motivated, energized, focused
    C. 3 ways to maintain a positive attitude
        1. Find something positive in my work—even something small
        2. Take one class in my major each term if possible
        3. Use positive self-talk; use reframing to change negative to positive

OUTLINING AND OTHER NOTE-TAKING STRATEGIES

Courtesy of Nicole S. Williams

NAME: **Nicole S. Williams**

SCHOOL: *Indiana University–Purdue University Fort Wayne*

MAJOR: *Business Management*

CAREER GOAL: *Financial Adviser or Accountant*

> **" I've found the outlining technique to be a very effective note-taking strategy."**

I've found the outlining technique to be a very effective note-taking strategy for me. I always use bullet points, main points, and subpoints. I came across this strategy in high school. My high school teacher really didn't write many notes on the board. She talked most of the time. So, when she did write on the board, I knew the information was important, and I chose it as the main point in my outline. Then I usually added the things she said afterward as my subpoints. I've been using this technique ever since.

Outlining is clear and flows nicely for me. I'm an organized person, so I need my notes organized and in order so I can make sense of them. This strategy helped me in many courses, especially those in big lecture halls, such as psychology and anthropology.

I'm always ready to take notes. I always read assignments and books with a pencil in my hand so I can write down information. Also, I listen closely to speakers in class because they don't always write down the key points. As a matter of fact, most of the important concepts are verbally stated, so you have to be an active listener.

I also review my notes for clarity, although I admit that I don't review as much as I should or would like to. But with a test coming around — say that my test is next week — I'll usually try to review my notes for at least an hour, then take an hour break, and then go back and review them again. I try to do this for the whole week until the test comes up. Then, if I have questions about my notes, I'll go to professors at least three days before the test. That's how I usually review.

YOUR TURN: Have you used outlining to take notes? If so, what benefits has this method offered you? What challenges has it presented? If you haven't used outlining, what's the reason?

Charting

A chart is a series of rows and columns designed to organize main ideas, key concepts, and supporting details. Charts allow you to record information in a way that's easy to study from later. Consider the sample chart from a first-year experience class shown in Figure 7.3. The main topic is found in the left-hand column, and the other two columns highlight defining features and strategies related to the main topic. Charts work particularly well in classes where your instructor always presents course content in the same way. You can sketch out a rough draft of the chart before you go to class and then fill it in during the lecture.

FIGURE 7.3 Using Charts to Take Notes

Motivation Comparison Chart, First-Year Experience 101 Sept. 23 page 1

Topic	Features	Strategies
Self-efficacy	• Related to my belief that I can perform the actions needed to meet a goal • Strong sense of self-efficacy means I'm more likely to manage setbacks effectively	• Experience success • Watch successful others • Get support/encouragement • Have just a little stress as a motivator
Relevance	• When I believe that achieving a goal will make a positive difference • Helps motivate me to reach for goals	• Pick a topic of interest in each class • Connect class to long-term goals • Build transferable skills in all classes • Keep things practical • Focus on love of learning
Attitude	• Benefits include becoming resilient, enjoying successes, and learning from mistakes • Motivation and positive attitude are connected	• Always look for the positive • Take a class in my major each term, if possible • Use positive self-talk and reframing

Cornell System

The **Cornell system** organizes each page of your notes into sections: Your initial notes go on the right, key points go in a cue column on the left, and a summary section goes at the bottom of the page (see Figure 7.4). This system helps you study because after attending class or reading, you return to your notes to expand on the material you just learned. To create notes using the Cornell system, follow these steps.

1. **Divide the page.** Draw a horizontal line about two inches from the bottom of the page. The space below the line is the *summary section*. Next, draw a vertical line about two and a half inches from the left side of the page, meeting the horizontal line across the bottom. The area on the left is the *cue column*. The area on the right is the *notes section,* where you'll write notes during class or while you complete your reading.

2. **Take notes.** Record information in the notes section in any form you like, such as an outline, a series of paragraphs, or bullet points. Don't try to write down everything from the instructor's lecture or your reading material. Instead, focus on key concepts, supporting details, dates, formulas, and examples. Leave some space between each idea in your notes. You can add information here later, or just use the space to keep your notes clean and easy to read.

3. **Write cues.** Once you finish taking notes, add cues to the cue column. Cues can be main ideas, key words, formulas, questions, diagrams, or examples that correspond to the notes you've already taken, or answers to any purposeful reading questions you've developed. (See the reading chapter.) Line up your cues with the corresponding content in the notes section. When it's time to study your notes, use the cues to find information quickly or to create flash cards, with the cue on one side of the card and the content from your notes on the other side.

4. **Summarize.** After you've created your cues, write a brief summary at the bottom of the page that restates the main ideas from your notes. To summarize, you have to understand the material, so writing the summary proves that you've grasped what you've read or heard. When it's time to study, use the summary as a quick review of the ideas from that page of notes.

Mapping

A *map* is a graphical depiction of course material. It includes *nodes* and *branches* that show the connections among concepts. Detailed maps also incorporate symbols and other markings that further describe the content (see Figure 7.5). Some students sketch their maps before class with main ideas from a textbook chapter and then fill in additional content while listening to the lecture. For others, maps work best as study tools. The key to effective mapping is to create a consistent system and focus on including key words rather than trying to cram in too much detail. With practice, you can learn how to use nodes, branches, and symbols to organize material and make concepts come alive.

- **Nodes.** Nodes represent the main topics and key ideas from the lecture or reading assignment. Create a system of nodes that works for you, either with one main node (topic) in the center of the page or several large nodes on each page. When you create one central node, you can add smaller nodes to represent concepts that support the center node's main topic. For instance, in Figure 7.5 "Motivation" is the central node, and "Self-Efficacy," "Relevance," and "Attitude" are smaller nodes that introduce supporting concepts.

FIGURE 7.4   Taking Notes Using the Cornell System

First-Year Experience 101, Sept. 23, Page 1

★ Get motivated = succeed in college	Motivation — connected to my study and homework completion • 3 key components of motivation
Bandura = psychologist = self-efficacy	Self-efficacy — belief that I can perform actions needed to meet goal • Albert Bandura: 4 things build self-efficacy
Me = Strong self-efficacy for speaking in class, weak self-efficacy for writing papers. Visit writing center??	• Experiencing success • Observing successful others (models) • Getting support/encouragement from others • Using a little stress to motivate (but not too much)
Relevance = the "R" in SMART!	Relevance — if things are important to me, I'm more likely to be motivated • Find a topic of interest in each class • Connect coursework to long-term goals • What transferable skills can I get in each class? • Practical things are more relevant • Remember that I love to learn
Positive attitude = powerful motivator	Attitude — having a positive attitude can help me stay motivated • Benefits: being resilient, enjoying success, learning from mistakes
"I've studied hard, so I'm confident I'll do well on this test."	• Always look for the positive • Take a class in my major each term, if possible • Positive self-talk and reframing are tools I can use

Summary:
A person's level of motivation can affect his or her success in college. Motivation includes three key components: self-efficacy (belief in one's ability to perform certain actions), relevance, and a positive attitude. Students can use a variety of strategies to strengthen self-efficacy, make tasks relevant, and stay positive.

- **Branches.** Branches represent supporting details, such as examples, formulas, and dates. Branches might be smaller circles, squares, or simply a straight line pointing to information. Their shape and location show how the details connect to specific nodes and how different pieces of supporting information relate to one another. For instance, in Figure 7.5 the rectangular branches indicate strategies that can help strengthen

each of the three components of motivation.

- **Symbols.** You can use symbols such as stars or exclamation points to emphasize important concepts in your map. For example, a number inside a box might represent an important date; a smiley face might indicate an important person (see Figure 7.5). You can also use different kinds of lines to reflect the nature of connections among details or associations between nodes and branches.

FIGURE 7.5 Sample Notes Map

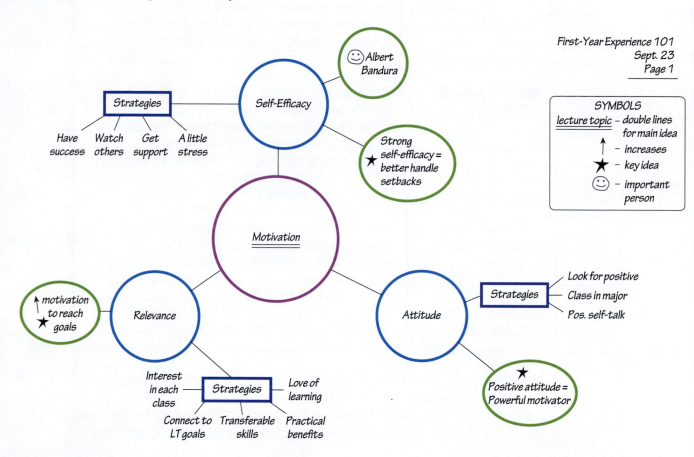

Note-Taking Tips for Math, Science, and Online Classes

The basics of note taking apply in most learning situations: You need to prepare, focus, record, and review information whether you're taking computer science or composition. But science, math, and online classes have unique characteristics, so additional, specialized strategies can come in handy. By adjusting your strategies to account for these differences, you can record the information you need efficiently and effectively.

Taking Notes in Math and Science Classes

Whether you take one math or science class or ten over your college career, try these strategies for taking good notes.

- **Be ready to record formulas and equations.** Formulas and equations are sentences written in mathematical notation. When you write down a formula or an equation, carefully record and label each of the components or steps in the process. Where appropriate, also note how the formula or equation is used.

- **Leave space in your notes.** Leave enough room in your notes to draw diagrams, write formulas and equations, and copy down problems. Also leave space to record each step as you solve problems and to show your work (see steps 1–4 in Figure 7.6).

- **Use good scientific laboratory practice.** If you think you've made a mistake in a formula, an equation, or a diagram, don't erase or scratch out everything you've written. Instead, draw one or two lines through the part containing the mistake. These lines will help you trace your thinking later and find errors that need fixing. To create a clean version, rewrite the material on a new page of notes.

- **Keep writing if you get off track.** If you fall behind the lecture when writing down a problem or a diagram, mark where you got off track and keep writing down what your instructor is saying. You want to record as much of the information as possible—you can always go back later to fill in what you missed.

- **Learn the shorthand.** In your math or science classes, learn the shorthand for those fields. For instance, if you know that Hz = hertz and d = distance in physics, or that BTU = British thermal unit in chemistry, you'll take notes faster and better understand what the information means.

- **Ask for help when you need it.** If you don't understand a concept, talk with a tutor or your instructor to get clarity. Because math and science classes tend to be linear (meaning information builds from class to class), you need to clear up any confusion immediately to stay on track. Moreover, forming a good relationship with your instructors will help you succeed in these classes.[5]

Taking Notes in Online Classes

The note-taking strategies you use for traditional classes are the same for online classes and *hybrid* classes (a blend of face-to-face and online). But online classes don't meet as regularly as face-to-face classes, so students sometimes fall behind and cut out time to take notes. To avoid this scenario, make sure you spend as much time taking notes in your online class as you do in your other classes. For example:

- When you watch videos or listen to audio recordings of lectures, take notes.

- When you read online, take notes.

- When someone makes an important point on the class's discussion board, take notes.

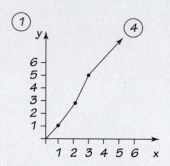
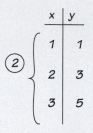

FIGURE 7.6 Sample Page of Math Notes

Math and science notes include lots of diagrams and problems. Give yourself plenty of space to write things out and show your work, and if you make a mistake, neatly cross it out. Carefully written notes can be useful when you run into problems and need to ask for help — others can see what you've done and help you identify the correct answers.

And don't forget to manage your time. When your instructors post recorded lectures online, resist the impulse to spend less time (or no time) taking notes, on the assumption that you can always go back and view the lectures again. You can — but it's more efficient to view lectures just once and take good notes rather than to watch them several times because your notes are incomplete.

Take Notes like a Professional

Good note taking is a crucial skill to have in school, but it's also a valuable transferable skill. Here are three reasons that taking stellar notes will set you up for professional success.

- **Accuracy and Attention to Detail.** How an employee captures detailed information can make or break an organization—and can even have life-and-death consequences. Think about it: If a nurse writes down incorrect details about a patient's drug allergies, then that patient could become very ill or even die if prescribed the wrong drug. If a baker mistakenly writes down that a bride wants a chocolate wedding cake instead of vanilla, then that unhappy bride could write a negative online review—driving potential new customers away. For almost all employees, the ability to capture information accurately is a key job requirement.

- **Transforming Information.** Have you ever explained something computer related to a relative who has no experience with technology? Have you ever studied with a friend and found yourself explaining a complex idea in a way that made the concept more understandable? In scenarios like these, you're *transforming* information by restating it in a way that others can understand. You practice this skill every time you paraphrase while taking notes. Transforming information is particularly useful in *STEM* fields (science, technology, engineering, and math), but it's also useful in sales, education, and many other careers.

- **Using the Information You Record.** At its heart, note taking involves accurately recording, organizing, and managing information so you can learn from and *use* it. In the work world, you might use information captured

in notes to create slide presentations, business plans, and other documents. In doing so, you get a chance to communicate what you've learned in a clear, understandable, and creative way.

Good Notes, Good Care. Emily works in an emergency room. When patients arrive, she interviews them and writes down their symptoms, medications, and allergies. By taking detailed, accurate notes, she helps provide the right care for patients. ERproductions Ltd./Getty Images

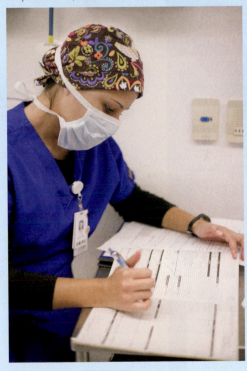

my personal success plan

Are you inspired to set a new goal aimed at improving your note-taking skills? If so, the Personal Success Plan can walk you through the goal-setting process. Read the advice and examples; then sketch out your ideas in the space provided.

To access the Personal Success Plan online, go to LaunchPad Solo for *Connections Essentials*.

1 GATHER INFORMATION

Think about your strengths and weaknesses related to taking notes. What strategies have worked for you in the past? What could you do differently? Revisit your Note Taking score on ACES and review the relevant sections of this chapter for additional ideas.

2 SET A SMART GOAL

Use the information you've gathered to create a SMART goal, making sure to use the SMART goal checklist.

SAMPLE: I'll use the Cornell system to take notes for the next two weeks.

3 MAKE AN ACTION PLAN

Outline the specific steps you'll take to achieve your SMART goal, and note when you'll complete each step.

SAMPLE: By Wednesday, I'll format twenty pages of notes using the Cornell system. I'll use these pages to take notes in class for the next two weeks.

4 LIST BARRIERS AND SOLUTIONS

Think about possible barriers to your action steps; then brainstorm solutions for overcoming them.

SAMPLE: If I have any trouble getting used to the Cornell system, I'll remind myself that it takes practice to get comfortable with a new note-taking method.

5 ACT AND EVALUATE OUTCOMES

Now that your plan is in place, take action. Record each action step as you take it. Then evaluate whether you achieved your SMART goal, and make any adjustments needed to get better results in the future.

SAMPLE: I used different formats (outlines, paragraphs, bullet points) to record information on my Cornell pages. That ended up being confusing, so I'll use a more consistent format from now on.

6 CONNECT TO CAREER

List the skills you're building as you progress toward your SMART goal. How will you use these skills to land a job and succeed at work?

SAMPLE: I want to become a nurse practitioner, so I'll need to collect information from patients about their health concerns and present it in reports to health care providers. Using the Cornell system will help me do that effectively.

1 my information

_____
_____
_____
_____
_____

2 my SMART goal

_____
_____
_____
_____
_____

☐ **S**PECIFIC ☐ **M**EASURABLE ☐ **A**CHIEVABLE ☐ **R**ELEVANT ☐ **T**IME-LIMITED

3 my action plan

_____
_____
_____
_____
_____

4 my barriers/ solutions

_____
_____
_____
_____
_____

5 my actions/ outcomes

_____
_____
_____
_____
_____

6 my career connection

_____
_____
_____
_____
_____

Chapter 7 Review

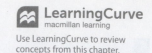

CHAPTER SUMMARY

- To take good notes, you need to follow a four-step process: prepare to take notes; actively listen, watch, read, and participate to focus on the information you're hearing or reading; record information; and review your notes.

- Outlining is a structured way to take notes that involves recording information at different levels using letters and numerals or bullet points.

- Charts organize a large amount of information in a series of rows and columns.

- In the Cornell system, you record notes, cues, and summaries on a single page. You first make notes and then go back to write cues and summaries that will be useful for studying.

- Mapping presents information visually. Nodes, branches, and symbols help you organize and depict relationships among ideas.

- To take good notes in math and science classes, you need to be thorough in noting formulas, equations, and diagrams. Learning math and science shorthand will help you take notes quickly and accurately.

- When taking notes for online classes, keep up with class material, schedule enough time for note taking, and take notes on all the information you're exposed to (such as recorded lectures, videos, and discussion board posts).

CHAPTER ACTIVITIES

Adopting a Success Attitude

BUILDING CONFIDENCE IN IDENTIFYING KEY POINTS

It takes time to build strong note-taking skills. This activity focuses on building your confidence in one component of note taking: identifying key points of a message.

First, in a notebook, create three headings across the top of a page: "Advertiser," "Product," and "Key Selling Points." Under the headings, add numbers 1 through 10. Now watch a series of television commercials. For each commercial, write down the name of the advertiser, the product, and the key points the ad is making to interest you in the product. For example, the advertiser may be an insurance company that's trying to sell car insurance, and the key selling points are the company's low-cost premiums and fast processing of claims. If you're watching TV with other people, ask them to help. Have fun with it!

Applying Your Skills

IMPROVING YOUR NOTE-TAKING SKILLS

Select a note-taking method described in this chapter (outlining, charting, the Cornell system, or mapping) that you haven't used before but would like to try. During the next week, use this method in a specific class to take notes during lecture, for reading assignments, or both. After each note-taking session, review your work within twenty-four hours and respond to the following questions:

- What are the main ideas of the lecture or reading you took notes on? What material was unclear? What questions do you have? (Talk with your instructor to clarify any confusing concepts.)

- Overall, what did you like about this note-taking method? What challenges did you encounter?

- Will you continue to use this method? Why or why not? If not, what other method will you try instead?

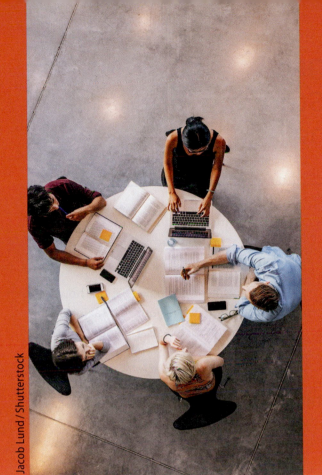

Jacob Lund / Shutterstock

8

Memory, Studying, and Test Taking

Learn How Your Memory Works

Study Basics: Set Yourself Up for Success

Prepare for Tests

Learn Test-Taking Strategies

Follow Up after Tests

MY PERSONAL SUCCESS PLAN

Picture a student sitting in the library, eyes half-open, staring blankly as he slowly turns pages of handwritten notes. He seems to be studying, but his mind isn't focused, and he's just going through the motions. How well do you think this student will perform on his upcoming exam? Chances are, he'll be disappointed with the results: When you don't think actively about what you're learning, it's hard to remember that information and use it to demonstrate mastery of material. Information doesn't magically end up in your brain. That's why you need study and test-taking strategies that help you remember and perform well on exams — strategies you'll learn in this chapter.

Does the thought of taking college tests give you butterflies? If so, let's put exams in their proper perspective. Yes, doing well on them matters, but

exams are *not* measures of your worth as a human being. They're *not* broad indicators of your intelligence. A single exam will *not* dictate the future direction of your life. Rather, an exam is a snapshot of your ability to answer a specific set of questions on a given topic. It's an opportunity to demonstrate that you've studied and that you can apply your new knowledge to the questions posed on the test. As such, tests let you "show what you know."

With these points in mind, we start this chapter by exploring the basics of memory. Then we consider strategies that help you study smarter, as well as specific techniques you can use to prepare for exams and manage test anxiety. Finally, you'll discover tactics for approaching the types of exams you'll encounter in college and for reflecting on your performance once the exam is over.

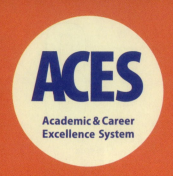

ACES

Academic & Career
Excellence System

MY ACES SCORE

☐ High
☐ Moderate
☐ Low

MY ACES SCORE

☐ High
☐ Moderate
☐ Low

REFLECTION:
Memory, Studying, and Test Taking

Take a moment to reflect on your Memory and Studying score and your Test Taking score on ACES. Find your scores on both of these scales and add them to the boxes on the left.

Your Memory and Studying score measures your beliefs about how well you study and remember information, while your Test Taking score measures your beliefs about how well you take tests. Do you think these scores are accurate snapshots of your current skills in these two areas? Why or why not?

- **IF YOU SCORED IN THE HIGH RANGE** on one or both of these scales and you're confident that these scores are accurate, then memory, studying, and test taking may be strengths for you. That's great news. Remember, though, that even strengths can be improved. For instance, maybe you routinely create review sheets — a tool that helps you study and remember information so you're prepared for your tests. If you learn how to create other kinds of do-it-yourself study tools, too, you'll be in a much better position to switch tools as needed to suit the subject matter or the settings in which you're studying.

- **IF YOU SCORED IN THE MODERATE OR LOW RANGE,** take action. This chapter — in fact, your entire college experience — gives you a powerful opportunity to build your memory, studying, and test-taking skills. You can strengthen these skills with time and practice, and this chapter is filled with ideas to help you do so.

ACES Journal

Do you ever stop to think about how your memory works? About the process of learning in class, studying that content, and then performing on an exam? Write a short paragraph about a situation in which the process of remembering, studying, and taking an exam went very well. Think about the steps you took to remember the information and study it. Next, write a short paragraph about a time when remembering, studying, and taking an exam didn't go well: What steps did you take (or *not* take) that negatively affected your performance?

Learn How Your Memory Works

Think of memory, studying, and test taking as partners who walk hand in hand. After all, if you can't remember the information you're studying, you won't learn it. As a result, you won't be able to use it later to take exams and get work done for class.

Memory involves three processes:

1. *encoding,* or taking in information and changing it into signals in our brain;
2. *storing* the information in our memory; and
3. *retrieving* the information when we want to remember it.

To get a basic sense of how these processes work together, consider what happens when you run out of milk. You open the door of the fridge, and you see a milk carton on the shelf. You pick it up and realize it's almost empty. This information from your senses of sight and touch is *encoded* into your brain as an idea: You need to pick up milk on the way home. You repeat this thought several times as you head to class ("Don't forget to buy milk"), and this repetition *stores* the idea in your memory. Later, on your way home, you *retrieve* your memory about the milk and stop at the store to pick up a carton.

This process of making memories is incredibly complex, and scientists have many theories about exactly what occurs and why.

According to one common model, which we'll focus on here, there are three stages of memory: sensory memory, short-term/working memory, and long-term memory.[1] The processes of encoding, storing, and retrieving connect the three stages together. In the following section we'll look at how this relationship works—and how it helps us remember what we learn.

Sensory Memory

In the first stage, **sensory memory**, you take in information through your five senses and form fleeting memories based on those experiences. In college, for example, information can come in through your ears (when you listen to lectures) and your eyes (when you read textbooks). In some classes you might also use touch as you perform experiments or use equipment. A few lucky students, like those of you taking culinary classes, will also get to smell and taste in class. As you absorb information through your senses, you form sensory memories of these experiences.

But sensory memories last only a split second. Our senses are constantly bombarded with information, and our brains can't take in everything.[2] It's only when we pay attention to information that it is *encoded* and moves to the next stage of memory: short-term/working memory (see Figure 8.1).

FIGURE 8.1
The Basics of Memory

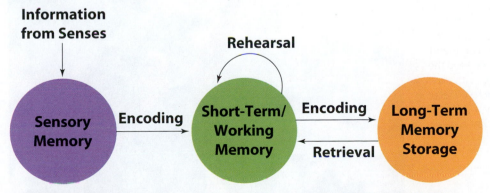

Adapted from David G. Myers and C. Nathan DeWall, *Psychology in Everyday Life,* 3rd ed. (New York: Worth Publishers, 2014), p. 194.

Short-Term / Working Memory

Our **short-term memory** is quite limited in how much information it can hold and for how long. Research shows that most people can hold about four to seven things in their short-term memory at once, and that information lasts for only twenty to thirty seconds.[3] Have you ever met someone new, only to forget his or her name when you started chatting? If so, blame your short-term memory.

To make information "stick," you need to put effort into remembering it. For example, when you are first introduced to another student, you might repeat (or *rehearse*) his name in your head five times as soon as you hear it. In addition, you might make a mental note to ask him if he wants to be your study partner for the next exam. When you put this kind of effort into remembering someone's name, you're engaging your **working memory**—the part of your short-term memory that actively processes memories and information. Thinking about, applying, rehearsing, and connecting new information to your existing memories are all ways to use your working memory, and they help your brain encode the information and move it to the next stage: long-term memory.

Long-Term Memory

Unlike sensory or short-term memory, the storage capacity of your **long-term memory** seems limitless, and memories here can last forever (although they don't always).[4] This is where you *store* the record of your life, such as your earliest childhood memories, your tenth birthday party, and your wedding day. Long-term memory is where you keep the facts, ideas, procedures, and skills you learn in college, such as the circumstances that led to the American Revolution and the process of cell division. It's also the place from which you *retrieve* your memories when you need them—for instance, when you're taking a history or biology quiz or when you run into a new acquaintance and greet him by name.

Putting It All Together

How do the three stages of memory work together? To understand this, it's helpful to compare them to the process of creating a spreadsheet. Suppose you're trying to save money to pay next term's tuition, so you decide to create a spreadsheet showing how much you spent last month. You take the following steps.

- First, you gather information about your income and expenses, such as paycheck stubs and credit card statements. When you see the information in front of you, you create a *sensory memory* of the facts and figures.

Unforgettable Experiences. Many years from now, the memories you have of graduation day—of putting on your cap and gown, getting your diploma, and celebrating with family and friends—will be stored in your long-term memory. Long-term memory is where you keep the record of your life, and it's also the place from which you retrieve your memories when you need them. Image Source TAC/Getty Images

- Next, you create a spreadsheet file on your computer and enter your expenses into it. The process of typing numbers is similar to your memory's *encoding* process—it's how information gets into the file. As you're typing, you realize that you haven't saved the spreadsheet on your computer. The unsaved spreadsheet is like your *short-term/working memory*: Until you make the effort to save it, you could lose the information if you had a power outage or your hard drive crashed.

- Finally, you save the spreadsheet file, which is like *storing* information in your *long-term memory*. Later, you open the file and *retrieve* the data.

Of course, your brain is much more complex than any computer program. For example, a computer shouldn't "forget" information unless it experiences a mechanical failure, but a human brain can forget with normal aging wear and tear. Still, this analogy gives you a basic idea of how the memory processes and stages work together.

Why You Forget

We've seen how memory works, but what happens when it *doesn't* work? Why do we forget? Forgetting occurs when there's a breakdown in one of the memory processes. Imagine that you meet a new acquaintance named Julio and that, when you run into him a week later, you can't remember his name. What happened? There are several possibilities. If you didn't hear his name when he first told you, then that information never made it into your sensory memory. Or you might have heard his name, but it slipped away because you didn't pay enough attention to keep it in your working memory. This represents an *encoding failure*: The information got lost or wasn't in your mind long enough to move to your long-term memory.[5] The other possibility, and certainly the more frustrating one, is that you did create a long-term memory for Julio's name but you still can't remember it. This is a *retrieval failure*.[6]

When you learn material for your classes, the ability to encode, store, and retrieve information is crucial, and doing this involves making an effort. Think about it this way: What would happen if you read a chapter only once and then tried to remember that information while taking a test a few weeks later? If you don't put effort into studying the chapter, you won't create strong memories of what you read, and you'll have trouble remembering the information when you need it. By contrast, actively thinking about the new information, making meaningful memories of the information, and repeatedly accessing the information by studying and reviewing it will move that information from your sensory memory to your short-term/working memory and from there to your long-term memory. In this way, you'll remember what you've learned, both at test time and far into the future.

Memory Mastery. If you find yourself remembering what you've learned in class, don't be surprised — or scared. Congratulate yourself: You've mastered major memory skills. For example, you've transformed short-term memories into long-term memories by actively reviewing information. Now you can retrieve what you've learned when you need it!
Marty Buccella / www.CartoonStock.com

"Want to hear something scary? This is the third time this week I've gotten off the bus and still remember what I learned."

Study Basics: Set Yourself Up for Success

Now that you understand how memory works, let's shift our focus to study strategies that help you remember and use your new-found knowledge. But first, ask yourself: How effective are your current study strategies? Are they working? Could you benefit from some new ideas? In this section we describe tried-and-true study strategies for mastering course material. Check out the wide array of suggestions and try out those that appeal to you most.

Manage Your Time Wisely

To study for classes effectively, you have to be in control of your time. Here are two strategies that you can use to schedule your studying effectively and make the most of every minute.

- **Space out your studying.** What's the most productive way to learn new material? As you saw in the learning chapter, it's when you space out your studying across multiple days or weeks and study in small blocks of time.[7] The more you work with the material, the more you remember about it. By contrast, trying to "cram" large amounts of information into your brain all at once (especially late at night) leads to poor performance on tests.[8]

- **Maximize study opportunities.** To make the most of study opportunities, identify brief periods of time that are going to waste and turn them into quick study sessions. For instance, if you have thirty minutes between classes, use that time to review your chemistry notes. If you have a fifteen-minute break at work, use it to look over flash cards. Thanks to mobile technology, studying anywhere is easier than ever: You can put your notes on your smartphone and quickly review them while you're waiting in the doctor's office or commuting on the bus.

Join a Study Group

Have you ever heard the saying "There's strength in numbers"? When it's time to study, working with other students can help you learn and improve your performance on tests.[9] There are several types of study groups. Many schools offer **Supplemental Instruction** for especially difficult classes, which consists of study groups led by students who did well in those classes in the past. Your instructors might also set up study groups for their classes to encourage students to work together. Alternatively, you can create your

Strength in Numbers. Joining a study group is a great way to master material. Group members can help one another grasp difficult course content. And when you explain a topic to other members, you deepen your understanding of that topic. That deeper understanding will pay off during tests. Stephen Simpson/Getty Images

own study group with classmates who want to support one another and work together. If you set up a study group yourself, create an agenda to help the group focus on particular topics at each meeting.

Before attending a group meeting, spend time studying on your own and identify specific questions you'd like help with. And be prepared to teach others in the group about topics you understand well. One of the most powerful ways to truly understand material (not just memorize it) is to teach it to someone else, and a study group gives you that opportunity.

Make Connections

You can make lasting memories by linking new information to what you already know or to personal experiences you've had (see the motivation and learning chapters). For instance, Cecily is studying for a midterm exam in Introduction to Biology, and she needs to remember the main parts of an animal cell. As she studies, she sees that one part of the cell, the Golgi apparatus, is made up of flat, oblong structures that are connected and stacked on top of each other. Their function is to process carbohydrates and proteins and sort them for transportation throughout the body. To Cecily, the Golgi apparatus looks a lot like stacked pancakes. She thinks about her favorite breakfast: pancakes and bacon, which provide the body with carbohydrates and protein. Now that she's made an association between that breakfast and the Golgi apparatus, it will be easier for her to remember what she learned when she takes the midterm.

When you make connections and apply information to other situations, you're using a powerful process called **elaborative rehearsal**. In elaborative rehearsal, you associate the meaning of new information with other information already stored in your memory,

Remember Material with Mnemonics

If you've ever tried a mental trick to remember something, like when you met someone new and associated their name with an animal they resemble, then you've used a **mnemonic** (pronounced "neh mon ik"). Try the following popular mnemonic strategies to remember information in your classes.

- **Acronyms.** Make an *acronym*, a word created from the first letter of each word you want to remember. For example, in your Introduction to Psychology class, the acronym OCEAN can help you remember the five major personality traits (openness, conscientiousness, extraversion, agreeableness, neuroticism). In this class, the acronym SMART can help you remember the steps of the goal-setting process (specific, measurable, achievable, relevant, and time-limited).

- **Associations.** Create associations between new information and things you already know. Let's say you want to memorize a list of Greek gods for your art history course. You start with Zeus, king of the gods, whom you associate with your uncle, who happens to be a large and powerful man. Zeus's wife, Hera, you associate with your aunt Helen. (Both names start with *H*, which is easy for you to remember.) Next you associate Ares, the son of Zeus and Hera, with your cousin. You might take the association even further and imagine how all of these gods would interact at your family reunion. As you create these associations, you're practicing elaborative rehearsal and building long-term memories of this new information.

- **Acrostics.** An acrostic is a phrase or sentence in which the first letter of every word corresponds to a word beginning with that letter in a list of words you want to remember. Acrostics are especially useful when you want to memorize words in a particular order: For example, in music you can use "Every Good Boy Does Fine" (E, G, B, D, F) for the order of notes on the lines of the treble clef. Can you think of what the acrostic "My Very Energetic Mother Just Served Us Nachos" represents? Here's a hint: We all live on "E."

making it easier to recall the new information later. As an added bonus, making connections requires critical thinking—a vital skill that helps you evaluate, learn, and use new information at school and at work.

Create Your Own Study Tools

You've spent hours sitting in class or responding to posts online, reading your textbooks, and taking countless pages of notes. When you create your own study tools, you bring all these efforts together to learn on a deeper level, strengthening your comprehension. Creating study tools is like using your working memory to encode information in your long-term memory: You *actively* process course material to make new memories, which you can use later on tests and projects. Consider these ideas to make your own study tools.

- **Review sheets.** To manage all the information from reading and lectures, try creating a review sheet by condensing pages of detailed notes into a one-page document. When you condense material, you include only the information you really need—such as the main ideas from your notes, annotations you made while reading a textbook chapter, problems from your math class, or dates from your history class. Give yourself some flexibility, though: If one page is too limiting, create a separate review sheet for each chapter that will be covered on a test.

- **Purposeful reading questions.** If you've created and answered purposeful reading questions while taking notes on a textbook chapter or other reading assignment (see the reading chapter), you have a ready-made study tool. Review the questions in your notes, cover up the answers, and answer the questions out loud to yourself or with a study partner.

- **Practice tests.** Answering practice test questions is a great way to get ready for an exam and increase your confidence, and it can have a significant impact on your performance.[10] As you saw in the learning chapter, one easy way to test yourself on concepts is to use flash cards. You can also design a practice test that looks more like an exam your instructor would give.

To create a practice test, first figure out the most important information you'll need to know for the exam. Review your notes from class, your textbook, and notes you took while reading to identify key topics for practice test questions. You might create matching questions for dates and events in history class, essay questions for economics class, multiple-choice questions for accounting or biology, and practice problems for chemistry or math. Create answers for each question; then take the test yourself.

Study for Math and Science Classes

Many of the study strategies you've already learned in this chapter can be used in all your courses, but several additional suggestions will be particularly helpful in your math and science classes.

- **Get plenty of practice solving problems.** Complete all the problems in your textbook, even if your instructor doesn't assign them, and do any problems provided by your instructor. Many Web sites also offer practice math, physics, or chemistry problems. Your textbook may even come with access to such online practice problems (see Figure 8.2).

- **Check your answers when solving problems.** Do your answers make sense? Are they what you expected? For example, if you're calculating the amount of force acting on a moving object, it wouldn't make sense to have a negative value as an answer. In addition, evaluate whether you're making similar or repeated mistakes when you solve problems so that you have time to correct these mistakes before an exam.

- **Write down units when solving problems.** As you work on a problem, make sure you're using the correct units of measure. If your

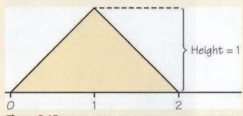
FIGURE 8.2

Solving Practice Problems

Completing plenty of practice problems, like the ones shown here, is a great way to study for math and science classes. So try your hand at all the problems provided in your textbook—even those your instructor hasn't assigned—and check out Web sites that offer practice problems. COMAP, *LaunchPad for For All Practical Purposes: Mathematical Literacy in Today's World,* 9th ed. (New York: W. H. Freeman, 2015).

---

solution is supposed to be in hertz (Hz) and instead it's in seconds, you know you've made a mistake.

- **Create lists of theorems, formulas, symbols, and vocabulary.** Review these lists during your study time.

- **Explore Khan Academy (www.khanacademy .org).** This free online resource provides brief lectures and demonstrations of many math and science concepts.

Study for Online Classes

Whether you're studying for online classes or traditional face-to-face courses, most of the same techniques can help you master material in either environment. The following tips, though, are particularly useful in studying for online courses.

- **Study all class materials.** In an online class, you may have to watch recorded instructor lectures or online videos. Add the notes you take during these lectures or videos to your study materials for the class.

- **Set up an online study group.** Create an online discussion group with your classmates to share information or practice questions. Your online course-management system might offer video-conferencing so that you can hold a virtual study group.

- **Explore online study resources at your school.** Your school may have online tutors, extra recordings of lectures, or other resources specifically designed for students taking online classes. Investigate your options.

Prepare for Tests

According to an old saying, "Success is 90 percent preparation and 10 percent perspiration." The idea that preparation leads to success isn't a new concept—throughout this book we've stressed that investing time up front helps you learn and retain more information—but that idea is equally relevant in this chapter. Why? Because taking the time to prepare is one of the most *crucial* parts of taking tests successfully. The study strategies we've already introduced are great tools for preparing for exams. In addition, you can use the specific test preparation strategies presented below.

Know the Exam Format

Knowing the exam format is critical to getting ready for a test. It also takes some of the anxiety out of the test-taking experience. Early in the term, find out what kinds of questions your instructors will include on their exams. Some instructors put this information in the syllabus; in other classes, you may have to ask. In addition, figure out whether the exams are **cumulative** (covering all the material you've learned so far in the course) or whether they include only new material you've learned since the previous test. This information will affect how you prepare.

Review Previous Exams

If your instructors provide their previous exams as a study aid, use them to get some practice and familiarize yourself with the types of questions you'll see on tests. Your instructors may make these tests available online, in a study guide, or in their offices. If your instructors don't mention previous exams, ask them if these exams are available—the worst they can say is "no." Also, even if an instructor doesn't let students review previous exams, he or she may review test material during the class period before the exam or host a study session. Take advantage of all of these opportunities.

Healthy Test Prep. As tempting as it may be to gulp down caffeine and cram late into the night to prepare for a big exam, this behavior could leave you tired and unfocused at test time. To keep your energy levels up, stick to your normal routines: Get plenty of rest, eat right, and keep exercising. That way, you'll deliver your best possible test performance. PeopleImages/Getty Images

Stay Healthy

The week leading up to an exam can be stressful, and you may find yourself skimping on sleep, devouring junk food instead of taking time to prepare meals, and cramming for the test rather than hitting the gym. These behaviors may be understandable, but they can backfire and sap your energy. As a result, when test day comes, you may deliver a less-than-stellar performance.

Resist any urge to change your routine right before a test. Instead, make a plan to stay healthy. Try to stick to your normal exercise, dietary, and sleep routines—going into a test well rested is vital to performing your best. Also, give yourself a wake-up insurance policy: If your exam is first thing in the morning, set your regular alarm plus a second alarm as a backup.

Talk with Your Instructor

Your instructors want to help you succeed—that's why they teach—so visit them during their office hours if you have questions or concerns about exams. Sometimes students feel intimidated by in-person visits, but office hours are designed so that students can meet and talk with instructors and learn one-on-one.

To get the most from these visits prepare a list of questions beforehand. For example, you might ask, "What will the exam format be?" or "How much time will we have to complete the exam?"

Most instructors' office hours are first come, first served, so consider making an appointment before you go. Also, if you can't make it to office hours, don't give up: Ask your instructor if he or she is willing to meet with you before or after class so that you can get the answers you need.

If you're taking an online class, you may not be able to visit your instructor in person, but you can still find ways to communicate. Some professors hold "virtual" office hours during which they're available to chat or answer questions online. Alternatively, use e-mail or contact your instructor to schedule a phone call.

Manage Test Anxiety

If you experience some level of **test anxiety** (nervousness or worry) before or during an exam, guess what? You're normal. Research has found that between 25 percent and 40 percent of students have experienced test anxiety.[11] In fact, a mild level of test anxiety is actually a *good* thing: It helps you stay attentive and focused while you prepare for and take the test. Intense test anxiety, though, can cause damaging, obsessive thoughts of failure ("I'm going to bomb this test"; "I know I'll fail this class"). It can also spawn feelings of doom and dread following the test ("I just know I gave the wrong answer on

Your Happy Place? If you have test anxiety, visualizing a place that relaxes you and imagining yourself in that place can help calm your nerves. You can "visit" this place anytime you want—when you're studying hard for an exam and starting to feel anxious, or even during the test if your stomach suddenly twists into knots. S-F/Shutterstock

question 9"). If you have intense test anxiety, you might experience physical reactions such as sweating, nausea, shortness of breath, or headaches. Your mind might even "go blank" during the exam.

The good news is that you *can* manage test anxiety and its negative effects. To do so try these tactics:

- **Breathing.** Breathe in for the count of three ("one, two, three") and breathe out in reverse ("three, two, one"). Repeat this pattern several times. Note how calm you feel as you exhale.

- **Muscle relaxation.** Choose a muscle group, tense those muscles for a count of ten, and then relax them. For example, curl your toes tightly and then relax. Repeat or move on to another muscle group, such as your lower leg muscles and then your upper leg muscles.

- **Preparation.** If you feel especially anxious about tests when you're not sufficiently prepared, add more time to your study schedule. Take practice tests to get comfortable with the test format.

- **Reframing.** Reframe any negative thoughts about failing the test as positive thoughts. For example, if you're thinking, "I'm going to freeze up," write that down; then rewrite it as "I've worked hard, and this test will let me demonstrate my knowledge." (See "Think Good Thoughts" for more on the power of positive thought.)

- **Visualization.** Envision a place that relaxes you—a beach, a meadow, a forest—and visualize yourself in it. "Visit" this place in your mind to relax before or during an exam.

- **Worry journal.** Record all your worries in a journal. Write down what you're afraid of, along with the emotions and physical sensations you're experiencing. Then close your journal to symbolize that you're setting aside your worries for the rest of the day. Or when you're done writing, rip the page out of your journal, crumple it up, and "throw away" your worries.

- **Campus resources.** Talk with a counselor about test anxiety or any other issues affecting your ability to succeed in school. If you experience test anxiety because you have difficulty understanding course material, work with a tutor to establish a regular study schedule and boost your confidence.

Think Good Thoughts

Not surprisingly, people who suffer from test anxiety tend to get lower scores on exams than those who don't experience test anxiety.[12] And those with test anxiety often have negative feelings and expect to perform poorly. But there is good news: According to one study, you can combat these effects by harnessing the power of positive thought.[13]

Researchers asked 118 students to engage in a brief writing task and then take a quiz. They asked students in one group to write about a recent successful experience, focusing on a time when they overcame a challenge and felt good about themselves. They asked students in another group to write about what they did in a typical morning. Students in both groups then answered questions about their feelings, how they manage stress, and any anxiety they felt about the upcoming quiz. Finally, they took the quiz.

What were the results? As it turns out, students in the positive-thoughts group had more positive feelings, a more optimistic attitude, and less test anxiety than students in the routine-thoughts group. They also had greater confidence in their stress-management skills than students in the routine-thoughts group, and they performed better on the quiz than students in the routine-thoughts group.

The bottom line? Positive thinking is a powerful thing. Simply remembering successes and thinking positive thoughts can help you reduce anxiety and perform better on exams.

PREPARING FOR TESTS AND OVERCOMING TEST ANXIETY

Courtesy of Stephanie Young

NAME: **Stephanie Young**

SCHOOL: *Oklahoma City Community College*

MAJOR: *Diversified Studies*

CAREER GOAL: *Dental Hygienist*

When I was taking college algebra, I learned that I need to breathe. I would hold my breath through a portion of my tests because I had test anxiety, and one night I just told myself I have to get over this—it's not going to work. Now, before an exam I make sure to set aside ten minutes just to look over my notes, to assure myself that what I've been studying isn't anything to be afraid of. During this time, I calm myself down by breathing easily and slowly. I also run a lot, and I feel calmer when I run. I try to stay positive because I know I'm not going to do well if I tell myself I'm not going to do well.

When I first started school, I would cram before tests, and it wouldn't work. Cramming made my anxiety issues worse. I would also feel really burnt out, and then I wouldn't do well. Now, I break up my studying. If there are ten things I have to learn for a test, I'll focus on two things each day. Also, I'll rewrite my notes and read over them throughout the day. If I can tell my husband how something works, then I feel comfortable about it, and I move on. I'm a mom and I have a four-year-old who needs my attention, too, so it works for me to study in small amounts.

I have a study buddy, and that makes preparing for tests a lot easier. I also use the biology lab at school. The lab assistants there are students, too, and are really knowledgeable. It's reassuring to know that they're learning what I'm learning and that I can move on like them. They'll sit and tutor you, too, if you need a tutor. It's hands-on in the biology center, and I really like that. Mingling with other students in the lab helps because sometimes what they're learning is being taught in a different way.

YOUR TURN: If you experience test anxiety, have you used any of the strategies for managing it that Stephanie describes? If so, which ones? How have they worked for you? What (if any) other strategies have you found helpful?

> **" I calm myself down by breathing easily and slowly."**

Learn Test-Taking Strategies

When test day rolls around, you can go into the exam knowing that you've spent time preparing, and now it's time to perform. Most of your success depends on the hard work and learning you've done before the test, but during the test you can use the strategies in this section to maximize the benefits of this preparation.

Start Smart

It's "go" time: The exam is in your hands (or on your screen). Get a solid start by taking these steps.

- **Write your name or student ID.** Depending on the instructions, put your name or student ID number on the test documents. These documents might include the test questions, an electronic answer sheet, or a booklet in which you'll write essay responses.

- **Read the directions.** Instructors design their tests in different ways, so read the test instructions carefully before answering any questions. For example, some instructors discourage guessing by giving *negative* points for an incorrect answer and *zero* points if you leave the answer blank. Find out what the rules are before you start.

- **Preview questions and budget your time.** Quickly review the types of questions on the test and the points assigned to each. For instance, a 50-point test may have ten multiple-choice questions worth 1 point each and two essay questions worth 20 points each. Knowing this will help you budget your time and might reduce your feelings of anxiety.[14] If you have fifty minutes to complete the 50-point test, spend no more than one minute on each multiple-choice question and about twenty minutes on each essay question. Also, use all the time provided. If you finish early, take advantage of the remaining time to check your answers.

- **Start with easy questions.** Tackle the questions you know the answers to first. Responding to questions that are easy for

you can help you gain confidence. Be sure, though, to keep in mind the overall points; leave enough time to answer the high-value questions, whether they're hard or easy.

- **Manage any test anxiety.** If you tense up as you start the test, use the relaxation techniques described earlier. In particular, remind yourself that you're prepared, and it's time to show what you know.

Answer Common Question Types

As a college student, you'll likely encounter five common question types when you take exams: multiple-choice, matching, fill-in-the-blank, true/false, and essay questions. This section spotlights strategies you can use to answer each question type successfully.

Multiple-Choice Questions. Exams during your first term and those in larger classes will likely contain multiple-choice questions. To answer them, you have to accurately recall information, evaluate multiple options, and eliminate poor choices. Try these strategies to improve your performance on multiple-choice questions.

- **Read the directions carefully.** Often, you'll be prompted to pick the single best answer for a multiple-choice question, but occasionally you may have to select more than one response. In addition, sometimes you'll need to identify which of the options is *incorrect*. Finally, check whether your instructor gives negative points for incorrect answers.

- **Answer the question in your mind *before* reading the answer choices.** Before you look at the response options, answer the question in your mind if you can. Then look through the options for a choice that matches your answer. If you find one, you can be relatively confident it's correct.

- **Mark any questions you skip.** If you don't know the answer to a question and want to come back to it, clearly mark the question you skip so you can easily find it later.

- **Cross out all wrong answers.** As you read through each answer option, eliminate all choices that you know are incorrect. Crossing out wrong answers will help you focus on the options you're seriously considering.

- **Read all the options.** Before marking your response, read all the answer options carefully. Instructors may use tricky language to make sure that you're paying attention and that you really know the material. They may also include several items with similar wording.

- **Look for mismatches in how the question and the answer options are worded.** Response options that don't match the question in some way may be incorrect. For instance, if the question contains a singular noun, options that are plural nouns are likely incorrect. Or if the question names a category and one of the answer responses contains something that doesn't fit in that category, that response is likely wrong.

- **Look for clues in other questions.** From time to time you'll find the answer to one question in the wording of another question.

- **Look for conditional and unconditional language.** Answers that use conditional language (such as *frequently*, *mostly*, and *typically*) tend to be correct. Answers with unconditional language (such as *always*, *forever*, *totally*, *never*, and *only*) are often wrong.

- **Consider "all of the above."** If at least two of the answer options are correct, then "all of the above" or "all of the choices" is often your best response.

- **Look for the longest answer option.** All things being equal, if you don't know the answer to the question, then choose the longest answer option. Test-question writers tend to make the correct responses longer than incorrect responses.

Matching Questions. Matching questions require you to connect test items in one list with the correct answer in a second list. These questions allow instructors to cover a great deal of information in a single test question.

Tools for Tackling Tough Test Questions. A potent set of strategies can help you tackle difficult test questions. For instance, with a multiple-choice question, unconditional language (such as *always* and *only*) often indicates an incorrect statement. And no matter what type of test you're taking, always read the directions carefully and preview the questions before you begin to work. David Schaffer/Getty Images

One challenge of these questions is that if you get one pair wrong then it keeps you from getting another right. Try some of these ideas to answer matching questions.

- **Read the question prompt very carefully.** Be sure you know exactly what the question is asking you to match.

- **Read through all the options.** Take time to read all the items in both lists to ensure that you know everything the question covers.

- **Start at the top of one list.** Matching questions are most commonly presented as two columns. Start with the first item in one of the columns, and search through the other column to find the correct answer. After you find the answer, move on to the second item in the column. If you don't find the correct answer, skip it and move to the next item, and so on.

- **Answer questions you know first.** First make any matches you're confident are correct. Skip over the ones you're not sure about.

- **Match all the items.** Matching questions usually have the same number of items in each column. Make sure you match all the items.

- **Draw a line between items.** If you're taking a written test rather than an online test (and you have a pencil that you can erase), draw a line between answers in the two columns. This approach allows you to see which items you've matched and which options remain. It also prompts you to match all the items.

- **Double-check your answers.** After you've matched all the items, briefly review your answers to make sure you've used all the items and you haven't duplicated any answers.

Fill-in-the-Blank Questions.

Fill-in-the-blank questions can be more challenging than multiple-choice questions because you don't have several responses to choose from. Instead, you have to produce the answer yourself. The following strategies can help.

- **Think about the key concepts, dates, and main topics of the class.** These are often the answers to fill-in-the-blank questions.

- **Write something.** Unless there is a penalty for guessing, write something in each blank provided in the question.

- **Check grammatical fit.** If the blank in the sentence requires a noun, make sure your answer is a noun. If the blank requires the past-tense form of a verb, be sure your answer takes that form.

- **Check your work.** After you've filled in all the blanks in a sentence, reread the sentence to make sure your responses make sense and are grammatically correct.

True / False Questions.

True/false questions can be challenging to answer, particularly when they're long and include language that seems designed to trip you up. On the positive side, you always have a 50 percent chance of being correct. Consider these strategies for answering true/false questions.

- **Look for conditional and unconditional language.** As with multiple-choice questions, conditional terms (including *sometimes*, *often*, *generally*, *seldom*, or *some*) suggest that the statement is probably true. Unconditional language (such as *all*, *only*, *invariably*, or *entirely*) often indicates a false statement.

- **Choose "false" if any part of the answer option is incorrect.** For example, the statement "The noble gases include helium, neon, argon, krypton, xenon, radon, and hydrogen" is false because hydrogen is not a noble gas.

- **Guess "true."** If you have no idea whether the item is true or false (and your instructor doesn't deduct points for guesses), select "true" as your response. As instructors, we can tell you that it's easier to write test items that are true than those that are false.

Essay Questions.

You'll often encounter essay questions on college tests, particularly in upper-level and smaller courses with fewer students. Most essay questions require you to describe topics in detail, make arguments, or analyze information. For these questions, you need to use your critical-thinking skills. In fact, your answers may need to show a mix of the levels of learning represented in Bloom's taxonomy, which range from knowledge, comprehension, and application to analysis, synthesis, and evaluation. Here are some suggestions for answering essay questions effectively.

- **Read the question carefully.** Essay questions often include one or more of the following terms: *define, summarize, apply, explain, compare/contrast, critique, illustrate, justify, outline, describe, review.* Circle these terms in the question, and make sure you're answering the question that's being asked. For example, if a question asks you to compare and contrast two theories and your response merely defines them, you're not answering the question.

- **Budget your time.** If you have thirty minutes and three essays to write, give yourself ten minutes for each.

- **Organize your response.** Before you start writing, briefly outline your response. Decide on a main point and supporting details for each paragraph in your essay. Use your outline to ensure you're answering

the question completely. Also, leave space at the end of your answer in case you have time to return to the essay and want to add a few more supporting details.

- **Proofread.** If possible, leave yourself time to proofread each essay so that you can fix any problems with grammar and spelling, flow of ideas, and accuracy of content. Draw a line through any problem areas, and neatly write your revision above the crossed-out material.

Take Math and Science Tests

In addition to the common question types we've just examined, you'll also need to be prepared for tests that focus on solving problems. Given frequently in math and science classes, these types of tests might ask you to show a proof, solve for a variable in an equation, or draw the electron configuration of a copper atom. Consider these strategies when you answer problem-solving questions.

- **Show your work.** Write out each step of your answer. This will help you double-check your work and show your instructor how you arrived at your answer.

- **Check for basic errors.** Review your work to catch and fix simple mistakes, such as mixing up positive and negative signs, rounding a number incorrectly, or calculating operations out of order.

- **Tackle hard problems last.** If you encounter a difficult problem, skip it and do the easier ones first. Return to the hard one later.

- **Answer all the questions.** Write down something for each question. Even if you can't solve an entire problem, you might get partial credit for the work you do show.

- **Make your answers legible.** Make sure any diagrams and proofs you write are clear and neat. Sloppy or unreadable work will hurt your grade.

Take Tests Online

During your college experience, you'll probably take at least a few exams online. Even traditional classes that meet face-to-face may

"No Comment"? No Dice. When you answer essay test questions, you won't get away with just jotting down careless or silly responses. Instead, you need to review the question's wording and use critical thinking to generate a strong answer. Martha Cambell/www.CartoonStock.com

"Will Mr. 'No Comment' please remain after class."

have online tests. Use the following strategies to take online exams successfully.

- **Use your notes sparingly.** Most of your online tests will be open book/open note, but they'll also be time-limited. During an open book/open note test, you can use the book and your notes as a resource. However, you won't have time to look up the answer to every question. Study as you would for any other type of test, and use your notes and book to verify answers for just a few questions.

- **Check your browser.** Make sure that your computer's browser works with the test-taking platform. Your instructor may recommend a specific browser, or you may need to check the login procedure to confirm you can access the test-taking system.

- **Test your Internet connection.** Before starting the exam, check that you have a secure, stable Internet connection. If you lose your Internet connection during the test, don't close the browser. Instead, reestablish the connection and try to continue. A broken connection or closed browser may cause the system to mistakenly conclude that you've finished taking the test. If this occurs, contact your instructor immediately and explain the situation.

- **Reserve a quiet space.** Find a quiet, distraction-free space to complete the exam. If necessary, make arrangements ahead of time with roommates or family members.

- **Don't start until you're ready.** Most online exams are *forced completion*, meaning that once you start you can't stop and return later to finish. Wait until you're ready; then begin.

- **Enable pop-ups.** Sometimes questions appear as pop-ups, so before you start make sure your browser will allow pop-ups during the exam. Use the browser's Help feature to find out how to disable the pop-up blocker.

- **Record your answers.** If your instructor allows it, write down your answers as you complete the exam. That way, if your answers somehow get lost, you can use your saved responses to re-create them.

You've Got Integrity

Throughout your college career you'll have many opportunities to act with **integrity** by being honest and demonstrating behavior that reflects your values. You'll take personal responsibility for and ownership of your education, which you likely value highly. For example, you'll spend time studying when you'd rather do something more fun, and you'll do your own work on papers and projects. Taking tests is another critical opportunity to act with integrity — again, by doing your own work rather than cheating.

Students decide to cheat for a variety of reasons: They're overwhelmed by college demands, they don't have enough time to prepare effectively, they're not sure how to study for tests, or they simply don't want to put in the effort to succeed. But cheating comes with some high costs. For one thing, if you cheat, you're cheating *yourself* out of the opportunity to learn, so you're wasting your tuition money. You're also being unfair to all the students who put in the effort to learn the material. And if you decide to cheat and you get caught, you may fail the exam, fail the entire course, and have a written record of the event permanently attached to your student file. You might have to go in front of a student panel at the college, or you could even be expelled. These risks just aren't worth the possibility of scoring a few more points on an exam by cheating.

Also take care to avoid any *appearance* of cheating during exams. For instance, if you're taking a closed-book exam, pulling out your phone or rummaging in your bag for scratch paper is asking for trouble. If you need to do any of these things, let your instructor know. Don't put yourself in a position to be questioned.

Follow Up after Tests

Have you ever taken a test, walked out of the classroom, and then never thought about the experience again? As tempting as that might be, once you've completed a test, you have a valuable opportunity to follow up by thinking critically about your approach and using your insights to make improvements in the future.

Evaluate Your Approach

Right after you take a test, reflect on the experience and how prepared you felt. It might take some time before you receive your exam results, but immediate self-reflection can help you get a sense of your performance. Ask yourself:

- Was the test harder or easier than I expected?
- Did the test cover the material I studied?
- Did I spend enough time studying?
- Which of my study and preparation strategies helped me the most with this test? Which helped me the least?
- What new types of strategies would I like to try when I prepare for my next test?

You can use your responses to these questions to determine your next steps. If you're confident you did well on the test, reflect on what led to this success. If you feel you didn't do as well as you hoped, identify the reasons, and take steps to do better next time—for example, by changing your study strategies and trying something new.

Get Hard Evidence

In addition to self-reflection, after-test follow-up involves finding out your results on the exam. In most classes instructors hand back graded exams so you can see how you did on each question. If tests aren't handed back, visit your instructor during office hours and ask if you can look at your exam. And be sure to discuss your performance and test-taking strategies with your instructors. By talking with them, you show that you want to understand what's being assessed.

Learn from Your Mistakes

What if your exam grade is less than you hoped for or expected? First, realize that at some point this happens to everyone. Take a few deep breaths, and acknowledge that it's perfectly natural to feel disappointed or upset. Next, remind yourself that a test evaluates your performance on one set of questions, on a specific day. One poor test result doesn't reflect your overall ability to succeed in college. By identifying what led to the disappointing results you can figure out how to do better next time.

If you feel you did everything right and still had a poor outcome, seek out resources on campus. Explain to your instructor how you prepared, and get his or her feedback on what you might do differently next time. Work with a tutor or a study group. And definitely make use of the Personal Success Plan—for example, write a goal focused on improving your test results next time.

Tap into Your Instructors' Insights. Talk with your instructors about your performance and the test-taking strategies you used. They can offer ideas for preparing more effectively for exams and tackling different types of test questions. Hill Street Studios/Getty Images

my personal success plan

MEMORY, STUDYING, AND TEST TAKING

Are you inspired to set a new goal aimed at improving your memory, studying, or test-taking skills? If so, the Personal Success Plan can walk you through the goal-setting process. Read the advice and examples; then sketch out your ideas in the space provided.

To access the Personal Success Plan online, go to LaunchPad Solo for *Connections Essentials*.

1 GATHER INFORMATION

Think about your strengths and weaknesses related to memory, studying, and taking exams. What strategies have worked for you in the past? What could you do differently? Revisit your Memory and Studying score and your Test Taking score on ACES and review the relevant sections of this chapter for additional ideas.

2 SET A SMART GOAL

Use the information you've gathered to create a SMART goal, making sure to use the SMART goal checklist.

SAMPLE: To reduce my test anxiety, I'll practice breathing techniques and visualization for ten minutes each night.

3 MAKE AN ACTION PLAN

Outline the specific steps you'll take to achieve your SMART goal, and note when you'll complete each step.

SAMPLE: Starting tonight, I'll use breathing techniques for various amounts of time and visualize different kinds of images until I find the right combination.

4 LIST BARRIERS AND SOLUTIONS

Think about possible barriers to your action steps; then brainstorm solutions for overcoming them.

SAMPLE: Muscle relaxation didn't work for me before. If these new techniques don't work, I'll visit the counseling center to get more help with relaxation skills.

5 ACT AND EVALUATE OUTCOMES

Now that your plan is in place, take action. Record each action step as you take it. Then evaluate whether you achieved your SMART goal, and make any adjustments needed to get better results in the future.

SAMPLE: The visualization / breathing combination worked great. When I tense up, I picture a waterfall, breathe deeply, and start to relax.

6 CONNECT TO CAREER

List the skills you're building as you progress toward your SMART goal. How will you use these skills to land a job and succeed at work?

SAMPLE: I'm learning to relax in difficult situations, so things will go more smoothly when it's time for me to interview for a job or give a big presentation.

1 my information

2 my SMART goal

☐ **S**PECIFIC ☐ **M**EASURABLE ☐ **A**CHIEVABLE ☐ **R**ELEVANT ☐ **T**IME-LIMITED

3 my action plan

4 my barriers/ solutions

5 my actions/ outcomes

6 my career connection

Chapter 8 Review

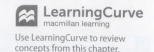

LearningCurve
macmillan learning

Use LearningCurve to review
concepts from this chapter.

CHAPTER SUMMARY

- Memory involves three processes: encoding, storing, and retrieving information. Creating a memory begins with taking in information through your five senses (sensory memory). Information resides briefly in your short-term memory, and you can use your working memory to move it into your long-term memory.

- Basic study strategies include managing your time wisely, joining a study group, and using elaborative rehearsal. You can also build your own study tools and use specific techniques to study in math, science, and online classes.

- Key test preparation strategies include learning the exam format, reviewing previous exams, staying healthy, talking with your instructor, and managing test anxiety.

- You can use a wide variety of strategies to take tests with multiple-choice, matching, fill-in-the-blank, true/false, and essay questions. You can also use specific strategies to prepare for problem-solving tests in math and science and for online tests.

- After taking an exam, you can assess the effectiveness of your approach to preparing for and taking the test. If needed, you can change your approach in the future.

CHAPTER ACTIVITIES

Adopting a Success Attitude

FINDING MOTIVATION TO STUDY

Motivation is a study aid: It can help you stay focused and accomplish tasks efficiently and effectively. Your attitude can affect your level of motivation: When you feel negatively about a class, a test, or studying in general, you risk setting yourself up for failure. Select one class that you find challenging; then respond to these questions to adopt a more positive attitude toward studying for that class.

1. What long-term goals do you want to achieve by attending college? How will studying for this class help you achieve your goals?
2. What is one positive statement you can tell yourself over and over (a mantra) to get through this class?
3. What are some specific good things that will come from studying for this class? What knowledge, attitudes, or relationships will you build as a result?
4. In what ways are you in control over how and when you study for this class?

What are the benefits of having this control?
5. What negative thoughts or beliefs do you have about studying for this class? Play devil's advocate and challenge each thought or belief.

Applying Your Skills

ANTICIPATING ESSAY QUESTIONS

In college, you'll need to anticipate the types of essay questions you'll see on a test. Let's practice.

Pretend you'll be taking an essay exam on this chapter. Review the chapter and your notes, looking for important concepts that could be turned into essay questions. Then create six of your own essay questions, with each question using one of the following verbs: describe, summarize, explain, compare/contrast, critique, and outline. To get you started, here's an example: "*Explain* how the test-preparation skills presented in this chapter can help you manage test anxiety." Finally, test yourself on chapter concepts by answering two of the questions you created.

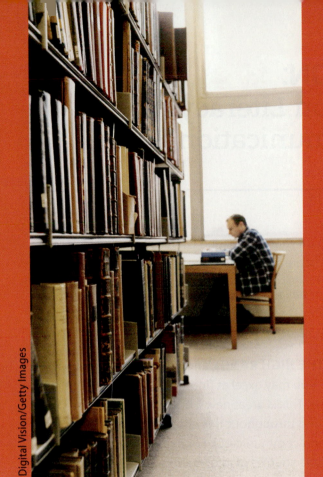

Information Literacy and Communication

9

Develop Information Literacy
Communicate Information through Writing
Present in Class with Confidence
MY PERSONAL SUCCESS PLAN

When you start working on class assignments, is the information you need already in your head? When you sit down to write, do the words flow easily onto the page? When you deliver a presentation, do you calmly stroll up to the front of the room and then wow the crowd? These scenarios might happen occasionally (and isn't it great when they do!). For most people, though, finding information and communicating it through writing and speaking are often difficult. Maybe you have trouble locating useful sources for a paper and clarifying your thoughts in writing, or you suffer from "stage fright" when giving presentations. If so, here's good news: Although finding information and communicating it through writing and speaking take work, you can build these skills. Here's even better news: College is the perfect place to do it.

As a college student, you'll use these skills all the time. For example, you'll probably have to write papers with references to outside sources and give class presentations. You'll also use these skills in your job. Police officers, for instance, need to write reports and speak with authority during daily briefings. Civil engineers must record the results of structural tests or explain the design needs of a new bridge. To excel in almost any job, you'll need to work with information and communicate your ideas effectively through speaking and writing.

The ability to find, evaluate, and communicate information is called *information literacy*. In this chapter we start by focusing on the first two components of information literacy: locating information and evaluating its quality. Then we move to its third component: communicating that information through writing and speaking. We explain how to navigate the writing process and avoid plagiarism, and we conclude the chapter by exploring how to give strong class presentations.

ACES
Academic & Career Excellence System

To find your **Information Literacy and Communication score,** go to LaunchPad Solo for *Connections Essentials*.

MY ACES SCORE

☐ High
☐ Moderate
☐ Low

macmillan learning

Take a moment to reflect on your Information Literacy and Communication score on ACES. Find your score and add it to the box on the left.

This score measures your beliefs about how well you can find and communicate information. Do you think it's an accurate snapshot of your current skills in this area? Why or why not?

- **IF YOU SCORED IN THE HIGH RANGE** and you're confident that this score is accurate, you may excel at finding and communicating information effectively. This is great news, but don't stop there: Use the information you find throughout this chapter to become an even stronger researcher and communicator. For example, learn how to track down new, reliable sources of information for research papers; take steps to sharpen your writing skills; or try out new tips for delivering a persuasive presentation.

- **IF YOU SCORED IN THE MODERATE OR LOW RANGE**, seize the day! Use the strategies from this chapter and this course to grow as a researcher, writer, and speaker. With time, practice, and a positive attitude, you can build your skills and develop confidence in each of these three areas.

ACES Journal

How do you become informed on a topic? What are the sources of your knowledge? Once you learn something or form an opinion on a certain subject, how do you convey that information to others? Take a few minutes to write about the different ways that you take in and use new information. In your discussion, address how you evaluate the quality and accuracy of that information, as well as the different ways you communicate your ideas to others.

_____

_____

_____

_____

Develop Information Literacy

Meet Destiny, who is several weeks into her first term of college. She has two weeks to write a short paper for her political science class, and the paper must reference five academic sources. She isn't sure where to start, so she Googles "dictatorship." Instantly, she has pages and pages of information at her fingertips. As the options fill her screen, Destiny's confidence grows—she's well on her way to getting this paper done!

Destiny copies paragraphs from the first five Web sites that show up in her search results and pastes them into her paper. Since she knows that copying someone else's work is cheating, she rewrites the paragraphs in her own words. She includes references to the sites where she got her information, as well as a few images to jazz things up. She feels good when she hands the paper in, but later she receives the bad news: She got a D. Confused and upset about what happened, she asks herself: What did I do wrong?

To answer this question, Destiny needs to understand **information literacy**. Information literacy includes a number of elements, but we'll focus on three of the most essential: finding information, evaluating its quality, and effectively communicating it to others (see Figure 9.1).

Destiny had trouble with all three elements. First, she didn't locate the type of information the assignment required (academic sources). Instead, she used the first sources that showed up in her Internet search, without considering whether they were appropriate for an academic paper. Second, she used the information without checking whether it was reliable. Third, the patchwork of paragraphs she stitched together from five different Web sites and then rephrased didn't communicate a clear, smoothly flowing message.

Destiny wasn't information literate, so she made some serious mistakes in her paper. But you don't have to go down the same road. Let's look closely at each element of

FIGURE 9.1
Key Elements of Information Literacy

information literacy, beginning in this section with the first two: where to find information and how to evaluate it.

Find the Information You Need

To write a paper or create a presentation, you need to track down information. Where should you start? Try the library. Although the Internet may make libraries seem outdated, they're hugely valuable: Not only do they contain countless resources, including many electronic ones, but they also have staff who can answer questions and help you find what you need.

Keep in mind that you don't have to be *in* the library to take advantage of its resources. Whether you're sitting in the library itself, at your desk, or at your kitchen table, you can access the library's Web site. From there, you can explore a wealth of physical and electronic resources you'll need to write papers and complete assignments, including the following:

- **Books.** Books provide more depth and detail than many other information sources. Prominent book authors are usually experts in their subject matter, and they add credibility to your writing when you acknowledge, or **cite**, their ideas in a paper.

- **Journal articles.** Instructors and other experts often publish research findings, theories, and literature reviews in professional journals. Journal articles are typically *peer reviewed*, meaning that other experts review, comment on, and approve the articles before they're published. Peer review is part of the scientific process, and it helps to ensure that the journal's information is useful and trustworthy. Journals are a good source for facts and other information you need. However, you might find it more difficult to read articles than books because articles are generally written for other professionals in the field.

- **Newspapers and magazines.** Information in newspapers and magazines is often timely because these periodicals are published more frequently than books or journals. Look to newspapers and magazines for descriptions of recent events or in-depth reporting. These articles have less technical detail than what you'll find in journal articles, but they're easier to read.

- **Encyclopedias, archives, and historical documents.** Encyclopedias provide broad overviews of many topics and are a good starting place for gathering basic information. Archives and historical documents can also be valuable sources of information. For instance, to write her paper on dictatorships, Destiny might have quoted from or described part of the Declaration of Independence.

- **Databases.** Using databases on your library's Web site, you can find collections of journal articles, magazine and newspaper articles, videos, government reports, and images on specific topics. If Destiny had started with databases rather than with Google, she could have found articles about dictatorships from highly respected sources such as the *Journal of International Affairs*.

- **Course reserves.** Some instructors create a set of physical or electronic readings for a course that students can access through the library's Web site. When your instructor puts extra time into making these materials available, you know that he or she considers the information important, so be sure to take advantage of them.

Evaluate the Information You've Found

In some ways, evaluating the quality of the information you find is like examining the quality of ingredients when you're baking. Just as you wouldn't put a rotten apple into a pie, you don't want to include weak or questionable information in your papers. Recognizing bad information isn't as easy as picking out a rotten apple, but the strategies in this section can help.

Basic Quality. Ask some simple questions about the basic quality of the information. When looking at a book, check the name of the publisher. Have you heard of the company? Does the publisher have a well-developed Web site? With the rise of self-publishing, anyone can write and print a book.

If you're examining a journal article in the library, see if it includes a list of professionals who edit and review articles for the journal. If you've found an article through your library's Web site or another online database, do a

Online Articles: Trustworthy — or Not? It's important to think critically about any information you read, but it's especially important to evaluate information published online. Why? Because anyone can post anything they want — without undergoing a peer-review process. So put extra care into assessing an online article's trustworthiness. Marty Bucella/www .CartoonStock.com

"I just read an online article that says you should never believe anything you read online."

quick search to make sure the journal is peer reviewed.

When you're evaluating Web sites, trustworthy sources will clearly state who maintains the site and will often be linked to other well-known, respected sites. Sites ending in *.edu* or *.org* may be more appropriate for research purposes than *.com* sites.

Author Credibility. To determine an author's credibility, investigate the answers to these questions: Do you recognize the author's name? Has your instructor referred to the author in class, or does the author's name appear in your textbook in a list of citations or the index? What can you find out about the author's background and credentials? Is he or she an expert on the topic? As you read the source, ask yourself how well the author has covered the topic. Does he or she seem well informed?

Objectivity. Quality sources maintain objectivity by presenting all sides of an issue. If the author has a particular bias, he or she should make that known. For instance, politically conservative or liberal writers should be up-front about their views. A bias doesn't mean that the author's writing is flawed or useless, but you do need to be aware of it and consider how well the author has supported his or her views. If the author merely states a biased view without backing it up, you probably shouldn't include this information.

Currency. Check the publication date of books and journals. How current is the information you're evaluating? How current does it need to be? A description of the Internet written in the mid-1990s might be a great resource for a project on the history of the Internet but not for a project focused on today's Internet-related issues. Also check the dates of the citations in articles or books. If the dates of the citations are close to the article's or book's date of publication, the authors were using current information. With Web sites, look for the dates when articles were posted and for references to more recent events so that you can see whether the content is refreshed regularly. However, don't assume that older content is worthless; a thirty-year-old book for a geology class might still be a good source if it's an important work in the field.

Wikipedia: Friend or Foe?

Do you use Wikipedia for research in your everyday life, but you've been told to avoid the site when completing coursework? If so, you're not alone: Using information from Wikipedia in papers and presentations has long been a controversial topic on college campuses, and many instructors don't consider it an acceptable academic source.[1]

Why so much controversy over a site that's so popular? Wikipedia is an information source created by thousands of volunteer editors, so anyone who wants to can contribute content to the site.[2] This combined brainpower means that a huge volume of information is available on Wikipedia, which is an advantage. But it also means that the site's information might be inaccurate or purposefully misleading, since the people making revisions may not be experts on the content they're altering. With peer-reviewed journal articles or edited textbooks, people who are experts on the subject matter have read and reviewed the information. Peer review doesn't guarantee complete accuracy, but it does make the information more trustworthy than content in Wikipedia articles.

Before you use Wikipedia, follow two rules of thumb. First, investigate the wealth of electronic resources available through your library: In using these resources and in consulting with a librarian, you'll find content you know you can count on. Second, ask your instructors for their thoughts about the site, and follow their lead. They'll let you know whether they consider Wikipedia an acceptable starting point for research — provided you confirm your information through other sources — or a site that you should stay away from altogether.[3]

Communicate Information through Writing

As you've likely seen for yourself, almost every college course includes some type of writing assignment, from essay questions and research papers to creative writing and lab reports. *Why* do instructors assign so much writing? It's not to torture you—remember, they have to read all the papers they assign! Rather, writing assignments help instructors answer two important questions: (1) Do my students understand the key concepts we're covering in class? and (2) Can they think critically about the material? You use all aspects of critical thinking—gathering, evaluating, and applying information, as well as reviewing outcomes—when you write in college. The strategies in this section can help you apply those skills to your writing assignments.

Prepare to Write

Preparing effectively for your writing assignment will help you stay on track later when you write the first draft and make revisions. As you read this section on preparation, think back to Destiny's experience. If you had fourteen days to write a paper on dictatorships, how would *you* prepare?

Clarify Your Purpose. When you understand *why* you're writing—your purpose—you can more easily organize the information and ideas in your written piece and focus on the points you want to convey. Consider these different purposes for writing:

- **To inform.** One reason for writing is to inform the reader about a particular topic. Most of your papers in college will serve this purpose, including research reports, annotated bibliographies, review papers, and lab reports.
- **To persuade.** In persuasive writing, you might start by conveying information about a topic and then seek to persuade

The Magic of Writing. Anything you write has a purpose, such as informing, persuading, or entertaining. When J. K. Rowling wrote the Harry Potter series, she set out to entertain her readers. And entertain she did—so much so that people waited in line until midnight to get the next volumes in the series. Some fans, like this one, even dressed up as characters from the books. Lisa Maree Williams/Stringer/Getty Images

your reader to view the topic in a particular way. Editorial assignments in a journalism class, policy papers in a government course, or advertising plans in a marketing course fit into this category.

- **To express or entertain.** In expressive writing or writing for entertainment, you convey your thoughts and ideas or tell stories to enlighten an audience. Examples include writing poems or short stories for a literature course, plays for a theater course, and song lyrics for a music course.

Make a Plan. Writing assignments often take longer than you expect, so schedule plenty of time to complete them. Plan out each part of the process: preparing, writing your first draft, revising, and polishing. While not everyone spends the same amounts of time on each task, significant chunks of time are usually required for each step. Building a plan helps you manage and get the most from that time.

Choose a Topic. For some writing assignments, your instructor will give you a topic. For others, you can choose a topic. If you can choose your own topic and need inspiration, think about what you've found interesting in class, ask your instructor for ideas from previous terms, or talk with your classmates about how they chose a topic. You can also explore different ideas for paper topics by rereading your textbook and looking for the articles and books it cites or by reviewing suggested readings listed in your course syllabus.

Conduct Research. Researching your topic gives you a chance to put your information literacy skills to work by finding information and evaluating it. When you're researching, tap into the wide range of sources described earlier in this chapter, and use your critical-thinking skills. Remember to evaluate what you're reading by asking yourself:

- Does the author's argument make sense?
- Is it credible?
- Are there alternative arguments worth considering?

When you evaluate information you've found through research, you point out problems with an argument or provide alternative arguments. Then, when you write your paper, you can include your questions and evaluation in the draft.

For example, let's say you're writing a short paper on drowning deaths for a public health class. You've found an article whose author claims that eating ice cream causes drowning. The author backs up this claim with numbers showing that ice-cream consumption and drowning rates increase together. If you neglected to use your critical-thinking skills, you might say, "Makes sense—people eat ice cream, get cramps, and drown." But if you had your critical-thinking hat on, you would

be open to alternative explanations, such as this one: Both swimming (and hence drowning) and eating ice cream increase during the warmer summer months. So, although it may appear that one event causes the other, something else—the warm weather—is actually causing both events to increase. The point? Don't unthinkingly accept the viewpoints you come across in your research. Rather, think critically before you take what you read as fact.

Create an Outline. An outline helps you organize your ideas before you start writing. In fact, in one study, students who created an outline before they began writing wrote longer papers, spent more time writing, wrote faster, and produced higher-quality papers than students who didn't create an outline before writing.[4]

You can use an outline to sketch out the structure of your entire paper and ensure that you have all the required components of the assignment, such as an introduction, citations (if required), main and supporting ideas, and a conclusion. The sample outline in Figure 9.2 has two levels of headings, but you can add as many headings and as much detail as you want. You can also include examples or quotations that you plan to use in your paper—or you can keep it simple and leave such details for the writing step.

Write Your First Draft

Once you've taken time to prepare, you're ready to write your first draft. For some students, all the preparation makes this part easy. For others, writing a draft can be intimidating or overwhelming. If you find it challenging to get started, think of writing like rolling a boulder down a hill: The hardest part is the first push to get the massive object moving. Once you put those first few words on paper, the rest of the process comes more easily.

Develop a Thesis Statement. A thesis statement is the main idea or argument you want to convey, and it sets the stage for your

Title: The Value of Writing SMART Goals
I. Introduction
   A. Personal example of setting goals
   B. Outcome of goal setting
II. Value of Goal Setting
   A. Research by Smith and Smith (2012) documenting the positive effect of goal setting
   B. Goal setting leads to intentional actions
III. SMART Goals
   A. Specific
   B. Measurable
   C. Achievable
   D. Relevant
   E. Time-limited
   F. Research by Jones and Marquez (2012) demonstrating positive effects of SMART goals
IV. Conclusion

FIGURE 9.2
Sample Outline

entire paper. You can create your thesis at various points in the writing process. You might draft it during your research to organize your thoughts and include it in your outline to provide clarity to that document. Or you might choose to write a thesis statement once your research and outline are done.

How you word your thesis depends on your writing purpose. For example, if you write a thesis statement about SMART goals, it might vary according to purpose.

- **To inform:** Learn how to set and achieve your goals using SMART criteria.

- **To persuade:** You should try SMART goals to improve your note-taking skills.

- **To express:** This is how I used a SMART goal to improve my note-taking skills and succeed in college.

Craft an Engaging Introduction. Grab your reader's attention right from the start by creating a compelling introduction to your paper. Imagine, for example, that you're writing an essay on hunger. A perfectly serviceable—but dull—introductory sentence might read: "Hunger is a serious problem in the United States." Compare that statement with this one: "One out of the next six people you meet will go to bed hungry tonight." Wouldn't that second sentence make you want to keep reading much more than the first?

Think Critically. You'll have the opportunity to demonstrate your critical-thinking skills many times as you write your draft. Here are just a few examples of how you can incorporate critical thinking into the writing process.

- **Provide evidence.** Incorporate citations and ideas from your sources into your draft. A paper on poverty that simply says "poverty is bad" shows you haven't really thought about your topic. But if you include statistics on the number of children in poverty who go to school hungry each day, you'll demonstrate that you found and applied evidence. Just be sure to credit others when you use their ideas to support your point.

- **Interpret information and draw conclusions.** As you write, interpret and draw conclusions from the information you're working with, and incorporate these into your paper. For instance, suppose that a key source for your paper is an article about how national economies have become increasingly interconnected. You could think up three of your own examples showing the impact of globalization and work these into your draft. Then, at the end of the paper, you could identify what you see as the positive or negative effects of globalization.

- **Compare and contrast.** If appropriate for the writing assignment, describe similarities and differences between topics. For instance, for a political science class, you might compare and contrast the reasons the United States entered the wars in Iraq and Afghanistan.

- **Generate new ideas.** For some writing, you'll have an opportunity to generate original ideas—for example, in forms such as poetry, essays, or short stories in an English class or by brainstorming new ways to use an existing product or tool in a design or an engineering class.

First Steps to a First Draft. Writing a first draft can be intimidating, but the best way to get started is just to begin. Once the words start to flow and you feel increasingly confident in your writing, you can focus on making sure your draft contains all the right elements (including a thesis statement, an introduction, and a conclusion) and presents important evidence to support your main points. James Woodson/Getty Images

Structure Your Paragraphs Carefully.

When you're writing, pay attention to how you structure each paragraph. The most common approach is to start with the main idea and then follow it with supporting ideas, examples, facts, or details. Focus on only one main idea in each paragraph; start a new paragraph as soon as you begin writing about another main idea.

Add a Conclusion. End your draft with a conclusion that pulls your thoughts together. A strong conclusion restates your thesis, revisits the major findings or recommendations of your paper, or summarizes your argument. To come full circle, you might even connect the concluding paragraph to the catchy introduction you created at the start of your paper.

Revise and Polish Your Paper

Once you've written a first draft of your paper, it's time to revise and polish it.

Consider these ideas for editing and finalizing your work.

- **Include transitions.** Transitions connect your paragraphs and smooth the flow of ideas throughout your entire work. (For instance, the first sentence under the heading "Revise and Polish Your Paper" serves as a transition from the preceding section.) If your paper sounds choppy, adding transitions between paragraphs can help.

- **Use a formatting and style guide.** The MLA (Modern Language Association) and APA (American Psychological Association) have established guidelines for formatting papers and citing sources. These style guides will help you with some of the "nuts and bolts" of writing a paper—such as the format to use for the title page, line spacing, margins, paragraph indents, headings, page numbers, and citation style. Including citations is especially important for avoiding *plagiarism*, which occurs when you use someone else's work and call it your own (see "Avoid Plagiarism" for more). Ask your instructor or check your syllabus to determine which style guide you should use.

- **Read your paper out loud.** You can identify language that sounds awkward and then revise as needed to make your writing more fluid.

- **Have someone else read your paper.** Ask a friend or classmate to give you honest feedback. Someday you can return the favor.

- **Use campus resources.** Use any resources your school offers to help with writing. Make an appointment at the writing center, work with a tutor, or ask your instructor to review a draft of your writing.

- **Polish and proofread.** Once you've revised your draft several times to address macro-level issues of structure, flow, and clarity, give your written piece a final polish. Then step away from your paper and take a break, returning with fresh eyes to revisit and proofread it carefully. Fix any spelling, grammar, and punctuation errors, and make sure it reads just as you want it to.

Write in Online Classes

You can use the strategies we've just explored to write papers in both face-to-face and online classes. However, some additional techniques can be especially helpful for writing online. Online classes are more likely to include writing assignments such as blog posts or written comments on other students' posts. Your posts and comments will be graded, so you want to make sure they're high quality. To do so, try these tips.

- Write in complete sentences. Shorthand and slang are fine for Facebook and Twitter, but use more formal and thoughtful language when writing for your online classes.

- Writing posts in online classes can feel conversational—there is a back-and-forth exchange of information—but remember that in online conversations you don't have nonverbal cues and tone to provide context, so the tone you had in mind doesn't always come through. As you type posts for online classes, read them out loud and listen to how they sound. Could readers interpret your tone in a more negative way than you intended? If so, rephrase your comments so that they're more constructive.

- Pay attention to your emotions and how quickly you respond in these classes. If you're having a heated discussion on a controversial topic, consider writing out your post on a piece of paper and coming back to it twenty minutes later to make sure it conveys your message appropriately.

Avoid Plagiarism

When it comes to writing, honest students take care to avoid **plagiarism**. Plagiarism occurs when one person uses another person's words or ideas and presents them as his or her own. In some cases, plagiarism is intentional: for example, when a student takes a paper off the Internet and turns it in or knowingly copies information into a paper without putting it in quotation marks and citing the original author.

But plagiarism isn't always intentional. Let's say a student copies a sentence from a source and puts it in his paper, planning to go back later to credit the author, but then forgets to do so. Is this plagiarism? At many schools the answer would be "yes"; often, instructors don't distinguish between intentional and unintentional plagiarism. If you do get caught plagiarizing, you may have to rewrite your paper. Even worse, you might automatically fail the course, have to meet with the dean of your college, or even be expelled.

We assume that since you're in college, you value your education and will honor your values by not plagiarizing intentionally. But what's your best defense against accidental plagiarism? Develop good research and writing habits: Find out how your instructors want you to use citations in your paper; use a style guide; and apply the following strategies.

- **Take notes in your own words.** Avoid copying large sections of material. Instead, paraphrase your sources by taking notes in your own words, and then use these notes to write your paper. Give credit to the original author by citing the source where you got the information.

- **Use quotation marks for direct quotations.** If you use someone else's exact words, which you should do only in moderation, always use quotation marks and cite the source.

- **Keep track of where your information comes from.** Be consistent so that you always know which notes and ideas are yours and which are others'.

- **When in doubt, give credit.** If you aren't sure whether you need to cite a source, err on the side of caution and include a citation to the original work.

- **At the end of your paper, include a bibliography or reference list.** This list shows that you're giving appropriate credit for the ideas in your paper.

- **Seek guidance.** If you have any concerns, ask your instructor or someone from the campus writing center to review your paper before it's due.

Student Voices of Experience

GETTING FEEDBACK ON YOUR WRITING

Michael J. Wicht

NAME: Ashley J. Willey

SCHOOLS: *Highland Community College; University of Nebraska*

MAJOR: *Advertising and Public Relations*

CAREER GOAL: *Copy Writing*

I've learned that the best way to become a good writer is to read good books. These books inspire me to try to emulate as many styles as possible until my own style shines through. I find myself playing around with different narration styles that I would typically never have used. I'm also blessed to have had a very good English professor, who taught me how to appreciate the knowledge I've gained and encouraged me to use methods of revision that have been amazing learning tools for me.

One of the best things I've done as a writer is to attend creative writing workshops. I enjoy being critiqued by as many people as possible, and I find it helpful to gain multiple perspectives. It's important to go to your professors for their opinion and not only to other students. Your professors are professionals who can provide you with the most experienced, educated opinion. I follow their advice to the best of my ability, until I get feedback that my work is creating the impression that I was aiming for. This allows me to learn from my mistakes and perfect my craft.

I'm comfortable building professional relationships with my professors and going to them after hours for advice. I'm not ashamed to ask for help because I know that my professors are there for me. Many students fail to take advantage of the many resources available in the college setting because they're closed off and are so focused on their goals that they miss out on opportunities. I'm getting my degree not for me but, ultimately, for my daughter. In order to go to college, I first had to obtain my GED without the help of my daughter's father, who was not supportive of my obtaining my education. I began community college as a single mother and am now attending the University of Nebraska. I want to set the bar as high as I possibly can for my daughter.

YOUR TURN: Have you used any of the approaches that Ashley describes for improving your writing? If so, which ones? How useful have these approaches been? Have you found any other approaches helpful?

> "I enjoy being critiqued by as many people as possible, and I find it helpful to gain multiple perspectives."

Present in Class with Confidence

Speaking in front of a group is a skill that colleges consider part of a well-rounded education and that employers appreciate.[5] As valuable a skill as public speaking is, however, for many people it's utterly terrifying. What can you do if the thought of standing in front of the class gives you stomach butterflies and sweaty palms? You can practice and build your skills to increase your confidence. It won't happen overnight, but any student can become a successful public speaker.

Know Your Purpose—and Your Audience

To begin, give yourself plenty of time to plan your presentation. Use that time to figure out the purpose of the presentation and the major points you want to make. For example, if you have to demonstrate a medical procedure in your nursing class, you may design your presentation to *inform* your audience about how to perform the procedure.

Delivering a Slam-Dunk Talk. Top-notch speakers know their audience. Here, a basketball coach is surrounded by reporters, but he knows they're only part of his audience. The other part is made up of people who read articles in which he's quoted, listen to his comments on the radio, or watch video of him on news outlets. Is he nervous? Probably a little. USA Today Sports Images

If you're going to show a new smartphone application you developed in your mobile computing class, your purpose may be to *persuade* classmates that the app is worthwhile. You might even perform a one-act play to *entertain* classmates in your drama course.

To plan your presentation, you also need to consider your audience. Ask yourself:

- **How many people will be there?** If you're presenting to fewer than thirty people, you can move around the room and involve your audience. You can pose questions, have listeners complete tasks and report back to the larger group, or even stimulate discussion among audience members. With larger groups, this interactive style is more difficult, so you may decide to spend your time addressing the audience as a whole.

- **How much do they know about your topic?** If your topic is new to the audience, share what you've learned while researching your presentation. If your topic is covered in the textbook, your listeners probably know the basics, so use your presentation to provide new information or discuss the topic in more depth.

- **How can you capture the audience's interest?** Brainstorm ideas for grabbing your audience's attention at the start of your presentation— for example, by developing a funny (and tasteful) anecdote or joke, a personal story, or an example that will engage the audience while also setting the stage for your topic.

Craft Your Presentation

Many of the same strategies you use to write papers can also help you create presentations. Like written work, most presentations have a thesis statement, an intriguing introduction, a well-structured multipart argument, and a clear conclusion. As with papers, you'll develop several drafts of your presentation as you work to create the finished product.

Presentations usually use more visual aids than written pieces do, so consider how visuals can strengthen your message. You can use slides with text and images (PowerPoint and Prezi are popular slide-creation tools) or physical objects that demonstrate a process (such as taking blood pressure) or clarify a concept (such as how electrons move during a chemical reaction). Keep in mind that visual aids work best when they convey main ideas and aren't overly complex.

Present like a Pro

On the days leading up to your presentation, take time to practice repeatedly so you're as comfortable as possible (see "Practice, Practice, Practice!"). Then, when the big day arrives, use these tips to present successfully.

- **Look the part.** Even if your appearance isn't factored into your official grade for the presentation, your instructor and audience will notice what you're wearing. So, approach class presentations as you would a job interview. Ditch the shorts and flip-flops in favor of business casual or nicer clothes. Professional apparel gives you an air of credibility and conveys that you take the assignment seriously.

- **Arrive early.** By arriving early, you'll have time to get set up and organize your notes and any materials you plan to use.

- **Breathe and visualize.** Take deep breaths and visualize yourself being successful. Settling your nerves in advance will help you deliver a smooth presentation.

Harness the Power of Technology: Present Online

Increasingly, online classes require students to prepare presentations and deliver them using technology tools such as videoconferencing. This means you may have to master some new technology skills to make your presentation a success—for example, adding narration to a slide presentation or setting up conferencing tools such as Skype or WebEx on your laptop. If you have any concerns about delivering your online presentation, ask your instructor for help. And be sure to schedule some extra time during the preparation phase to try out any technology and make sure it's running smoothly.

Practice, Practice, Practice!

Fear of speaking in public is very common,[6] and practicing your presentation is the best way to become more comfortable, confident, and calm. Rehearse several times to polish the following elements of your talk:

- **Time.** Work to stay within the time limit. If you have twenty minutes to speak, for example, try keeping your talk between fifteen and seventeen minutes as you practice. That way, you'll have a few minutes left for questions from your audience.

- **Voice volume.** Make sure you're speaking loudly enough. If you'll be using a microphone, practice talking at the same volume you'd use when sitting next to another person. If you won't have a microphone, practice speaking loudly enough so that people at the back of the room can hear you. And vary the volume and pace of your voice—speaking in a monotone is a surefire way to put your audience to sleep.

- **Body language.** Practice showing confidence and authority through your posture and other body language. Stand up straight, make eye contact, and imagine conversing with your audience—glancing only briefly at your notes or slides if needed. Also practice using hand gestures to emphasize points, and avoid nervous gestures that will distract your audience (like tugging at your hair or wringing your hands).

To practice your presentation, consider asking trusted friends or classmates to watch you. They can provide feedback on how you can improve. Or record your practice sessions on your smartphone and critique your own performance. It may be hard to hear critical feedback or watch yourself on video, but these techniques will help you strengthen your presentation—and boost your confidence.

my personal success plan

INFORMATION LITERACY AND COMMUNICATION

Are you inspired to set a new goal aimed at improving your information literacy and communication skills? If so, the Personal Success Plan can walk you through the goal-setting process. Read the advice and examples; then sketch out your ideas in the space provided.

To access the Personal Success Plan online, go to LaunchPad Solo for *Connections Essentials*.

---

1 GATHER INFORMATION

Think about your strengths and weaknesses related to information literacy and communication. What strategies have worked for you in the past? What could you do differently? Revisit your Information Literacy and Communication score on ACES and review the relevant sections of this chapter for additional ideas.

2 SET A SMART GOAL

Use the information you've gathered to create a SMART goal, making sure to use the SMART goal checklist.

SAMPLE: I'll create an outline for my economics paper that's due next week.

3 MAKE AN ACTION PLAN

Outline the specific steps you'll take to achieve your SMART goal, and note when you'll complete each step.

SAMPLE: I'll spend one hour this Sunday night writing my outline.

4 LIST BARRIERS AND SOLUTIONS

Think about possible barriers to your action steps; then brainstorm solutions for overcoming them.

SAMPLE: Outlines have always been hard for me. If I get stuck, I'll take my outline to the writing center on Monday and get feedback.

5 ACT AND EVALUATE OUTCOMES

Now that your plan is in place, take action. Record each action step as you take it. Then evaluate whether you achieved your SMART goal, and make any adjustments needed to get better results in the future.

SAMPLE: For this big paper I didn't leave enough time to develop my outline, so for my next assignment I'll build more time into that phase of the writing process.

6 CONNECT TO CAREER

List the skills you're building as you progress toward your SMART goal. How will you use these skills to land a job and succeed at work?

SAMPLE: Using outlines will help me organize my writing. When I become a public-relations specialist, I'll use them to write effective press releases.

1

my
information

_____
_____
_____
_____
_____

2

my
SMART
goal

_____
_____
_____
_____

☐ **S**PECIFIC ☐ **M**EASURABLE ☐ **A**CHIEVABLE ☐ **R**ELEVANT ☐ **T**IME-LIMITED

3

my
action
plan

_____
_____
_____
_____
_____

4

my
barriers/
solutions

_____
_____
_____
_____
_____

5

my
actions/
outcomes

_____
_____
_____
_____
_____

6

my
career
connection

_____
_____
_____
_____
_____

Chapter 9 Review

CHAPTER SUMMARY

- Information literacy is the ability to find, evaluate, and communicate information through writing and speaking.

- Information sources include books, journal articles, newspapers, magazines, encyclopedias, databases, and course reserves. Evaluating the quality of a source's information involves considering whether the source is credible, objective, and current.

- Preparing to write includes clarifying your purpose, making a plan, selecting a topic, researching, and creating an outline.

- A well-written piece has a clear thesis, an engaging introduction, focused paragraphs, and a strong conclusion. It prompts critical thinking, is properly formatted and cited, and is free from grammatical errors.

- By developing good research and writing habits, you can avoid plagiarism.

- Creating a strong classroom presentation involves planning what you want to say, crafting the content, practicing thoroughly, and taking steps to prepare yourself the day of the presentation.

CHAPTER ACTIVITIES

Adopting a Success Attitude

OVERCOMING WRITER'S BLOCK

For some people, negative thinking and self-doubt can create a mental block, making it difficult to even begin writing an assigned paper. If this happens to you, try using freewriting to break through this writer's block.

Sit down at a computer and type your topic at the top of a page (or write it on a piece of paper). You may want to choose a topic that relates to a writing assignment for another class. Set a timer for ten minutes, and then type or write whatever comes to mind about this topic—thoughts, feelings, questions, and so on. Type or write as fast as you can, and don't stop until the timer goes off. Now review what you wrote. Did you generate any new ideas that might help you with your writing assignment? If not, it's okay—you may need to try freewriting a few more times to start seeing results. Don't give up on this technique after only one try!

Applying Your Skills

FINDING AND CITING SOURCES

For many college assignments, you'll need to find information in various sources and accurately cite those sources. This activity gives you practice developing these skills.

1. Identify a topic you find interesting.
2. Locate four sources related to your topic (for example, books, magazine or newspaper articles, research articles, and Web documents).
3. Provide citations for the information sources you found. Depending on your instructor's preference, use either MLA (Modern Language Association) or APA (American Psychological Association) style to cite each source.

For example, let's say you chose the topic "Should Performance-Enhancing Drugs Be Accepted in Sports?" You identify as useful resources the book *Steroids: A New Look at Performance-Enhancing Drugs* by Rob Beamish and the newspaper article "There Are No Sound Moral Arguments against Performance-Enhancing Drugs" by Chuck Klosterman. Your instructor requires APA style for citations, so you cite these sources as follows:

Beamish, R. (2011). *Steroids: A new look at performance-enhancing drugs*. Santa Barbara, CA: Praeger.

Klosterman, C. (2013, August 30). There are no sound moral arguments against performance-enhancing drugs. *The New York Times*. Retrieved from http://www.nytimes.com

Sam Edwards/Getty Images

10

Connecting with Others

Enhance Your Communication Skills

Build Emotional Intelligence

Resolve Conflict

Grow and Sustain Healthy Relationships

Embrace Diversity

MY PERSONAL SUCCESS PLAN

I magine how you would respond to the following scenarios:

- Your significant other is talking and your mind starts to drift. He or she wants a response, but you aren't sure what was just said.
- Your psychology instructor assigns a group project. You look around and don't see anyone you know in the class.
- You're angry and frustrated at your roommates. You feel like you're the only one who ever cleans the kitchen!

If you can easily imagine an effective way to respond to these scenarios, you may have a natural ability to connect with other people — and maintain those connections. If you had difficulty responding to these scenarios, you can learn how to build and strengthen connections, even in challenging or emotionally charged situations. In fact, no matter how confident you are in your abilities, there is always room for growth, and it's worth investing the time to strengthen your skills: Healthy connections form the foundation of a successful, satisfying life, both while you're in school and after you graduate.

With that in mind, this chapter begins with a look at two vital aspects of effective communication: listening actively and speaking effectively. We then explore how to strengthen your *emotional intelligence* (including how to recognize, understand, and manage emotions in yourself and others) and manage conflict. Finally, we examine how connecting with others can enhance your existing relationships, help you build new ones, and strengthen your relationships with people from different backgrounds.

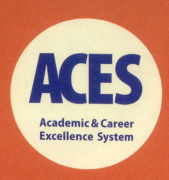

ACES
Academic & Career Excellence System

To find your **Connecting with Others score**, go to LaunchPad Solo for *Connections Essentials.*

LaunchPad Solo
macmillan learning

REFLECTION:
Connecting with Others

Take a moment to reflect on your Connecting with Others score on ACES. Find your score and add it to the box on the left.

This score measures your beliefs about how well you connect with others. Do you think it's an accurate snapshot of your current skills in this area? Why or why not?

- **IF YOU SCORED IN THE HIGH RANGE** and you're confident that this score is accurate, you may be great at making connections. Still, consider how you can strengthen this skill. You can probably think of at least one interpersonal interaction — a job interview, an argument with a loved one — that you could have handled more effectively if you had better understood and managed the emotions that arose during that interaction. In this chapter, you'll learn new techniques you can use to build on your current connection skills.

- **IF YOU SCORED IN THE MODERATE OR LOW RANGE**, take action: This chapter is filled with tips and strategies you can use to connect more effectively with others. Use these approaches to boost your confidence and build rewarding relationships with the people in your life!

ACES Journal

Flip through the pages of this chapter and look at some of the major headings. As you can see, connecting and maintaining relationships with others necessitates many specific skills and attitudes — listening, speaking, managing emotions, resolving conflict, networking, and embracing diversity. Discuss two of your strengths in connecting and maintaining relationships and explain how you could use these strengths to help others in this class. Then discuss two of your challenges in connecting and maintaining relationships. How could others in this class help you build these skills?

_____

_____

_____

_____

Enhance Your Communication Skills

Communication is at the heart of connecting with others. When we communicate, we engage in a back-and-forth exchange that helps us learn information and build relationships with the people around us. In college you might clarify concepts with an instructor, discuss project plans with a classmate, or exchange first-year survival tactics with a friend. Communication experts call this active exchange of information between two people (or more) **interpersonal communication**.

Interpersonal communication is a two-way street where each person takes turns speaking and receiving. When you're the speaker, your goal is to convey your message clearly to the person on the receiving end. When you're the receiver, your goal is to listen actively to the speaker's message and to provide short responses called *feedback* that show you've heard and understood the message—or to ask for clarification if you haven't. The roles of speaker and receiver may quickly reverse if the receiver has something more substantial to contribute to the conversation.

In this section we focus on your role as the receiver of information, including how to listen and how to respond when barriers to a conversation prevent you from hearing or understanding the full message. Then we touch on ways you can communicate your message effectively when you're the speaker—a topic we continue to explore throughout the chapter.

Become a Better Listener

Strange as it may seem, one of the best ways to become a good communicator isn't to speak—it's to listen. Through *active listening* you pay close attention to a speaker and focus on his or her message. Active listening involves communicating nonverbally and providing verbal feedback.

Nonverbal Communication.
Your body language says a lot about how well you're listening to another person, and the following techniques can help you stay attentive.

- **Make eye contact.** Maintain an appropriate amount of eye contact with the person who's talking. Preferred levels of eye contact vary according to culture or context, but most Americans prefer eye contact of moderate intensity—enough to show

"I'm Listening." When you're listening to someone else, your body posture, verbal responses, and other cues communicate how well you're receiving the speaker's message. Look at these two people: Are they listening to each other? Is their conversation going smoothly? What clues indicate how effectively they're communicating? Linda Winski/PhotoEdit, Inc.

interest, but not so much that the person feels that you're staring.

- **Maintain open body posture.** Convey attentiveness by using an *open posture*—face the speaker, sit up straight, relax your shoulders, and keep your arms at your sides or folded in your lap. Avoid any temptation to cross your arms because this *closed posture* may convey irritation, anger, discomfort, or disagreement with the speaker or his or her message.

- **Watch your body movement.** Lean slightly toward the speaker to show that you're ready to listen or want to hear more. Nod occasionally to encourage the person to continue or to convey your understanding of (or agreement with) what he or she is saying.

- **Stay focused.** Maintain your focus on what the other person is saying; for instance, try not to glance at your phone or give in to other distractions.

Provide Feedback.
In addition to nonverbal communication, you can show that you're listening to someone and that you understand his or her message by providing verbal feedback.[1] Here are several ways to provide feedback effectively.

- **Give brief encouragement.** When used occasionally, brief responses such as "yes," "uh-huh," and "okay" indicate that you're paying attention to the message. (Although when used too frequently, they may give the impression that you want the speaker to hurry up and stop talking.)

- **Paraphrase.** If you summarize or *paraphrase* what the speaker said by restating it in your own words, you can check your understanding of the message ("So, what I hear you saying is . . .").

- **Manage barriers.** Interpersonal communication isn't perfect, and sometimes barriers—everything from noise to confusion to distractions—can cause communication to break down. To overcome barriers, address them tactfully by asking a follow-up question, providing information, or sharing your own insights (see Table 10.1).

Become a Better Speaker

Feedback shows that you're listening to a conversation, but what do you do when you want to communicate something more substantial—to become the speaker yourself? Throughout the rest of this chapter we'll look at specific techniques that will help you express your message thoughtfully, effectively, and honestly—during both pleasant and not-so-pleasant conversations. We begin by discussing emotional intelligence, which you can use to speak with others openly and sensitively.

TABLE 10.1 Using Feedback to Manage Communication Barriers

Communication barrier	Examples of possible feedback
You couldn't hear what the speaker said because of a loud noise.	"Sorry, but I couldn't hear what you said. Can you explain again?"
You didn't understand what the speaker said.	"I'm not sure I get what you're saying. Can you clarify what you mean?"
You zoned out for a minute and lost track of the conversation.	"I apologize. I lost focus for a second. Could you repeat what you just said?"
The speaker seems distracted.	"I may be wrong, but you seem a bit distracted. Do you want to pick this up later, when things have calmed down?"
The speaker is telling you one thing, but his or her expression conveys something else.	"I know you're telling me that everything's fine, but you look sad."

Build Emotional Intelligence

Emotional intelligence—the ability to recognize, understand, and manage your own and others' emotions—is a critical part of communicating and connecting effectively with others (see Figure 10.1).[2] It can also help you learn about yourself and better manage how you respond to others. Thus emotional intelligence is both *interpersonal* (between people) and *intrapersonal* (within ourselves).

To see how emotional intelligence works, let's say your friend just broke up with his significant other. You *recognize* that he's sad because his shoulders are slumped, and you seek to *understand* the reason for his sadness by asking "Did you think things were going better than they really were?" You might then try to help your friend *manage* his sadness by offering a sensitive response: "I'm so sorry. That must be hard. Is there anything I can do to help?"

And during conversations, recognizing, understanding, and managing your *own* emotions can also help you communicate more effectively. For example, suppose a coworker tells you excitedly that she just received the employee of the month award. You feel strongly that you deserve the award more than your coworker, who spends all day on her phone and takes too many breaks.

However, you recognize that you feel unappreciated, and thanks to this understanding, you can manage your emotions and politely congratulate your coworker. Later, you can look up the criteria for the award and schedule a meeting with your boss to discuss his perceptions of your work performance.

Let's take a closer look at how you can handle situations like these in healthy ways by mastering the three key elements of emotional intelligence.

Recognize Emotions

The first step in exercising emotional intelligence is recognizing emotions—identifying what you or another person is feeling and labeling it.[3] Is it sadness? Excitement? Anger? Embarrassment? Joy?

Your Emotions. To better recognize your own emotions, there are a number of strategies you can try, including the following:

- Find and use words that designate emotions. Google "feeling word list," and select specific words that describe how you feel. Avoid generic words such as *happy, sad, mad,* and *glad*—instead choose words that depict the intensity of your emotions. For example, if you're unhappy, would you describe yourself as *slightly disappointed* or *completely devastated*?

- Consider how your body is reacting physically to an emotion. Is your heart pounding? Are you sinking in your chair? Are you becoming hot? Clenching your teeth? Getting teary eyed? Physical responses can provide clues to our feelings.

In some cases, you might have various conflicting feelings about the same situation, and that's okay—feelings are complicated. However, denying feelings (especially negative ones) can cause problems, so it's important to acknowledge that these feelings exist. (See "The Dangers of Suppressing Your Emotions.")

FIGURE 10.1
Components of Emotional Intelligence

Source: Synthesized from the work of Mayer and Salovey (2008; 1997).

Name That Emotion. When you're trying to recognize which emotions other people are feeling, look at their gestures, facial expressions, and other clues. What emotion do you think the people in the photo on the left are experiencing? What about the person on the right? What cues led you to arrive at your interpretations? *Left:* DreamPictures/Blend Images/CORBIS *Right:* antoniodiaz/Shutterstock

Others' Emotions. There are also strategies you can use to recognize emotions in other people. For example:

- Ask the person what he or she is feeling.
- Pay attention to what others tell you. Notice when someone says he or she is feeling "excited," "thankful," "sad," or "frazzled."
- Notice what the person's body language seems to be saying. If a friend says he's "fine" but he's wringing his hands, you might conclude that he's actually feeling nervous or worried.
- Pay attention to **paralinguistics**—changes in the voice that convey emotion. When people are angry or anxious, for example, their throat muscles may tense up, giving their voice a higher pitch. If they're excited, their voice might get louder.

Understand Emotions

Once you've recognized your own emotions or those of another person, the next step is to understand why these feelings are occurring.

Your Emotions. Understanding where your feelings are coming from can help you think before you act. That way, you can manage the emotion and respond constructively to the situation. For example, suppose you received a D on your English paper and you feel upset. To better understand yourself, ask "Why do I feel this way? What's making me angry?" If you conclude that you're actually angry at *yourself* for not putting more effort into your work, you'll probably adopt more effective strategies for talking to your instructor about your grade—rather than storming into her office and demanding to know why she doesn't respect you.

Others' Emotions. When you understand another person's emotions, you have **empathy** for that person, even if you haven't had the same experience that triggered that person's emotion. For example, suppose your sister tells you she just completed her first marathon. You hate running and have never completed a marathon. But by imagining yourself in her shoes or recalling an experience you've had that gave you a similar sense of accomplishment, you can feel some of the same pride and excitement that she is feeling. And that empathy can help you respond appropriately, with feedback such as "That's great news! You must feel fantastic about achieving your goal!"

Manage Emotions

In the personal and financial health chapter, we explore how to manage stress, depression, and anxiety so that they don't affect your academic performance. In this section we focus on managing the emotions you might have toward a speaker, as well as the emotions of those around you.

Your Emotions. How can you manage your own strong emotions? If you find yourself getting angry with someone because of something he or she said, what can you do? Once you *recognize* your anger and *understand* where it comes from, you can manage it using a number of techniques.

- Take a deep breath and count to ten.
- Use empathy to put yourself in the other person's shoes, or ask the other person questions to try to understand his or her perspective.
- Calmly let the person know you're reacting intensely to what he or she is saying.
- Take a brisk five-minute walk to regain your focus.

These tactics can help dial down the intensity of your emotion, enabling you to think more clearly and respond more appropriately to the situation.

Others' Emotions. When you see other people experiencing strong emotions, you can help them manage these feelings in a sensitive and respectful way. Your goal is not

Boiling Mad? If you don't effectively manage your emotions, they can boil over — triggering unproductive responses that just worsen the situation that initially upset you. Are you "boiling mad" about something someone said? If so, adopt the emotion-management strategies that work best for you — even if it's just taking a quick walk to let off steam. KC Slagle/Shutterstock.com

to change or control what they feel but to provide empathy and, if appropriate, to help them work through their feelings or connect them with professional resources. The following strategies may be useful.

- Let them know you recognize that they may be having a hard time.

- Invite them to share their feelings with you, and listen to them actively.

- Put yourself in their shoes and provide a compassionate response.

- If you've had a similar feeling or experience, share it and let them know what helped you through it.

- Instill hope that their situation can change.

- Offer assistance and connect them to appropriate campus or community resources if needed.

Managing emotions is a key step toward resolving interpersonal conflicts and restoring healthy connections between yourself and others—a topic we'll turn to in the next section.

The Dangers of Suppressing Your Emotions

As psychologists, we've seen firsthand what happens when people try to suppress persistent negative emotions: Similar to lava inside a volcano, these emotions can intensify over time, and without any release, they'll eventually blow. Have you ever lashed out at someone for something very minor? Upon reflection, you may find that it wasn't that one small thing that caused you to become angry; it was weeks and weeks of small things that accumulated and festered. Ignoring or denying your feelings (especially negative ones) can cause problems. You may begin to feel overwhelmed or unmotivated, and you may experience physical consequences.

Research confirms a link between chronic stress and illness. A national study found that 60 to 80 percent of all primary care doctor visits had a stress-related component.[4] Other research found that chronic stress can suppress the immune system, leaving you more vulnerable to illness, infection, and disorders such as asthma and diabetes.[5] Chronic stress can also alter the acid concentration in your stomach, leading to ulcers, and cause plaque buildup in the arteries, leading to heart problems.[6]

Recognizing your emotions is the first step in doing something about them. Our bodies often give us warning signs that we're getting upset or stressed, so reflect on the emotions you're experiencing and do your best to understand where they're coming from.

Also consider strategies you can use to manage your emotions. You may find talking to a friend or a counselor helpful, for example. Or you may prefer to do something physical as a release, or find quiet contemplation through journaling, yoga, or meditation useful. Watching a funny movie can also be a great way to let go of negative emotions. Experiment!

Resolve Conflict

Conflict arises when two or more people disagree. Disagreeing with a friend about which movie to see, disputing your grade on a pop quiz, receiving a customer complaint—these and many other types of disagreement can lead to conflict, which makes it an inevitable—and normal—part of life. But not all conflict is the same. In cases where the disagreement is minor, the incident may end with a quick compromise. In cases where you feel that compromising would go against your values, the conflict may be harder to resolve.

Conflict can be scary, and we all deal with it in different ways. Some people deny there's a problem or give in to the other person to maintain harmony. On the opposite end of the spectrum are those who fight ferociously for what they believe in or compete to "win" every time. But the ideal outcome of any conflict is a resolution that's agreeable to everyone involved. Such resolutions often require collaboration among the parties.

As we saw earlier, communicating effectively and honing your emotional intelligence can help you work through difficult situations. But you can also use assertiveness and "I" statements.

Be Assertive

Being *assertive* means stating your thoughts, feelings, and opinions and advocating for yourself without disrespecting others or their views. Although being assertive can be daunting, it's good for your mental health and your relationships.[7] For example, by letting an instructor know you need help in his or her class, you can gain access to resources that will help you succeed. By telling your romantic partner you want more intimacy, you can start a conversation in which you both brainstorm ways to feel more connected.

Assertiveness differs from *passivity*, in which people keep their thoughts and feelings to themselves to "avoid causing trouble." Some situations call for passivity. For example, it would be inappropriate to express your negative opinions about someone at his or her funeral. However, your ideas, opinions, feelings, and needs matter. If you don't speak up for yourself in situations where doing so is appropriate, your needs may go unmet.

Assertiveness also differs from *aggression*, which involves humiliating, criticizing, blaming, attacking, or threatening others.

Assertiveness — or Aggression?
Assertive behaviors help you express your thoughts and feelings and pose questions in respectful ways. Assertiveness works far better than aggression in interpersonal conflict because it invites honest conversation rather than triggering defensiveness. Considering the aggressive stance these men have adopted, do you think they'll resolve their conflict productively?
gilaxia/Getty Images

Aggressive communicators provoke feelings of fear or dislike. By contrast, assertive communicators are respectful. They take responsibility for getting their needs met, address issues as they arise, and speak openly and honestly.

To be an assertive communicator, you must first value yourself and know and respect your own feelings and opinions. Not everyone will like what you have to say, but by being honest, you'll likely earn their respect. (For more, see "Don't Be a Doormat.")

Use "I" Statements

Statements beginning with "I" show that you're taking ownership of your thoughts and feelings—such as "I felt hurt when you didn't respond to my text" or "I think I'm confused by your behavior." By using "I" statements, you express your thoughts and feelings clearly, honestly, and constructively[8] and create a respectful environment in which you can explain how something the other person said or did has affected you. During disagreements or conflicts, "I" statements give the receiver the chance to respond to or clear up any misunderstanding and give the speaker a chance to request the receiver's help in finding a solution.

For example, suppose your housemate keeps leaving dirty dishes in the sink before heading off to work. You're angry, and your first impulse is to say, "You're such a slob" or "You're the most inconsiderate person I know." Such blaming or judging statements tend to make others defensive.[9] Instead, you might say calmly: "I get frustrated when you leave dirty dishes in the sink because I feel like I have to spend extra time scraping them off, and it's harder for me to get to school on time. I'd like to talk about this so we can find a solution." By sharing your feelings, your housemate has a chance to reflect on his or her behavior and how it affects you. He or she may feel motivated to start rinsing the dishes, but if not, you might respectfully suggest a solution: "Perhaps we could each be responsible for washing our own dishes. What if we agree to do this at least four times a week?"

Don't Be a Doormat

Are you familiar with the expression "being a doormat"? It refers to a situation in which you feel stepped on or used. If you ever find yourself feeling this way—like someone is taking advantage of you or not considering what you want or need—you can stand up for yourself by becoming an assertive communicator. Try the following assertiveness strategies:

- Before making a request, know what you want to ask for.
- Rehearse what you plan to say. You may even want to role-play the scenario with a friend.

- Show confidence in your feelings and opinions by making eye contact with others and demonstrating confident nonverbal behavior, such as maintaining an open posture.
- Speak clearly and concisely. Emphasize the key points you're communicating.
- If you're making a statement, end it with a downward inflection in your voice. Ending with an upward inflection will make your statement sound like a question, signaling uncertainty.

- If the situation is too fresh and you're feeling angry or emotional, wait a day or two to have the conversation when you feel calmer and more in control.
- If you didn't do anything wrong, don't apologize.
- Remind yourself that you have the right to say "no" and to change your mind.
- Take the strongest stance on issues that matter most to you. For less significant issues, practice the vital art of knowing when to let it go.

Use All Your Skills to Resolve Conflicts

Together, being assertive, using "I" statements, and drawing on the other skills you've learned about in this chapter (active listening, providing feedback, exercising emotional intelligence) can help you resolve conflicts. The following process, which incorporates each of these skills, shows you how.

1. **Identify the problem.** Use active listening to pinpoint the nature of the conflict. Then assertively state your perspective of it ("It seems to me that we disagree about who should do which parts of this project"). If several people are involved in the conflict, let all the participants provide their own perspective on what the problem is. Convey your understanding of their perspective by providing feedback.

2. **Understand your emotions.** Identify the feelings you're experiencing. If they're intensely negative, use your emotional intelligence to understand and manage them. Then provide an "I" statement to communicate your feelings ("I'm feeling frustrated by our inability to create a clear plan for this project because without a plan we could do sloppy work and miss the deadline").

3. **Understand others' emotions.** Empathize with others or ask questions to better understand the feelings of those who disagree with you ("What's causing you to feel upset by what I'm proposing?").

4. **Investigate others' viewpoints.** Ask questions to better understand others' perspectives ("How did you arrive at your thoughts about who should do the various parts of the project?").

5. **Find common ground.** Identify points of agreement ("I know we all want to submit a well-done project on time").

6. **Stay positive.** Frame the conflict as a problem that needs to be solved—not an indication of poor character or incompetence on the part of those who disagree with you ("Let's fix this situation together" versus "What's wrong with you people?").

7. **Involve others in creating the solution.** Ask everyone involved in the conflict to brainstorm possible solutions. List the potential solutions and talk about each one, with the goal of identifying one that everyone can accept and support.

8. **Compromise if necessary.** If it's impossible to arrive at a solution that pleases everyone, see which participants are willing to compromise for the sake of moving forward. Implement the compromise, and thank them for helping the group make progress.

Grow and Sustain Healthy Relationships

All the connection skills we've discussed so far—effective communication, emotional intelligence, conflict resolution—have an overarching purpose: helping you build and sustain healthy relationships while you're in college. These relationships are important because to succeed in school, you need a strong *social support network*—a group of people who encourage you when things get tough and join in celebrating your accomplishments. This network can include people outside of school, as well as classmates, faculty members, members of study groups, and people you meet in campus clubs, professional organizations, or even online. In this section we look at how to connect with the important members of your social support network.

Connect with Classmates

Getting to know your classmates can help you build a network of people who—whether they become good friends or just study partners—can keep you motivated and connect you to information and other resources you need to succeed in class.

Look for opportunities to get to know your classmates. In face-to-face classes, strike up a conversation before or after class. In an online environment, you may be required to introduce yourself in a discussion forum and respond to others' introductory posts.

Connect with Instructors

When you feel connected to your instructors, you'll feel more comfortable asking them for help. And when they know you, they'll be more likely to give you career advice, point you to internship or job opportunities, and write you letters of recommendation. So try chatting with your instructors before class, after class, or during their office hours—although take care to maintain an appropriate degree of professionalism in these conversations. Telling an instructor you saw a great concert last night is fine.

Describing how wild and crazy you got at the concert, on the other hand, is not.

And keep in mind that you communicate with your instructors not only with conversation but also with your nonverbal behavior. In a face-to-face class, getting to class on time, sitting near the front of the room, making eye contact, shutting off your phone (no texting), and taking notes shows your respect for your instructors and your interest in the class material. And in an online course, your instructor will assess other aspects of your communication, including the quality and frequency of your discussion board posts and your e-mail etiquette. Be sure to follow these guidelines when crafting e-mails to your instructors.

Getting to Know You . . . Meeting classmates is a great way to start building a network of people who can support you and connect you to the resources you need to succeed in school. So take every opportunity to strike up conversations with fellow students. Who knows? Some may become lifelong friends. John Giustina/Getty Images

1. Use the subject line to indicate the content and purpose of your e-mail ("Question about deadline extension for English literature paper").

2. Address your instructor formally by his or her appropriate title—for example, "Dear Dr. Jones. . . ."

3. If you don't know the instructor personally, explain who you are. For example, "I am a student in your 8:00 a.m. English literature class."

4. Be courteous in your tone, even if you're stating a complaint.

5. Use complete sentences, proper sentence structure, and correct spelling and grammar. Proofread your message and use the spell-checker before you hit "Send."

6. Keep your message brief. If something requires a long explanation, set up an in-person meeting.

7. Never use all capital letters in an e-mail. That's considered shouting.

8. Review your e-mail to make sure you've included all relevant details and any required attachments.

Connect with Your Campus Community

Connecting with the larger campus community is another great way to meet people and build relationships. Your school may have a number of student-led clubs and organizations to fit your interests, values, and affiliations—everything from a Ballroom Dance Club and a Campus Vegetarian Society to a Korean American Student Association and an Accounting Club. Additionally, you may want to get involved in student government to develop leadership skills or join other student organizations that provide services to the local community, such as Big Brothers Big Sisters. Your college may even offer classes that combine classroom instruction with volunteer experience in the

There's More to College than the Classroom

You may be thinking, "Joining a campus club sounds fun, but I need to focus on getting good grades." You absolutely need to fulfill your obligations, but research shows that getting involved on campus has benefits.

In one study, researchers at a large state college tracked the extracurricular activities of almost 15,000 first-year students to determine how active involvement on campus related to their grades and how long those students stayed in college.[10] The students were divided into two groups: those who participated in extracurricular activities (student clubs, student government, orientation) at least once during their college career and those who never participated in any extracurricular activities. The researchers discovered that students who participated in campus activities achieved higher cumulative GPAs than those who didn't. In addition, students who participated in campus activities remained in college at higher rates than those who didn't.

Why might this be so? Other research provides some clues. First, getting involved on campus can make college more fun and interesting, which motivates students to invest more time and energy in their studies.[11] Second, participation in campus activities can help students connect with others on campus, increase their social support network, and develop confidence and social skills—which in turn may make it easier for them to ask for help from instructors, advisers, or other college resources.[12] Finally, feeling like a valued member of the campus community may instill a sense of pride and belonging that further serves as motivation.

The bottom line? Participation can lead to good things! Getting involved on campus may help you connect to people and resources at your school—and may ultimately help you succeed.

community, called **service learning**. With so many opportunities, your options for meeting other people are endless!

Connect with Others Online

Joining online communities and networks that fit your interests and needs can also help you build relationships.[13] For example, through social media sites such as Facebook and Twitter and professional networking sites such as LinkedIn, you can meet others and stay connected through activities like wall posting, picture sharing, and instant messaging. If you want to meet people who share your interests, you can join an online discussion forum. If you want to make changes in your life, such as stopping drinking, you can join an online support group.

But use caution in your interactions with online communities. In particular, reflect on what you're posting. Five years from now, would you be embarrassed by the photo of yourself you just shared? If a potential employer saw the image, could it jeopardize your chances of getting your dream job? (Yes, some recruiters will search your name on the Web.) And if you arrange a face-to-face meeting with someone you met online, practice personal safety: Let someone else know about the meeting, get together in a public place, and consider bringing along a friend.

Stay Connected with Friends and Family

It takes time and effort to maintain relationships, but even as a busy college student you can use active listening, emotional intelligence, and assertiveness skills to show the people in your life *off* campus just how special they are. Here are a few strategies for preserving meaningful relationships with friends and family while in college.

- Stay connected with your loved ones through e-mail, texting, Facebook, phone calls, or face-to-face visits.

- Actively listen to any concerns or fears they might have for you.
- Share your hopes and dreams with them.
- Let them know how they can support you emotionally while you're in school.
- Invite them to campus or show them your online coursespace so that they feel they're part of your college experience.
- Communicate your needs assertively. Don't assume they can read your mind.
- Develop empathy—try to understand what it's like for them to spend less time with you.
- Let minor disagreements go.
- If tensions build, address the issue in a calm, respectful way using "I" statements.
- Try to negotiate mutually beneficial solutions to any conflicts that arise.

Keep in Contact. Nurture your relationships with friends and family members off campus by being a good communicator. Stay in touch by texting "hello," giving special people a call, and visiting in person when you can. Your loved ones will appreciate your efforts to stay connected. Caiaimage/Tom Merton/Getty Images

MAINTAINING RELATIONSHIPS

Courtesy of Samuel Caleb Stumberg

NAME:	**Samuel Caleb Stumberg**
SCHOOL:	*Montana State University, Billings*
MAJOR:	*History Education*
CAREER GOAL:	*Teaching*

Working part-time, going to college full-time, and maintaining a social life is anything but easy. Balancing my relationships, work, and school is what has helped me get through the tough times. Family and friends are extremely important; they provide support, love, and joy. However, maintaining relationships and doing well in school require good communication skills and the ability to make time for others.

I try to make as much time for my friends and family as I can. I like to get coffee with my friends in between classes or go on runs with them. Playing games is always fun — anything that can bring people together. I live far away from my family, so it's difficult to stay in touch with them. I try to call them once a week, for an hour or so, to catch up.

Maintaining relationships isn't all fun and games, though. Recently, some problems arose with my roommates. We said things that we didn't mean, and it seemed like our friendships would end. One of our main problems was that we weren't all in the same room; we were relying on texting for most of our communication. Texting is a terrible form of communication because you can't see the other person or communicate emotion.

Eventually, we were able to resolve our problem. We dropped the fighting and started to speak more assertively. We found that it was better to be respectful to the people with whom you're discussing an issue. Use your words wisely and aim your criticisms at the topic, not the person. When we started communicating like adults, we realized how childish our disagreement was. We apologized to one another, and things were settled. I learned that if you want to maintain friendships, sometimes you have to bite your tongue.

YOUR TURN: Have you ever had a disagreement with important people in your life, as Caleb did with his roommates? If so, what did you learn from this experience? What approaches seemed most (or least) useful for managing the disagreement and maintaining the relationship? Do you agree with Caleb that texting is a poor form of communication? Have you used it successfully?

> "Balancing my relationships, work, and school is what has helped me get through the tough times."

Embrace Diversity

In school and at work, you'll have many opportunities to build relationships with people who are different from you in any number of ways. Some of these differences might be visible, such as gender, skin color, age, and physical ability. Other differences may not be immediately apparent, such as income, religious affiliation, ethnicity, and sexual orientation.

The term **diversity** refers to characteristics or attributes that make us different from one another and that can be the basis for membership in a group. Differences make us unique, and they make the world a more vibrant and interesting place. Imagine how boring life would be if everyone was exactly the same!

In this section we explore many types of diversity. We consider the importance of respecting others' experiences and appreciating what makes them who they are. Finally, we look at how thinking critically about diversity can enrich your relationships.

Recognize Differences

If you were asked to describe yourself, what would you say? Would you talk about physical characteristics, such as your hair color or height? Would you mention your age, where you grew up, or your life goals?

When we describe ourselves, we can draw from many characteristics—physical appearance, personality traits, interests, family background, values, skills, and many more. All of us are *multidimensional*—we're defined by many different aspects of our identity. As you think about the diversity you see on your campus, at work, and in your personal life, reflect on the characteristics that make us unique and shape our experiences. Just some of the many characteristics are listed in Table 10.2.

Respect Differences

When you meet new people, remember that they bring with them diverse experiences, backgrounds, beliefs, and opinions. You can build relationships with and learn from them by practicing *tolerance*: acknowledging, valuing, and respecting what makes them different from you and from one another. When you're tolerant, you may not always agree with someone, but you try to understand his or her perspective by showing empathy and "agreeing to disagree." Being tolerant means treating people with dignity and respect, accepting that not everyone thinks or acts like you, and recognizing that diversity adds richness and color to life.

Unfortunately, some people look down on or even mistreat those who are different from them. Such reactions can occur if a person has inaccurate beliefs about a particular group or has had a negative experience with a member of a group and then generalizes that experience to the larger group. Lack of exposure to a particular group can also cause such reactions because people can be suspicious of what's unfamiliar. These reactions play a part in *stereotyping*, or assigning real, imagined, or exaggerated characteristics (negative or positive) to all members of a particular group—for example, "All American tourists are rude" or "Everyone from the East Coast is well educated."

When we have a fixed, overgeneralized belief about a particular group of people, we fail to see individual differences. Why is that a problem? Think about how you would feel if someone made assumptions about your values, beliefs, abilities, or behaviors solely based on your race, ethnicity, or gender. When we stereotype, we don't engage in critical thinking. Stereotyping is a lazy thinking process in which we place people in simple categories—sometimes even "us" and "them" categories. Our thoughts may then influence our behavior.

When we treat people less favorably based on their membership in a particular group, it is called **discrimination**. For example, it's considered discrimination if a manager avoids hiring well-qualified job candidates because of their age (*ageism*), race (*racism*), gender,

TABLE 10.2 Common Elements of Diversity

Element	Description	Did you know?
Race	A way to classify people into groups according to physical characteristics such as skin color, hair color, facial features, and body build.	Guessing someone's race based on physical features is risky because appearances may be deceiving. Further, many people are multiracial, which may not be clear from physical appearance alone.
Ethnicity	A way to identify a group of people with a common ancestral heritage and, often, a shared history and culture (language, traditions, food, clothing styles, values, beliefs, art, literature).	In the United States, people who identify as Hispanic or Latino (from places such as Mexico, Puerto Rico, and Cuba) are the largest and fastest-growing ethnic group.[14]
Gender	Refers to characteristics that a society or culture defines as masculine or feminine. Gender is different than *sex*, which refers to biological rather than cultural differences.[15]	Gender can also refer to one's own experience of being a man or a woman (gender identity), how a person presents him- or herself to the world (gender expression), or expectations others have for an individual based on their perception of the person's gender (gender roles).[16]
Sexual orientation	Refers to an enduring pattern of attraction to others, such as persons of the opposite sex (heterosexuality), the same sex (homosexuality), or both sexes (bisexuality).[17]	You may never know someone's sexual orientation unless the person tells you. If someone shares his or her sexual orientation with you, don't assume that it's been shared with everyone else.
Mental and physical ability	Refers to a person's ability to perform one or more major life activities, such as caring for oneself, walking, speaking, breathing, and thinking.	Mental or physical impairments, or disabilities, can limit someone's ability to perform major life activities. Sometimes it's clear that someone has a disability (such as when a person uses a wheelchair). Other times, the disability isn't so visible (such as when a person has dyslexia).
Religion	An organized system of spiritual beliefs, traditions, and practices agreed upon by a group of individuals.	Many colleges offer classes on world religions. These classes can be a great way to learn more about different belief systems.
Socioeconomic status	Refers to social standing or prestige based on income, occupation, or education.[18]	Visible status symbols, such as the way a person dresses, don't always accurately reveal socioeconomic status. Some wealthy people spend modestly, for instance, while some people in financial straits spend lavishly to build their image.
Age	Indicates how old a person is, which determines the social, political, economic, and technological events the individual is exposed to in his or her lifetime.	Terms such as *baby boomers* (born 1946–1964), *Generation X* (born early 1960s to early 1980s), and *millennials* (born early 1980s to early 2000s) are used to classify people who were born during different time periods.

Diversity's Power. Why should you embrace diversity and treat others who are different from you with respect and appreciation? By doing so, you can learn a lot and forge mutually beneficial connections. Those connections make life far richer—and more interesting—than it would be if you associated only with people who are exactly like you.

Tim Pannell/CORBIS

religion, or sexual orientation. Colleges and workplaces have established policies against all forms of discrimination, so report any incidents of discrimination you witness. Doing so will help make these environments safe places for diverse ideas, interests, beliefs, opinions, and lifestyles. If you've ever experienced discrimination, you know firsthand how important it is to combat it.

Think Critically about Differences

Thinking critically about yourself and others is vital to building relationships with people who are different from you. It can help you appreciate their perspectives, empathize with them, and develop new viewpoints. Let diversity enrich your relationships by using these strategies.

- **Know yourself.** Consider the components of your own identity. What makes you visibly different from other students? What differences would people learn about only by getting to know you? How have these differences influenced the person you are today?

- **Know your biases.** Ask yourself whether you feel uncomfortable talking or working with any groups of people. If so, what might have caused this discomfort? How might your own background and life experiences have influenced these feelings?

- **Gain information.** Learn more about people who are different from you, including how their group has been treated throughout history. For example, take a class such as Men and Masculinity or Comparative

Religions. Attend public events offered by your school, such as a Martin Luther King Jr. celebration. Learn how to create a safe space for lesbian, gay, bisexual, transgender, queer, and questioning (LGBTQQ) individuals by attending a Safe Zone Training Program.

- **Seek personal contact.** The more you interact with people who have different backgrounds, the more comfortable you'll feel. Talk together about the same things you would discuss with other friends. Explore what you have in common. Discover how you differ, and identify what's interesting or valuable about those differences.

- **Be open to feedback.** As you interact more with people who are different from you, you may unintentionally offend them through words or actions. If this happens, use active listening to understand their viewpoint, and remain open to their feedback. Apologize, and thank them for the opportunity to learn from the experience.

- **Advocate.** Use your assertiveness skills to stand up for others whom you see being treated unfairly because of something that makes them different. Let people know that you don't want to hear offensive language, jokes, stereotypical remarks, or insults directed toward a particular group of people, including any groups you're a member of. Report illegal discrimination, hate crimes, and other abuse to authorities.

my personal success plan

CONNECTION SKILLS

Are you inspired to set a new goal related to connecting with others? If so, the Personal Success Plan can walk you through the goal-setting process. Read the advice and examples; then sketch out your ideas in the space provided.

LaunchPad Solo
macmillan learning

To access the Personal Success Plan online, go to LaunchPad Solo for *Connections Essentials*.

1 GATHER INFORMATION

Think about your strengths and weaknesses in connecting with others. What strategies have worked for you in the past? What could you do differently? Revisit your Connecting with Others score on ACES and review the relevant sections of this chapter for additional ideas.

2 SET A SMART GOAL

Use the information you've gathered to create a SMART goal, making sure to use the SMART goal checklist.

SAMPLE: Starting next Monday, I'll use "I" statements whenever a disagreement arises between me and someone else.

3 MAKE AN ACTION PLAN

Outline the specific steps you'll take to achieve your SMART goal, and note when you'll complete each step.

SAMPLE: During all my interactions with others next week, I'll notice if I'm using blaming or accusatory language and will reframe my comments as "I" statements.

4 LIST BARRIERS AND SOLUTIONS

Think about possible barriers to your action steps; then brainstorm solutions for overcoming them.

SAMPLE: If I get so upset during a disagreement that it's hard to transform blaming language into "I" statements, I'll count to ten and try again.

5 ACT AND EVALUATE OUTCOMES

Now that your plan is in place, take action. Record each action step as you take it. Then evaluate whether you achieved your SMART goal, and make any adjustments needed to get better results in the future.

SAMPLE: Counting to ten didn't help me reduce my frustration as much as I had hoped. The next time my emotions get away from me, I'll try taking a short, brisk walk instead.

6 CONNECT TO CAREER

List the skills you're building as you progress toward your SMART goal. How will you use these skills to land a job and succeed at work?

SAMPLE: In any career I pursue, learning how to manage conflict effectively will help me work well with others and stay productive on the job.

1 my information

2 my SMART goal

☐ **S**PECIFIC ☐ **M**EASURABLE ☐ **A**CHIEVABLE ☐ **R**ELEVANT ☐ **T**IME-LIMITED

3 my action plan

4 my barriers/ solutions

5 my actions/ outcomes

6 my career connection

Chapter 10 Review

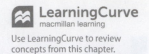
CHAPTER SUMMARY

- In interpersonal communication, ideally a speaker conveys a clear message to the receiver. The receiver hears the complete message, overcoming any barriers; interprets it; and then gives feedback.

- Exercising emotional intelligence involves recognizing, understanding, and managing your own and others' emotions.

- Assertive communication can help you constructively resolve conflicts by sharing your feelings in an honest, respectful way.

- "I" statements can also help you resolve conflicts effectively by showing that you take responsibility for your reactions.

- Communication skills, emotional intelligence, and the ability to work through conflicts with others can help you build and sustain healthy relationships.

- Knowing how to interact effectively with people from diverse backgrounds is valuable in college and the workplace because it helps you change and grow.

CHAPTER ACTIVITIES

Adopting a Success Attitude

BUILDING EMOTIONAL INTELLIGENCE

Everyone is entitled to feelings—good, bad, or ugly. When we have negative feelings, it's important to recognize them, understand them, and respond to them in healthy ways. From the following list of feeling words, choose three emotions that you experienced this week. Then respond to the questions below for each emotion. An example is provided.

Feeling Words

irritated	aggressive	resentful
provoked	disappointed	helpless
embarrassed	shy	distrustful
pessimistic	lonely	sorrowful
crushed	offended	anxious

What emotion did you experience?

I was embarrassed.

What caused this emotion?

I responded incorrectly to a question in class.

How did you respond?

I left class early and skipped the next class.

What was the consequence?

I missed a quiz and was given 0 points.

If appropriate, provide an alternate response.

If this happens again, I'll tell myself it's okay to be wrong and will remain in class to seek the right answers.

Applying Your Skills

COMMUNICATING ASSERTIVELY

Respond to the following scenarios by using an "I" statement to convey your feelings and your interest in reaching a solution to the problem.

1. You're working on a group project for class. You show up at the second group meeting with your part of the project complete. No one else has done any work yet. You feel angry.

   "I" message: _____

2. You like to bring your lunch to work, but the office refrigerator is disgusting! It's full of forgotten leftovers. You decide to speak to your coworkers.

   "I" message: _____

3. You have a big test tomorrow and need to study. No one else in the house seems to care. The television is blaring, someone's blasting a stereo, and the dog is whining to go outside.

   "I" message: _____

145/Eunice Harris/Ocean/CORBIS

11

Personal and Financial Health

Stress Less, Feel Better

Physical and Mental Health

Sexual Health

Financial Health

MY PERSONAL SUCCESS PLAN

Close your eyes, and create a mental image of what stress feels like to you. Perhaps you're picturing a 20-pound weight in your backpack, an itchy sweater that's three sizes too small, or a dark storm cloud following you around, ready to dump rain on you at any moment. Is your image as awful as any of these? Not as bad? Worse?

Now think about the relationship between feelings of stress and your personal and financial health. If you're like many people, there's a clear connection between how stressed you are and how good you feel — and even between how stressed you are and how well you manage your money. For example, if you're anxious about presenting in class, your blood pressure might rise and you might lose sleep. And high stress levels might prompt you to engage in a little "retail therapy" and splurge on things you can't afford in an effort to distract yourself from your troubles.

Conversely, your health choices can affect how stressed you feel. For instance, if you don't get enough sleep and never exercise, you'll probably experience stress in the form of exhaustion and anxiety. If you don't manage your money carefully, you may run out of funds for everyday expenses, further ratcheting up your stress levels.

The good news about this connection is that if you make the right decisions about your personal and financial health, you can control your stress levels — and this chapter shows you how. First, we examine stress in more detail. Then we explore key aspects of your physical well-being, mental health, and sexual health. Finally, we explore how to enhance your financial health through budgeting, understanding financial aid, and managing credit.

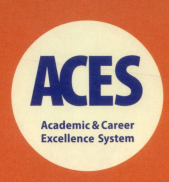

ACES
Academic & Career Excellence System

To find your **Personal and Financial Health score**, go to LaunchPad Solo for *Connections Essentials*.

REFLECTION:
Your Personal and Financial Health

Take a moment to reflect on your Personal and Financial Health score on ACES. Find your score and add it to the box on the left.

This score measures your beliefs about how healthy you are physically, mentally, and financially. Do you think it's an accurate snapshot of how you feel in this area? Why or why not?

- **IF YOU SCORED IN THE HIGH RANGE** and believe this score is accurate, then staying healthy and financially stable may be one of your strengths. Excellent! But remember: You can always work to improve strengths. For instance, if you're already getting enough exercise, explore how you could also improve your diet. Or if you've built an effective budget, identify ways you could reduce your spending to free up funds for tuition and other important expenses.

- **IF YOU SCORED IN THE MODERATE OR LOW RANGE**, use the suggestions in this chapter to better manage your health and to stay on track financially. Once you identify and implement strategies that work for you, you'll feel better physically and mentally, as well as more fiscally secure.

ACES Journal

How do you feel right now — physically, mentally, and financially? Begin this journal entry by describing something related to your health that you feel good about. For example, perhaps you snacked on carrots instead of cookies this afternoon or saved money by making coffee at home instead of buying it on campus. Next, write down a few quick and easy ways you might improve one aspect of your health in the next two weeks. What concrete steps can you take to make these ideas a reality?

_____

_____

_____

_____

_____

Stress Less, Feel Better

Why is stress such a major factor in our lives? To answer this question, let's explore how stress works and how it affects us. When you feel stress, your body releases stress hormones, such as cortisol and adrenaline.[1] Such hormones can speed up your heart rate and breathing. In addition, your muscles tense up, and your body readies itself for a fight-or-flight response—a primitive reaction in which you either combat the danger facing you or run away from it.

The fight-or-flight response was useful long ago in our evolutionary history. If a lion chased you, a surge of adrenaline would give you the strength to whack the animal over the head with a club or run away. Either move could boost your chances of survival. Today, many of us don't regularly face the kinds of perils that call for a fight-or-flight response. However, if we keep *experiencing* that response, we get bombarded with the resulting physical changes, which can lead to health problems such as anxiety, ulcers, fatigue, weight gain, and depression.[2]

How can you avoid these problems? Start by understanding your own personal stressors, which are events and situations that tend to upset you. To get a better sense of your stressors, look at this list of some common college stressors and check off any items you experienced during the last year.

___ Starting/Restarting College
___ Significant Change in Income
___ Disruption to Sleeping Pattern
___ Illness
___ Major Paper/Assignment/Exam
___ Start/End of a Dating Relationship
___ Problems with Family Members
___ Choosing a Major
___ Job Change
___ Making a Presentation in Class
___ Balancing School, Work, and Family
___ Other Stressors: _____

As you can see from this list, any event that intensifies your emotions and physical reactions—whether distressing or joyous—can be a stressor. For example, you can feel stress when you end a relationship or when you start a new one.

The good news is that you *can* manage stressors, and the most potent strategies for doing so involve keeping your mind and body healthy and your finances under control. First, let's turn to two vital components of personal health: your physical and mental well-being.

Nice Kitty. If this impressive tiger came your way, would his presence activate your stress response? It probably would! But it doesn't take the approach of a wild animal to put your body on high alert. Maybe you have a test tomorrow, your credit card payment is due, or you're going out on a first date with someone special. A variety of stressors can intensify our emotional and physical reactions—which is why we need strategies to keep ourselves healthy and our stress under control. AppStock/Shutterstock

Physical and Mental Health

Feeling unwell—physically or mentally—can hurt your academic performance by making it hard to go to class, pay attention, study, and get your assignments done. Do what you can to maintain your well-being—including eating right, staying active, and getting enough sleep—and you'll be ahead of the game.

Eat Right

Have you ever come home after a hard day and gobbled up a pint of ice cream or a giant bag of potato chips—only to realize that you felt just as stressed once all the goodies were gone? Guess what: What and how much you eat has a big impact on your health, your energy level, and even your mood.

That said, always eating healthy isn't easy in college. If you're on the go from morning until night, finding time to prepare nutritious meals may seem impossible. And if you live on campus, you may have access to an array of fast foods with high amounts of fat, salt, and sugar.

Let's consider some ideas for navigating these environments and discuss the consequences of eating too much—or too little.

Master Healthy Eating Tactics. When you make healthy dietary choices, you give your body the sustenance and energy it needs for you to function effectively. To learn about healthy eating, visit the U.S. Department of Agriculture's MyPlate program at www.choosemyplate.gov. An updated version of the food pyramid, MyPlate offers guidelines on issues such as what proportions of the different food groups should be included in every meal and how to eat healthy on a budget. There's even MyPlate On Campus, which spotlights strategies students can use to adopt a healthy lifestyle.

In addition, take advantage of other information sources to learn about healthy eating. For example, read the nutrition facts on foods you buy and ask dining services on campus for information about the calories, fat, sodium, and sugar in the available meal choices.

Finally, try these strategies for selecting foods that deliver a powerful, healthy-eating punch.

- Start your day with a light, nutritious breakfast, such as fruit and yogurt, instead of calorie-laden breads and meats.

- Keep healthy snacks in handy places, such as your backpack, car, and refrigerator or pantry at home.

- Eat more fruits and vegetables. If you change from fewer than three servings a

So Many Choices . . . You're at a buffet, ready to load your tray. You have countless options — so how can you pick the healthiest? Ask about the calories, fat, sodium, and sugar in the meal choices. And check out the USDA's MyPlate program to find out what portion of each food group should go on your plate. Mario Savoia/Shutterstock

day to more than five servings, you can cut your risk of heart disease by 17 percent![3]

- Stay away from processed foods and beverages. They have a lot of preservatives, sugar, and fat.

- Avoid supersized meals. Instead, take a smaller plate and say "no" when someone offers a larger portion. These easy steps will reduce your calorie intake.[4]

- Carry a water bottle with you, and keep drinking from and refilling it. You'll stay hydrated—essential for feeling well both physically and mentally.

Get Help for Eating Disorders. People often use healthy eating strategies as part of a plan to lose weight or maintain a certain weight. Managing your weight can be a good thing if you do so in a balanced, careful way. But if weight loss becomes your main focus in life and you start to engage in dangerous eating behaviors, you risk serious health problems. Severely restricting food intake and having an irrational fear of gaining weight are symptoms of *anorexia nervosa*. Engaging in binge eating followed by intentional purging (vomiting), obsessively overexercising, and abusing diuretics are symptoms of *bulimia nervosa*. These disorders can make you seriously ill—and even kill you.[5] If you show symptoms of these disorders, or you know someone who does, support is available: Seek help now at your campus's health and counseling centers.

Stay Active

Get more exercise! We've all heard this before, and there's a good reason why: Exercise helps build muscle strength and improves cardiovascular fitness. It's also a great way to manage the stress of being a college student.[6]

Every week, try to get at least 150 minutes of moderate exercise or 75 minutes of vigorous exercise.[7] If you have difficulty following an exercise routine or if you hate gyms, build an exercise schedule that works for you. For instance, break the 150 minutes into

30 minutes of exercise, five days a week. Or do a 45-minute workout two days a week and squeeze in several 10- to 15-minute walks to get the additional hour.

You can also take advantage of everyday tasks and events to get more exercise.

- If you have a car, park some distance away and walk to your destination.

- Take stairs instead of elevators.

- During study breaks, take a walk around the library or do jumping jacks in your room.

- Sign up for a fitness class at the recreation center.

- Ask a friend to work out with you. Having company can keep you motivated.

- Join an intramural sports team.

Don't Skimp on the Z's

Getting enough sleep affects our ability to function each day;[8] when we're overtired, dealing with stress is much more difficult. If you usually get less than seven to eight hours of good-quality sleep each night, you're probably exhausted. To get enough Z's and feel your best each day, try these strategies.

- Avoid late-night cramming. Organize your time so that you can get a full night's sleep before exams and can finish assignments on time.

- Stay away from caffeinated or energy drinks in the late afternoon or evening.

- Get enough exercise, particularly earlier in the day.

- Don't nap during the day; napping only makes it harder to fall asleep once you're in bed for the night.

- Establish a regular sleep schedule—then stick with it.

- If you have trouble falling asleep, try relaxation techniques such as deep breathing, tensing and releasing muscles throughout your body, or envisioning peaceful scenes.

Healthy Behavior Is Good for Your Grades

Do you get eight hours of good-quality slumber every night? Are you an "early to bed, early to rise" person? Do you have breakfast every day? If your answer to these questions is "no," then your health — and your academic performance — could be suffering, according to findings from a study of almost two hundred first-year college students.[9]

In this study, researchers asked students about their health-related behaviors during the first semester of college and then obtained their grade point average at the end of the term. When the researchers analyzed the data, they identified several significant relationships between health behaviors and grades. Higher grades were associated with

- Going to bed earlier and getting up earlier during the week and on the weekend
- Regularly eating breakfast

The researchers also discovered that the students who slept more on the weekends than they did during the week had lower grades. This finding suggests that using weekends to catch up on missed sleep is no substitute for being well rested all week long.

The bottom line? Taking care of your health pays off for your personal well-being and your academic performance: Behaviors like getting enough sleep and eating breakfast every day are linked to better grades in college.

gpointstudio/Shutterstock

Take Care of Your Mental Health

Taking care of your mental health is just as important as nurturing your physical health. If you're feeling down or worried, just going to class or reading a textbook chapter might seem as impossible as climbing Mount Everest. Depression, anxiety, eating disorders, substance abuse, and other mental-health issues are all too common among college students.[10] The good news, however, is that you *can* get better if you experience these challenges and there are people who can help.

In this section we look at depression and anxiety, two of the most common mental-health problems affecting college students.

Depression. Depression is common among college students, particularly since adjusting to college can result in feelings of loneliness, loss of previous friendships, or discomfort in being in a new environment. Left untreated, depression can affect your appetite, causing you to lose or gain weight; keep you awake at night or make it hard to get out of bed in the morning; and leave you feeling listless, with little interest in activities you used to enjoy.

Depression can range from very mild (feeling down a couple of days a month) to severe (feeling suicidal). If you experience symptoms of depression that last for more than two weeks or that make it hard for you to get through the day, or if you have experienced depression in the past and experience its symptoms again — including thoughts of hurting yourself — get help immediately. To manage feelings of depression, reach out to others who can help you: a therapist, a clergy member, friends, or family. You *don't* have to go it alone.

Student Voices of Experience

STAYING HEALTHY AND COPING WITH STRESS

Courtesy of Mathew W. Schneider

NAME: **Mathew Schneider**

SCHOOL: *University of Texas at Arlington*

MAJOR: *Biology*

CAREER GOAL: *Physician Assistant*

In my second year of college, I was struggling to balance my schoolwork, family life, and work. I also felt alone at school — I'm forty-three years old and almost retired from the military, so I felt different from this young crowd I now call my classmates. This was stressful. When I'm stressed, I find it difficult to accomplish things, I feel irritable, and I lose my appetite. Sleep becomes a huge issue for me; at night I'll just toss and turn and get rings under my eyes from not sleeping.

This semester, I was determined to change my sleep habits. In my Human Physiology class, I learned that sedentary activities, such as just going to class and studying, reduce energy levels and metabolism rates. When I found this out, I developed a goal of living healthier. This is an ongoing battle, but I've found that exercise helps me sleep better. It has also built up my energy level and helped me cut back from a pot of coffee a day to two cups (never after 6:00 p.m.). I've gone from restless sleep, which gave me no energy for the day, to quality sleep after exercise, which helped me feel fully functional and energized. Exercise has made a world of difference to me this semester.

In order to get control of my stress, it has also helped to get support. My wife has been supportive when I feel stressed out. When my stress is school related, my classmates, study groups, and student organizations have been the most comforting. I created a support group where I made friends and improved my grades. This tool helps me handle even my hardest and most stressful classes. I'm well known in the biology department as the study-group king, and I've found that so many others have been helped by this group as well.

YOUR TURN: To what degree do you identify with Mathew's experiences with exercise and with getting support for managing stress? For example, what role does exercise play in your life as a college student? Whom do you turn to for moral support when you're feeling overwhelmed?

> " **Exercise has made a world of difference to me this semester."**

Comfort Dogs. If you're like most college students, final exam time can intensify your anxiety to panic levels, so you need to take extra-good care of yourself. Students at the University of California at Riverside have an unusual resource available to them: specially trained "comfort dogs" brought by their owners to help students manage exam-week anxiety. Spencer Grant/PhotoEdit

Anxiety. If you experience excessive worry, dread, or fear, you may have anxiety. For some people anxiety is a general, all-encompassing sensation. For others it's more specific; for instance, they might feel anxious in social settings or while taking tests. Anxiety can also express itself as panic attacks, during which your heart starts racing in your chest for no apparent reason, you can't catch your breath, and you feel as though you're having a heart attack. If you suffer from anxiety that's far beyond everyday worry, reach out for help. The counseling center, an adviser, a clergy member, or another person you trust can connect you with the resources you need, on or off campus.

Don't Abuse Alcohol and Drugs

Alcohol and drug abuse are serious health problems on many college campuses. Why do students use drugs and alcohol? Some do so because they think it will help them manage stress. Others think that it's an expected part of being a college student and that "everyone's doing it." (Actually, many college students *overestimate* the amount of binge drinking that goes on at their school, so the assumption that "everyone's doing it" is wrong.[11])

At worst, abusing alcohol and drugs can lead to addiction and cause health problems (such as liver damage) and death from overdose. At best, it costs you money you could spend on other, more useful things. The healthy choice? Avoid illegal substances altogether; if you choose to use legal substances, adopt an "everything in moderation" mind-set. In addition, follow these rules to protect your physical safety—as well as your reputation.

- When you go out with friends, designate a responsible member of the group to stay sober and make sure that everyone gets home safely at the end of the night.
- Remember why you're in college and your goals for the future. You'll be less likely to let your partying get out of hand.
- Don't post photos online of yourself drinking or taking drugs. Potential employers may find them—and pass you over for a job.
- If your use of alcohol or drugs prevents you from attending or doing well in your classes, if you feel that you can't control it, or if important people in your life express concerns about it, you may have an addiction problem. Seek out confidential help at the counseling center.

Sexual Health

For students who choose to be sexually active, practicing safe sex helps minimize stress and promotes overall health. Reducing your risk of sexually transmitted infections and using effective birth control if you're not ready to start a family are two important ways to take control of your sex life and adopt healthy sexual behavior.

Avoid Sexually Transmitted Infections

There are many types of **sexually transmitted infections (STIs)**—illnesses spread through the exchange of bodily fluids during sexual activity.

If you're sexually active, how do you stay safe? Start by educating yourself. Table 11.1 shows the frequency, symptoms, and treatment methods for six common STIs. (As you can see, some STIs are curable; others aren't.) Then take steps to reduce your risk. For example:

- Have sex with only one partner at a time—a person you know well.
- Always use condoms.
- Get tested for STIs regularly, even if you don't have any symptoms. You can pass on an STI to someone else without even knowing you have one.
- Have your partner get tested regularly.

TABLE 11.1 Common STIs in the United States

STI	Estimated number of new cases per year	Symptoms	Treatment
Human papillomavirus (HPV)	14 million	There are many types of HPV. Men and women can experience warts in the genital area. HPV can also lead to cervical and other cancers.	No cure. Treatments exist for illnesses caused by HPV.
Chlamydia	2.86 million	Many people have no symptoms. Women can have vaginal discharge. Men can experience discharge from their penis or pain when urinating.	Curable. Treated with antibiotics.
Gonorrhea	820,000	Men may have a burning sensation when urinating or a yellowish, white, or greenish discharge from their penis. Women may have pain or discharge, but most have no symptoms.	Curable. Treated with antibiotics, but some drug-resistant strains are developing.
Genital herpes	776,000	One or more blisters near the genitals. Commonly mistaken for a skin infection.	No cure. Outbreaks are treated to shorten duration.
Syphilis	74,000	A sore on the skin or genitals is the first sign. Left untreated, rashes and sores then appear on other parts of the body.	Curable. Treated with antibiotics.
HIV/AIDS	44,000 (HIV)	Few or no symptoms early. Later, men and women may have weight loss, fatigue, cough, fever, or white spots on the tongue or throat.	No cure. Medications help people live with the disease.

Data from: Centers for Disease Control and Prevention, http://www.cdc.gov/std/healthcomm/fact_sheets.htm.

Issues of sexual health are very personal, but if you have any questions or concerns about STIs, talk with someone you trust who can advise and support you—for example, a counselor, a clergy member, your physician, or a mentor. This person can connect you with the information you need to stay safe and healthy.

Practice Birth Control

If you're a woman having sex with a man and you don't want to start a family now, practicing birth control can give you peace of mind and prevent the stress that can come with an unplanned pregnancy. If you're a man having sex with a woman, using a birth control method designed for men is a good idea, especially if you're not certain that your partner is using birth control. There are many birth control options. Some require prescriptions; others are sold over the counter; still others involve behavior choices. Most don't protect against STIs.

Physicians on campus or at community health centers can prescribe some of these options and share information about each method's risks and benefits, which can help you choose the options right for you.

- Birth control pill: a pill a woman takes orally at the same time each day.
- Patch: a skin patch a woman wears. She applies a new patch each week for three weeks and wears no patch during the fourth week, when she should get her menstrual period.
- Intrauterine device (IUD): a small device inserted in a woman's uterus by a health care provider. Some IUDs can be used for up to ten years.
- Vaginal ring: a small ring inserted in a woman's vagina for three weeks and removed during the fourth week, when she should get her menstrual period.
- The shot: an injection of pregnancy-preventing hormones that lasts for three months.
- Condoms: sheaths that are worn over the penis or inserted into the vagina.
- Abstinence: choosing not to engage in sexual intercourse.[12]

Talk to Your Doc. If you have questions about STIs or birth control, don't feel embarrassed: Contact a medical professional at your campus or community health center. He or she can talk with you about your options and provide useful information that will help you stay healthy.
sturti/Getty Images

Financial Health

If you're like most students, one big reason you're in college is to graduate, get a job, and make enough money to pay your bills and plan for the future. When you earn a college degree, you make a tremendous investment in yourself and your future financial health. As Figure 11.1 shows, people with an associate's degree earn, on average, $120 more per week than those with only a high school diploma, and those with a bachelor's degree earn $459 more per week. That translates into roughly $6,200 to $23,800 of additional income each year for the rest of your life, depending on the degree you get. Imagine what you and your family could do with that added income! Plus, as Figure 11.1 also shows, people with a degree are less likely to be unemployed.

As important as it is to your future to get a degree, you will likely face at least a few financial challenges while you work toward your goals. In fact, in a recent survey, seven out of ten Americans identified money as a significant stressor in their lives.[13] But if financial worries keep you up at night, you *can* take steps to take control of your finances—starting with creating a budget.

Create a Budget

A **budget** is a critical survival tool for your financial health. It is your financial plan: It documents your income and expenses over specific time periods (such as a week, month, or year). Creating and sticking to a budget lets you take control of your money, live within your means, and achieve your financial goals. To create a budget, follow these steps.

Step 1: Gather Information. For one month, collect your bank statements, loan and scholarship information, pay stubs, and any regular bills. Track *all* your spending over the course of the month, and keep all your receipts in one place, such as a desk drawer.

FIGURE 11.1

Earnings and Unemployment Rates by Educational Attainment

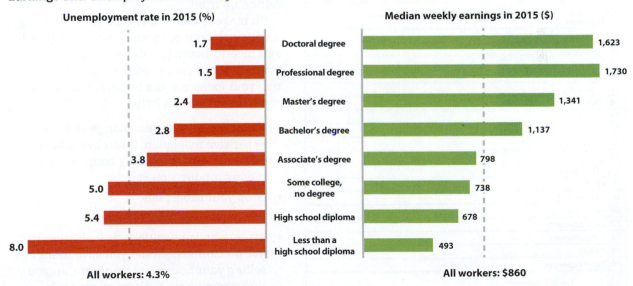

Unemployment rate in 2015 (%) / **Median weekly earnings in 2015 ($)**

Unemployment rate	Degree	Median weekly earnings
1.7	Doctoral degree	1,623
1.5	Professional degree	1,730
2.4	Master's degree	1,341
2.8	Bachelor's degree	1,137
3.8	Associate's degree	798
5.0	Some college, no degree	738
5.4	High school diploma	678
8.0	Less than a high school diploma	493

All workers: 4.3% **All workers: $860**

Note: Data are for persons age twenty-five and over. Earnings are for full-time wage and salary workers. Source: Current Population Survey, U.S. Bureau of Labor Statistics, U.S. Department of Labor, http://www.bls.gov/emp/ep_chart_001.htm.

Step 2: Record Your Income and Expenses. Using a form or spreadsheet like the one in Figure 11.2, enter in the "Last Month" column all the income and expense information you gathered for the previous month (in step 1). Then subtract your total expenses from your total income to obtain your balance for the past month. If your income was greater than your expenses (a financially healthy situation), your balance will be positive. If you spent more than you made (a financially unhealthy situation), your balance will be negative.

Step 3: Use Your Insights to Make Changes. If you discover that you aren't managing your money as effectively as you'd like, you can create a new budget reflecting the changes you need to make. For example, you might take a part-time job to earn more or cut back on unnecessary spending. Return to your budget, and record your expected income and expenses in the "Next Month" column.

Step 4: Track Your Results and Refine Your Budget Further. At the end of the next month, see how closely your actual income and expenses match what you budgeted for the month. Use any differences to further tweak your budget to bring your actual earning and spending in line with your goals. The sections that follow provide ideas you can try.

Reduce Your Spending

If you usually spend more than you make or you just want to save some money, try reducing your spending. You may find some easy ways to do this. For example, if you want to cut your spending by $50 a month, you can brew your own coffee each morning instead of buying coffee on the road. Other solutions may require more sacrifice. If your goal is to graduate with less than $5,000 in debt, you may have to take fewer classes per term so that you can work more hours and pay more tuition up front.

To make it easier to reduce your spending, distinguish between your must-haves (needs) and nice-to-haves (wants). Being honest with yourself about your needs and wants and cutting your expenses can be hard, but here are some ideas that can help.

- If you live on campus, change to a less expensive meal plan. If you live off campus, shop smart by using coupons and buying products on sale.
- Drop your cable plan.
- Find a cheaper Internet service.
- Explore housing options. Is it cheaper to live on campus? Would you save money by selling your house and renting? Can you find a roommate to share expenses?
- Cancel your gym membership and use campus facilities or exercise outdoors.

FIGURE 11.2

Recording Your Income and Expenses

	Budget Worksheet		
1			
2			
3	**Income**	Last Month	Next Month
4	Scholarships		
5	Work		
6	Support from family		
7	Loans		
8	Savings		
9	Other:		
10	**Total Income**		
11			
12	**Expenses**		
13	Tuition		
14	Books/supplies		
15	Housing		
16	Utilities		
17	Electricity		
18	Internet		
19	Cable		
20	Food		
21	Meal plan		
22	Groceries		
23	Dining out		
24	Phone		
25	Car payment		
26	Child care		
27	Debt payments		
28	Entertainment		
29	Other		
30	**Total Expenses**		
31	Total Income:		
32	– Total Expenses:		
33			
34	Balance:		

- Go an extra two weeks between haircuts.
- Explore options at your school for taking more classes each term. Full-time students can often take one or two more classes each term without paying more, which adds up to substantial savings. But take care that you don't get overloaded: Talk with your adviser and family about how to make this work.

Get a Job to Boost Your Income

Working is a fact of life for most college students. According to the National Center for Education Statistics, 41 percent of full-time students and 80 percent of part-time students work while attending college.[14] Working has important advantages. You make money, gain valuable experience, build your skills, apply what you're learning in class to the real world, and build your résumé.

However, there are potential risks associated with working, and it's good to be mindful of these as you schedule your time. Students who work more than fifteen hours a week and those who work off campus are more likely to have lower grades and leave school before graduating.[15] If you have a stressful job and work long hours, you might also have trouble putting enough time into your studies.

If you're balancing work and school effectively now, continue taking good care of yourself so that you don't get overwhelmed. If doing both is becoming problematic, consider taking fewer classes or getting more financial aid. You can talk about possible solutions with an adviser, your family, and your school's financial aid office.

Navigate Financial Aid

It's no secret that college is expensive and that financial aid is a lifesaver for students who couldn't otherwise afford to go. According to the U.S. Department of Education, 85 percent of full-time students at four-year schools and 78 percent of full-time students at two-year schools receive financial aid,[16] in forms such as public or private loans, grants, scholarships, or work-study programs.

Many sources of aid are available, but learning about and applying for aid can be stressful. A good place to start is with the basics: how to apply for aid, what types of aid exist, and how to keep your aid once you receive it.

FAFSA. If you're currently receiving financial aid, then you've already completed a form called the Free Application for Federal Student Aid (FAFSA). If you haven't yet applied for financial aid, start with the FAFSA. This tool assesses your (or your family's) financial situation and calculates how much the federal government believes you can afford to pay for college—which determines how much aid you qualify for. To learn more about the FAFSA, go to www.fafsa.ed.gov or visit your college's financial aid office.

Grants. One common type of financial aid is a *grant*, which is money provided by the government or your college that you're not expected to repay. The federal government gives grants based on financial need (such as Pell Grants) as well as military service (such as Iraq and Afghanistan Service Grants). Your state government might provide grants to in-state residents who earned a strong high school GPA or those who graduated in the top half of their class and attend a two- or four-year college in the state. Your college may also provide grants based on financial need or past accomplishments.

Scholarships. As with grants, you don't have to repay scholarships. Scholarships come from different sources and are awarded for different reasons, such as financial need, talents or accomplishments, membership in a cultural or religious group, or a student's area of study. Your high school or college may award scholarships, or you can earn them through your community, private organizations or businesses, and sometimes even your employer. Web-based services can help you find scholarships, but be sure to start with secure sites that don't charge a fee.

Student Loans. Many students take out a loan to help pay for college. However, if you borrow large amounts and choose a low-paying career or don't ever graduate, you could have trouble paying what you owe. So before you sign up for a loan, understand the pros and cons of borrowing that money. Research the different types of loans available to you, and talk with your adviser to make sure you're taking all the courses required for graduation. Spending an extra year, or even an extra term, in college may mean more loans. Visit the career center to learn how much you can expect to earn if you graduate with your intended degree. Will your future income be enough that you can repay your loans and still afford to eat? And remember: Whenever you borrow money, you have to pay interest on the loan. Often, the faster you pay off the loan, the less interest you'll end up paying in the long run, which can save you big bucks.

Here are some common loans available to students.

- **Direct subsidized loans.** The federal government provides these loans. They usually have a lower interest rate than other types of loans, and interest doesn't *accrue* (get added to the loan) while you're in school. Students qualify for these loans based on financial need.

- **Direct unsubsidized loans.** These government-provided loans tend to have higher interest rates than subsidized loans, and interest accrues while you're in school. All college students are eligible for unsubsidized loans, regardless of financial need.

- **Direct PLUS loans.** PLUS is a federal loan program that lets parents borrow money for the college expenses of a dependent student. PLUS loans have a higher interest rate and charge more fees than other federal loans.

- **Private loans.** These loans are issued by institutions such as banks, credit unions, or colleges. Compared to federal loans, they often have higher interest rates and fewer repayment options.

Work-Study Programs. If you receive a work-study award, you can apply for an on-campus job that's been set aside for someone with financial need. Positions fill up quickly, and placement isn't guaranteed, so talk with someone in the financial aid office if you want to explore what's available. Sure, the work-study job you get may not be perfect or exciting—you may find yourself making

I've Got Financial Aid—Now How Do I Keep It?

After all the time and energy you put into applying for and securing financial aid, take the following steps to keep it—or even increase it.

- **Fulfill requirements.** Understand and fulfill all the requirements for keeping your financial aid. For example, if your GPA falls below a certain level or if you drop a class and become a part-time student (which colleges and funding sources define differently), you may lose your aid.

- **If your financial situation changes, see if you qualify for more aid.** For instance, if you or a primary wage earner in your family loses a job, talk with your

school's financial aid office about what has changed and how that affects your aid eligibility.

- **Keep looking for aid.** You may qualify for different scholarships as you progress through college. For instance, a donor may have established a scholarship for junior and senior engineering students who want to go into public service. Regularly research emerging opportunities like these.

- **Apply for financial aid each year.** Be sure to complete the FAFSA and any other required applications on time so that you can keep your aid every year.

copies or delivering mail. Still, every job offers learning opportunities, and some work-study jobs can even give you experience in your field of study. See what you can find that fits your interests.

Control Your Credit Cards — So They Don't Control You

When you buy something with a credit card, you're taking out a short-term loan from the credit card company and promising that you'll pay for the purchase later. Like student loans, credit cards come with interest rates. You have to pay that interest if you don't pay off your credit card balance in full every month. But credit card interest rates can be shockingly high—as much as 20 percent or more.

To grasp how this high level of interest can affect your financial health, meet Jason. He has a $3,000 balance on his credit card, which charges 18 percent interest. If he makes only the minimum payment of $75 each month (and doesn't spend any more on the card), he'll end up paying more than $4,500 over five years!

If you have a credit card, look at one of your statements. Credit card companies are required to tell you how much you'll pay in the long run if you make only the minimum monthly payment on your balance. Once you start racking up big credit card debt, it's very hard to whittle it back down, so keep that number in the forefront of your mind.

If you're going to use credit cards, try these tactics for keeping your debt under control.

- Use only one card. If you have several cards, pay off and close all except one.
- Pay off the entire amount every month— on time.

- Consider getting a debit card. This functions like a credit card when you make purchases, but it's tied to your checking account and withdraws money that you already have.
- Check your credit report for errors. Each year, you can get a free copy of your credit report from each of the three credit-reporting agencies (Equifax, TransUnion, and Experian). To get your reports, go to www.annualcreditreport.com.

Combat Credit Card Debt. If you don't pay your credit card balance in full every month, the interest can start piling up. The accumulating interest makes it increasingly difficult to pay off the balance, and ultimately you can get buried under a mound of debt. High credit card balances can also hurt your credit score, making it hard for you to take out loans in the future. © CartoonStock

A credit card bill? Shoot, I just paid one of these a few weeks ago!

my personal success plan

PERSONAL AND FINANCIAL HEALTH

Are you inspired to set a new goal aimed at improving your personal or financial health? If so, the Personal Success Plan can walk you through the goal-setting process. Read the advice and examples; then sketch out your ideas in the space provided.

To access the Personal Success Plan online, go to LaunchPad Solo for *Connections Essentials*.

1 GATHER INFORMATION

Think about your strengths and weaknesses related to personal and financial health. What health- and money-management strategies have worked for you in the past? What could you do differently? Revisit your Personal and Financial Health score on ACES and review the relevant sections of this chapter for additional ideas.

2 SET A SMART GOAL

Use the information you've gathered to create a SMART goal, making sure to use the SMART goal checklist.

SAMPLE: Starting next week, I'll increase the amount of time I exercise from one hour to two and a half hours each week.

3 MAKE AN ACTION PLAN

Outline the specific steps you'll take to achieve your SMART goal, and note when you'll complete each step.

SAMPLE: Tomorrow I'll find out where the on-campus gym is located and go check it out.

4 LIST BARRIERS AND SOLUTIONS

Think about possible barriers to your action steps; then brainstorm solutions for overcoming them.

SAMPLE: I know gyms are often crowded, so I'll find out which time slots are least busy at the on-campus gym and schedule my exercise time for those slots.

5 ACT AND EVALUATE OUTCOMES

Now that your plan is in place, take action. Record each action step as you take it. Then evaluate whether you achieved your SMART goal, and make any adjustments needed to get better results in the future.

SAMPLE: I wasn't able to find enough non-busy time slots at the gym to increase my exercising to two and a half hours per week. So I'll add a few twenty-minute jogs around my neighborhood to fill in the gap.

6 CONNECT TO CAREER

List the skills you're building as you progress toward your SMART goal. How will you use these skills to land a job and succeed at work?

SAMPLE: Working out is great for stress management. Getting the recommended amount of exercise each day will help me manage stress when I start a new job after college.

1 my information

2 my SMART goal

☐ **S**PECIFIC ☐ **M**EASURABLE ☐ **A**CHIEVABLE ☐ **R**ELEVANT ☐ **T**IME-LIMITED

3 my action plan

4 my barriers/ solutions

5 my actions/ outcomes

6 my career connection

Chapter 11 Review

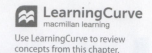

Use LearningCurve to review concepts from this chapter.

CHAPTER SUMMARY

- Safeguarding your personal and financial health can help you manage stress.

- Eating a healthy diet, staying active, and getting enough sleep can enhance your physical well-being and mental health.

- Knowing what your resources are and asking for help can be critical in managing anxiety and depression.

- If you're sexually active, protecting yourself against sexually transmitted infections and using birth control if you're not planning to start a family yet are critical.

- Budgeting can help you manage your money. You can also take steps to reduce spending and increase your income.

- Understanding your credit card interest rate and paying down balances are keys to managing credit.

CHAPTER ACTIVITIES

Adopting a Success Attitude

COPING WITH STRESS USING HUMOR

The phrase "laughter is the best medicine" is especially true when it comes to relieving stress. Laughing relaxes tense muscles; reduces blood pressure and heart rate; boosts your immune system; and triggers your body to release pain-fighting hormones. Plus, laughter boosts your mental health by distracting you from stress. With these advantages in mind, do the following:

1. Find a funny cartoon, joke, quotation, or picture, and put it somewhere you can easily see it when you need a chuckle.

2. Describe the item, where you placed it, and how often you glanced at it.

3. Explain what kinds of events made you want a laugh break. Then describe what impact, if any, these laugh breaks had on your stress levels.

4. Consider finding additional funny items and sharing them with others or even creating a scrapbook or Pinterest board of things that make you laugh.

Applying Your Skills

USING YOUR FINANCIAL RESOURCES

Many types of scholarships are available to help you pay for college. To learn about your options, choose two of the following sources of information and use them to search for scholarships you qualify for.

- Meet with a financial aid adviser or career counselor at your college.

- Search your college's financial aid Web site.

- Use the U.S. Department of Labor's free online scholarship search tool at http://www.careerinfonet.org/scholarshipsearch.

- Ask your employer if they offer financial assistance.

- Go to your state's Web site (for example, www.texas.gov) and search for "college scholarships."

- Inquire about scholarships through your membership in local religious, cultural, or community organizations.

- Contact professional associations related to your field of interest and ask about scholarships.

- Learn more about Reserve Officers' Training Corps (ROTC) scholarships through the Army, Air Force, Navy, or Marines.

Review the scholarship opportunities that you found and choose one scholarship that you'd like to apply for. Write down the title of the scholarship, the application criteria, and the application instructions. Then apply!

Academic and Career Planning

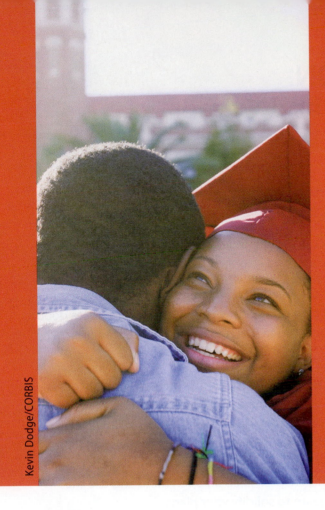

Kevin Dodge/CORBIS

Know Yourself

Develop an Academic Plan

Investigate Career Options

Launch Your Job Search

End-of-Term Reflection: Assess Your ACES Progress

MY PERSONAL SUCCESS PLAN

Think of people you know who have completed college and have launched their careers. If you asked them to describe their academic and career experiences, you'd probably hear a variety of responses. One person might say, "I always wanted to go into teaching, so it was easy to decide on my major." Someone else might say, "I thought I wanted be an anthropologist, but I ended up loving computer science." Another person may say, "I studied to get a job as an accountant, but then I wanted to try something new. I'm on my third career!"

As these responses suggest, everyone's academic and career experiences are different. You can think of going through college and entering the work world as a *general* path: You start school, choose an area of academic study, complete your degree or certificate, graduate, and then find a job. For some people, this process is straightforward,

but for others there are twists and turns along the way. Why? As you travel this path, you constantly learn about yourself and build new skills. You explore different areas of study and experiment with ideas about what careers interest you. Along the way, you grow and change. Consequently, your plans may change. In the end, your academic and career paths will be unique to you.

This chapter helps you start your journey by providing the information you need in order to think critically about your options. First, we explore how knowing your interests, values, and skills can help you start building academic and career plans. We then focus on the key components of academic planning, how to conduct career research, and how to search for a job. Finally, in a special concluding section, we do something a little different: We revisit your ACES results and reflect on your progress over the course of the term. Let's get started!

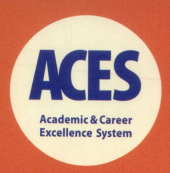

ACES

Academic & Career Excellence System

To find your **Academic and Career Planning score,** go to LaunchPad Solo for *Connections Essentials*.

REFLECTION:
Academic and Career Planning

Take a moment to reflect on your Academic and Career Planning score on ACES. Find your score and add it to the box on the left.

This score measures your beliefs about how familiar you are with academic and career planning and how confident you are that you can create good plans. Do you think it's an accurate snapshot of your understanding? Why or why not?

- **IF YOU SCORED IN THE HIGH RANGE** and you believe this score is accurate, you may be very knowledgeable about crafting academic and career plans and confident in your ability to do so. However, plans can change, and strengthening your planning skills can help you feel confident that you're continuing to make the best decisions for you. As you read this chapter, keep an open mind and use the new information you learn to solidify your plans.

- **IF YOU SCORED IN THE MODERATE OR LOW RANGE,** don't be discouraged. Many students question their ability to navigate the hundreds of courses their school offers, and many are anxious and unsure about choosing a major and a career. You'll have plenty of chances to strengthen your planning skills in this class, as you learn about degree options, course requirements, career possibilities, and ways to use insights about yourself to make these important decisions.

ACES Journal

Think about the different careers you've considered since you were young. What was it about those careers that caused you to be attracted to them? What was it about some of those careers that caused you to eventually remove them from consideration? Record your responses to these questions, and then write down the key factors you're using *now* to evaluate career options. Why are these factors so important?

_____

_____

_____

_____

Know Yourself

Your academic and career choices will be as individual as you are, so the best way to start planning for these two important aspects of your life is to know yourself. And that means thinking critically as you gather and interpret information about your own interests, values, and skills—and then use the resulting insights to start building future plans.

Explore Your Interests

Your interests are your personal preferences—for example, what you like to do in your free time, what course subjects you enjoy, how you like to work, and with whom. These preferences can shed light on what kinds of courses and careers you might find most satisfying. If you don't have a clear idea of your interests or you want to learn even more about yourself, the strategies in this section can help.

Take an Interest Inventory. One way to investigate your interests is to take an *interest inventory*, which is a survey of your preferences. A useful and free inventory is the O*NET Interest Profiler, which you can access at www.mynextmove.org/explore/ip or by searching online using the phrase "my next move interest profiler." Completing this inventory may take 10–15 minutes but it's worth it—your results will help you think about jobs or professions that may appeal to you. Plus, the inventory can help you with academic planning by giving you insight into what kinds of courses and majors you'd find most intriguing. Complete this inventory now, and then we'll discuss how to interpret your results.

Understand Holland's Interest Types. Once you have the results of your interest inventory, the next step is to look at what they mean. The inventory is based on the work of John Holland, a renowned career psychologist who developed a system that describes people and work environments using six categories: Realistic, Investigative, Artistic, Social, Enterprising, and Conventional.[1]

- **Realistic (R)** people enjoy working with their hands, working outside, using tools, installing and repairing things, or working with animals, and they enjoy studies that give them these opportunities. They're drawn to occupations in such fields as construction, veterinary and earth sciences, landscaping, forestry, physical education, athletics, personal training, and recreation or wildlife management.

- **Investigative (I)** people like analyzing and solving problems and enjoy science, technical, or medicine-oriented courses. They are drawn to careers such as laboratory assistant, medical technician, physician, and engineer.

- **Artistic (A)** people are creative, intuitive, sensitive, and expressive. Some gravitate toward art-related studies and work as art instructors, as dance therapists, or as graphic or fashion designers. Others write for newspapers or magazines or work as freelance writers.

- **Social (S)** people enjoy helping, coaching, teaching, or counseling others. They may be drawn to studies and careers related to teaching, child and elder care, or community leadership and social justice. They may become psychologists, physical therapists, social workers, or occupational therapists.

- **Enterprising (E)** people like to influence, lead, persuade, and manage others. They may enjoy business studies and may work as supervisors or managers in just about any industry, as fund-raisers or human resource workers, or as members of the legal profession.

- **Conventional (C)** people prefer structure in their school and work environments. They tend to be detail oriented, enjoy working with numbers or data, and are precise in their work. They frequently find satisfaction in the banking and finance industries, the computer sciences, or organizational departments such as payroll and purchasing.

Realistic Interest in Action? These women are working at a rehabilitation center for chimpanzees in Guinea. Their interests probably fall under Holland's Realistic type, which is characterized by a desire to work with one's hands, work outside, use tools, or work with animals. This interest may have strongly influenced their academic choices as well, including their degrees, majors, and classes. Dan Kitwood/Getty Images News

As you consider the results of your inventory, keep in mind that it's normal to have interests in more than one area. If your interests span two or three categories, the key is to consider which studies and occupations would let you combine your varied interest types. For example, in school, choosing more than one major might let you explore several academic interests, such as business and recreation. In the work world, being an art gallery director might let you express both your Artistic and Enterprising interests. Later in this chapter, we'll look more closely at how to use knowledge of your interests to explore possible careers.

Explore Your Values

Your values are what you consider important—really important. They stem from your experiences with your family, your community, or your faith. Because you're in college, your academic values probably include getting a good education; if you're the first in your family to go to college, they may also include making your family proud.

In addition to academic values, you also have **work values.** These are aspects of your work or work environment that you consider important. To learn more about your work values, examine the items on the list below and ask yourself: How important are each of these values to me?[2]

- **Achievement:** using your abilities and gaining a feeling of accomplishment
- **Independence:** trying out your own ideas, making your own decisions, and working without supervision
- **Recognition:** having opportunities to advance in your career, direct the work of others, and be recognized for your accomplishments
- **Relationships:** getting along with coworkers, doing things for other people, and not having to do things that violate your ideals
- **Support:** receiving helpful supervision, being treated fairly by your organization, and getting appropriate training
- **Working conditions:** being busy all the time, receiving appropriate pay, feeling secure in your job, and constantly doing different activities

Understanding your work values can help you identify careers, and academic programs related to those careers, you might find satisfying. It can also help you make trade-offs. For example, if you become an elementary school teacher, you may have relatively little opportunity for advancement, and you probably won't get rich. But you'll go to work each day knowing you're helping others learn.

Also note that some careers reinforce certain values and not others, depending on the setting or specialty. In the law profession, for instance, corporate lawyers typically earn a lot more money than public defenders do. If the law appeals to many of your work values but one of your strongest values is financial security, you might aim for a career in corporate law.

As you consider your work values, keep two things in mind: First, if you don't have much work experience, you may not have a clear picture of your work values just yet. That's okay: Your values will come into sharper focus as you get experience. Second, work values can change. For instance, someone who's raising a family may consider job security a critical work value. Once her children are grown, however, she may place more value on work that lets her feel that she's contributing to society. The upshot? Understanding your work values is an ongoing process, not a one-time event.

Explore Your Skills

As a college student, you probably excel at, and enjoy using, certain academic skills more than other skills. For instance, maybe you take detailed, accurate notes, but you find it more challenging to make class presentations. The same is true about the work world. Different positions will require you to use some skills more than others. By understanding which skills you enjoy and excel at most, you can find a job that emphasizes what you love to do. For example, perhaps you want to be a computer programmer, which involves writing computer code, solving problems, and

understanding your clients' needs. If you love writing code but dread meeting with clients, you can look for a position that focuses more on coding than on client relations.

When it comes to work skills, some are specific and are needed in only a few careers—such as writing computer code. Others are transferable and are used in many different careers—such as solving problems with logic and reasoning, listening to others, and managing your time. Your transferable skills let you cast your "career net" more widely, opening up a wider range of occupations that you could succeed in.

But you don't have to limit your options to work experiences that call for *only* your best skills. You can also seek out experiences that will let you develop new skills or strengthen your current skills. For instance, suppose you'd like to enhance your leadership skills. You could identify volunteer opportunities, leadership positions in campus clubs and organizations, and training opportunities with your employer (if you're currently working) that would help you become a more confident leader. You might even establish a goal to develop this skill over the next few months, which you can document in your Personal Success Plan.

Understand Yourself through Campus Engagement

As you've seen in this section, your interests, values, and skills play a key role in helping you identify a fulfilling academic and career path. But there's another factor that can help give you clarity about the future: becoming an active part of your campus community.

In one study, researchers measured student engagement in a group of undergraduates: For example, they looked at whether students participated in active or collaborative learning opportunities and whether they interacted with their instructors. The researchers also measured *vocational identity*, which is a person's understanding of his or her career goals, interests, and strengths. In addition, they recorded each student participant's GPA at the end of the term.[3]

When they reviewed the data they'd collected, the researchers discovered that students who were more engaged (meaning they interacted with instructors more frequently and participated in active and collaborative learning opportunites more often) had higher overall GPAs *and* stronger vocational identities than students who weren't as engaged on campus.

What do these results mean for you? They mean that now is a great time to become an active learner on campus. Interact with your instructors. Join campus clubs. Meet your classmates. Doing so could help improve your GPA and teach you more about your interests, values, and skills—all things that will help you succeed in college and in your future career.

Develop an Academic Plan

In college it's never too early to create an **academic plan**—a roadmap showing the steps you'll take to complete your degree or certificate. Recognizing your interests, values, and skills can help you create this plan, as can a solid understanding of your school's requirements—for instance, when you have to declare a major, the grade point average you need to be accepted into your chosen program, and whether you should document your plan electronically or on paper. To build your plan most effectively, you'll have to know what's expected—and when.

Your plan will also need to reflect your goals. For example, if you're attending a two-year college and you want to earn a four-year degree, it's crucial to determine which of your current classes will transfer to your next institution. And if you're attending school and want to get a job right after graduation, you'll focus on courses needed to obtain your degree and prepare for the job market.

Students have unique goals and schools have unique requirements, so your academic plan will likely differ from classmates' and those of students attending other types of institutions. This puts you in control—it's *your* academic plan, you own it, and you can make sure it works for you. If the idea of making these kinds of decisions right now seems overwhelming, trust that your critical-thinking skills can help you gather, evaluate, and use the information to make good choices and that many people at your school can help you do so. Your plan may change in the future, but developing a roadmap early gives you some initial clarity on your academic goals so that you can begin working to achieve them.

Choose a Degree or Certificate

To choose a degree or certificate you have to know your options—and there are many! Schools across the country offer a wide range of degrees and certificates. Generally, two-year colleges offer different types of degrees

than do four-year colleges, though not always. For instance, some colleges that traditionally offered two-year associate's degrees now offer four-year bachelor's degrees in high-demand fields. And some four-year schools offer select two-year degrees.

As you research the options at your school, pay attention to terminology. For example, your school may use different terms to describe associate's degrees that prepare you to transfer to a four-year college and associate's degrees that prepare you to enter the workforce directly.

In addition, remember that everyone's life circumstances are unique. Not all students graduate in exactly two or four years, even if they attend what's considered a two- or four-year school. For example, your time line may be different if you're going to school part-time (as do 37 percent of U.S. students[4]) or if you take foundational courses before you begin earning college credit. You can work with a professional adviser at your school to decide on a time frame and a degree or certificate program that make sense for you.

Choose a College Major

A **college major** is a collection of courses organized around an academic theme. A major enables you to understand one area of study or practice in depth. To select a major, you need to consider your own career goals and what's important to you and to understand some logistics—for example, by when your college expects you to make this decision.

Consider Your Career Goals and What's Important to You. If you have a particular career in mind, investigate what type of degree is generally required and whether that career requires a specific major. To enter fields such as nursing, engineering, education, and accounting, graduating with a specific major is critical. But other majors—such as sociology, English, psychology, and history—prepare you for a variety of careers by helping you build transferable skills valued by many employers. If your career of choice doesn't require a specific major, you can select a major based on other factors—for example, because of a class you enjoyed or because you're skilled in a particular area.

As you weigh your options, consider whether the career you have in mind calls for advanced schooling. Some careers (for example, doctor, lawyer, or school counselor) require a graduate or professional degree, so if you're planning to enter one of these fields, investigate whether related graduate programs recommend or require specific undergraduate majors. And if you're at a two-year school and plan to transfer to a four-year school, selecting certain majors may increase your chance of transferring, especially if you want to enter a specific program.

Consider Time Frame and Qualifications.

Many first-year students are undecided about which major to pursue, and that's okay—most schools have resources that can help students explore different academic and career pathways. However, you'll want to find out *by when* your school requires that decision to be made, so you can prepare yourself as best as possible.

In addition, you need to know your school's requirements for being admitted into a particular major—for example, you may need a certain GPA—so that you can plan how to meet those requirements.

Choose Your Courses

Depending on your school and program, you'll need a certain number of credits to graduate, and those credits usually come from two areas: courses required for your major and general-education (or *core*) course requirements.

To complete your major, certain courses will be required. For instance, if you major in outdoor education, you may have to take courses in teaching methods, child and adult development, and biology. Most majors also allow you to take *electives*—courses you choose to take based on your interests or career goals. If you're majoring in architecture, for example, you may decide to take electives in urban planning and art history.

General-education courses, which are common at both two- and four-year colleges, give students a broad liberal education in the natural and social sciences, humanities, arts, and mathematics. These courses are important because they help you develop critical-thinking skills, use and evaluate data

A Passion for Science. David, a science major, holds up a model of a molecule. He selected his major because he's interested in jobs involving scientific research, which require specific degrees and majors. But Gloria, who's also taking this class, registered for the course simply because she has always been interested in science and wants to learn more. Noel Hendrickson/Getty Images

and numbers, and communicate through writing and speaking—all transferable skills. General-education courses also introduce you to a wide range of ideas and topics. Exposure to new knowledge can help you gain insight into your interests and values—which in turn can help you pick a major. In fact, you might find that you enjoy a course in your general-education curriculum so much that you end up selecting that area as a major.

Conveniently, sometimes you can satisfy general-education course requirements by taking courses related to your major (such as an architecture major who takes an art course). An adviser can strategize with you about which general-education courses will help prepare you for a particular career.

Get Help from an Academic Adviser or a Counselor

As you can see, academic planning involves working with a lot of information. To make sure you're aware of everything you need to know, you'll want to meet with an **academic adviser** or, in some schools, a **counselor**—a highly trained professional who can help you

make effective academic decisions and refer you to valuable campus resources. Although ultimately you're responsible for your own academic plan, an adviser can provide the support and information you need to think critically about your options.

There are many types of advisers, and schools organize their advising programs in different ways. For example, some schools have a central academic advising office that specializes in working with first-year students, while at other schools this work is done in counseling centers. And in some cases, academic departments have advisers (some of whom are faculty members) who specialize in working with students who have declared a major.

Given the variety in how academic advising is structured, investigate your school's approach and find out which advisers are responsible for helping you right now. Schedule an appointment with an adviser at least once each term (including this term, if you haven't done so already) to assess your progress toward your academic goals, to get ideas for overcoming any challenges you encounter, and to refine your academic plan as needed.

Know Your Milestones

Creating your own personalized academic plan is critical to your success in college and beyond, and the four key items discussed in this section—selecting a degree or certificate, choosing a major, choosing courses, and asking an adviser or a counselor for support—are crucial in helping you establish an academic plan.

Along with the basics, however, there are additional things you can do to become better prepared to transfer to a four-year college, go to grad school, or launch a successful career. For example, exploring the relationship between your major and possible careers, documenting the skills you develop each term, and visiting your career center are all steps you can take to give yourself a competitive advantage when you're ready to move on to your next endeavor.

Your academic or career adviser likely has a timeline of milestones that is customized to your school—steps you

should take each year to make sure you're prepared for the future. To get you started, we've included a list of key milestones for your first year below. Compare and contrast this list with the milestones that are specific to your campus.

- Develop and practice the success skills discussed in this book.

- Focus on establishing a strong GPA.

- Begin to identify your career-related interests, skills, and values.

- Get involved in campus activities.

- Develop a preliminary résumé.

- Explore work or volunteer activities that will strengthen your résumé.

- Conduct one or more informational interviews.

SELECTING A MAJOR AND CHOOSING CLASSES

Tony Kao

NAME:	**Tony Kao**
SCHOOL:	*University of Kentucky*
MAJOR:	*Mechanical Engineering*
CAREER GOAL:	*Mechanical Design*

I'm a first-generation college student. My parents immigrated to the United States so I could get a better education. It was always assumed that I would go to college, and my parents and advisers have supported me throughout the process. I want to find a career path that I'll enjoy, but also one that will make them proud.

The people who know me can tell you that I'm a very logical and analytical kind of person. I always like to figure out how things work and how each component of a product contributes to the overall design, regardless of what it is. I thought that since I enjoy learning about how things work, why not make a career of it? I could continue to learn, put my own knowledge to the test, *and* get paid for doing something I love and enjoy.

Because of this passion and because of my aptitude in math and science, I chose mechanical engineering as my major. This degree will allow me to be creative but also develop my technical skills and knowledge. For example, I recently completed an internship in an automobile assembly plant, which taught me the importance of product reliability, construction, and installation.

My university also has general-education requirements. I've tried to find elective courses that will not only fulfill requirements but also be useful in my career or daily life. I chose Technical Writing and Personal Finance. I think these courses will apply no matter what job I get after graduating. I also wanted to take a course that was fun, so I enrolled in a tennis class. I really enjoy this class, and it gives me a break between my engineering classes.

I hope to find a job that will provide me with financial stability, the potential for growth, and fulfillment. I want a sense of pride from the work that I do.

YOUR TURN: Have you chosen a major? If so, how does the process you used to select your major compare with the one that Tony used to select his? If your school offers electives, do any appeal to you? If so, which ones — and why?

> **"I've tried to find elective courses that will not only fulfill requirements but also be useful in my career or daily life."**

Investigate Career Options

So far you've explored your interests, work values, and skills, and you've learned how to create an academic plan. What's next? You can use these insights to investigate career options by conducting online research, talking with experts, and getting direct experience that will help you discover more about careers of interest. You'll use your critical thinking skills to gather, evaluate, and use all this information in a way that makes the most sense for you.

As you gather information, try not to put too much pressure on yourself to pick the "right" career. For some students, making an initial career decision is a paralyzing process because it feels like this one choice could dictate the rest of their lives. In reality, career decisions are more flexible: You make the choice, evaluate how it feels for you, and change it if you don't like it! In fact, many people change careers several times during the course of their lives. So view the information-gathering experience as just one step toward a satisfying career.

Get to Know the O*NET

Probably the best place to start researching different occupations is the O*NET (Occupational Network), an occupational database maintained by the U.S. Department of Labor. (Go to www.onetonline.org, or search using the phrase "O*NET OnLine.") It's full of helpful job-related facts, including how certain occupations match people's interests, work values, and skills. Drawing on your self-knowledge, you can search for jobs that meet the criteria you consider most important. You can also use the O*NET to research what level of education and experience is required for a particular occupation (a category called the Job Zone), how much the occupation pays, and what the employment outlook will be when you graduate. You can also search for occupations by keyword, such as the name of your college major.

For a more detailed look at the O*NET, see Figure 12.1, which shows how to search for occupations using the results of the Holland interest inventory. An activity at the end of the chapter also gives you a chance to explore the O*NET firsthand.

Talk with Experts

As a college student, you have access to a wide range of experts who can help you with career planning, including career counselors on campus and people in the work world who can give you the "inside scoop" on particular types of jobs, employers, and careers.

Meet with a Career Counselor. Some students have a hard time defining a career path or feeling confident about the path they've chosen. Fortunately, many campuses employ **career counselors**, specially trained professionals who help students explore career options, make important career decisions, and manage any related stress they're experiencing. Career counselors, who usually work in the campus's counseling or career center, can connect you with all kinds of useful information. Services at these centers often include:

- Individual meetings with career counselors
- Workshops or groups designed to help you with specific concerns, such as how to structure your job search process
- Subscriptions to online career information resources (often based on the O*NET), which can include interest assessments and video interviews with people working in various occupations
- Tools for creating your résumé
- Tips for preparing for job interviews

Why not seize the day? Visit your school's counseling or career center this week to find out how counselors can help you investigate career options.

FIGURE 12.1   Example O*NET Occupational Search Based on Interests

These O*NET screenshots show a search for occupations by Holland interest type; a list of occupations sorted by Job Zone; and a summary report for a particular occupation. You can also search the O*NET by work values or skills.

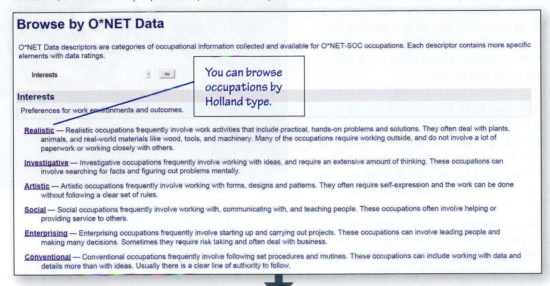

You can browse occupations by Holland type.

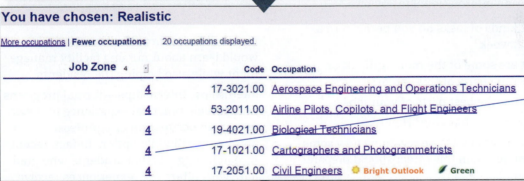

If you click "Realistic," for example, you'll get a list of jobs in this category. You can then sort the jobs by "Job Zone." (Zone 4 requires a college degree.)

Summary Report for:

17-2051.00 - Civil Engineers

Bright Outlook
green

Perform engineering duties in planning, designing, and overseeing construction and maintenance of building structures, and facilities, such as roads, railroads, airports, bridges, harbors, channels, dams, irrigation projects, pipelines, power plants, and water and sewage systems.

Sample of reported job titles: Bridge/Structure Inspection Team Leader, City Engineer, Civil Engineer, Civil Engineering Manager, County Engineer, Design Engineer, Project Engineer, Railroad Design Consultant, Structural Engineer, Traffic Engineer

Also see: Transportation Engineers

View report:	Summary	Details	Custom

Tasks | Tools & Technology | Knowledge | Skills | Abilities | Work Activities | Detailed Work Activities | Work Context | Job Zone | Education | Credentials | Interests | Work Styles | Work Values | Related Occupations | Wages & Employment | Job Openings | Additional Information

Tasks

5 of 17 displayed

- Inspect project sites to monitor progress and ensure conformance to design specifications and safety or sanitation standards.
- Compute load and grade requirements, water flow rates, or material stress factors to determine design specifications.
- Provide technical advice to industrial or managerial personnel regarding design, construction, or program modifications or structural repairs.
- Test soils or materials to determine the adequacy and strength of foundations, concrete, asphalt, or steel.
- Manage and direct the construction, operations, or maintenance activities at project site.

Once you click on an occupation, you can access a wide array of related information — everything from tasks involved to applicable skills and work values.

"Bright Outlook" jobs are those expected to grow rapidly in coming years. "Green Outlook" jobs are those that result from an emphasis on sustainability or that will change as a result of sustainability efforts.

Conduct Informational Interviews. You can also get valuable job information from someone currently working in a career that interests you. By conducting an *informational interview*, or conversation, with a person working in a particular field, you can get "insider information" about what a job is really like from day to day.

To find someone working in a field of interest, get referrals from friends and family or ask your instructors. When you first contact this person, be sure to explain that you're looking for an informational interview, either face-to-face or by phone. This is a fact-finding investigation—your purpose is not to job hunt but rather to find out what the work entails, what this person likes most and least about the job, and what benefits and opportunities for advancement this line of work offers. Consider asking the following questions during informational interviews.

- What kinds of tasks do you perform in a typical week?
- What are some of the more difficult or frustrating parts of this career?
- What are the best parts of your job?
- Is this career changing? How?
- Do you have any advice regarding how someone interested in this career should prepare?
- What types of advancement opportunities are available for an entry-level worker in this career?

Get Experience

Even while you're in college, you can gain experience that helps you learn more about careers of interest and start building the skills you'll need to succeed in those jobs. Consider these ideas:

- **Service learning.** Most colleges and universities offer *service learning* opportunities that pair a practical service experience with formal classroom discussions and assignments. For example, if you're interested in health care management and psychology, you could sign up for a service learning class working with senior citizens in a local

Growing Skills. The summer before Maria's second year in college, she planted strawberries as part of a paid internship at a community farm. The arrangement, financed by her college, helps Maria and other students build their skills. Meanwhile, the farm benefits from their energy, hard work, and fresh ideas. AP Photo/Steven Senne

nursing home. Through this experience, you would learn about nursing facility management while also helping the residents.

- **Internships.** Internships—formal programs that provide practical experience for beginners in an occupation or a profession—are another worthwhile option. In fact, recent research suggests that students who graduate with internship experiences receive more job offers and higher starting salaries than those without these experiences.[5] Check with a career counselor at your school to find out which nearby organizations offer internship opportunities.

- **Co-ops.** College co-op programs offer alternating periods of academic study and periods of work experience in fields such as business, industry, government, and social services. These programs are a great way to learn about specific careers while also making a little money.

- **Working.** Working while you're in college allows you to investigate career options as you build your skills and knowledge. The key is not to take on so many hours that you have difficulty juggling your coursework and your job.

Launch Your Job Search

Even though you just started college, you may be in the process of searching for a new job. Or you may be anticipating how you'll enter the job market once you finish your academic program. No matter what your situation, we've designed this section to walk you through the steps of writing a résumé, locating a job, and presenting yourself in a cover letter and on an interview. The job market is competitive. You may be applying for jobs alongside ten, a hundred, or even a thousand other people. Thus we don't just want to help you prepare for the job search; we want to help you stand out and successfully sell employers on your skills and abilities.

Write a Résumé

Your **résumé** is a summary of your education, work experience, and extracurricular activities. It gives potential employers a sense of your prior experience and qualifications for the position you're targeting. Recruiters will often skim a candidate's résumé for this basic information before deciding whether to read more closely, so it's important that these basics be easy to find in the visual layout of your document.

As you can see in Figure 12.2, your name and contact information should appear prominently at the top of your résumé. You might also include a link to your LinkedIn profile, Twitter feed, or another element of your online presence if appropriate. And remember that your e-mail address should be professional—you may want to obtain a new one for the job search process.

Many job applicants choose to open their résumé with a summary section. Think of this as a place to tell employers what kind of professional you are. This description should highlight the characteristics and skills that you would bring to a job, while citing previous accomplishments as support for these points. Note that each statement in this section of Figure 12.2 begins with a skill or quality that the student has chosen to emphasize.

Next, add your educational history. This should consist of all the institutions where you've completed undergraduate coursework, as well as any technical certifications you hold. On the first line of each entry, list the name of each institution, its location, and your dates of attendance. Underneath this, include your grade point average and area of study. Many students also choose to include their high school's name and location and their year of graduation; some students note the number of college credits they've earned, subjects in which they've completed substantial coursework, study abroad experience, scholarships, or even Honor Society membership.

After your education section, list your work and extracurricular experience in one of two styles: chronological or functional. On a **chronological résumé**, entries simply appear in reverse chronological order, with your current or most recent experience first. Figure 12.2 shows a chronological résumé, a style commonly used by college students. This format is a great choice for students who have taken on increasingly complex responsibilities over time, as it demonstrates this growth in a linear fashion. In a **functional résumé,** entries are grouped based on the nature of the experience they reflect rather than on the order in which they occurred. This style of résumé can be helpful when only some of your past experiences are directly related to the position you're seeking or when you're applying for different types of positions.

No matter which style you choose, you'll need to describe your responsibilities and accomplishments in each position you've held. As you can see in Figure 12.2, résumés use short phrases rather than complete sentences and begin each statement with an active verb. By describing what you accomplished in such vivid terms, you'll help employers visualize how your skills might apply to their open positions.

FIGURE 12.2 Sample Résumé

Marcus B. Student

2525 Market Street, #459
Springfield, WA 90546
403.555.1245

marcus.student@email.com
linkedin.com/marcusbstudent
@marcusontwitter

Qualifications Summary

Dedicated, hard-working professional with strong communication, leadership, and critical-thinking skills. Demonstrated ability to organize and lead teams in workplace and education settings. Strong interest in and extensive experience with computer hardware, software, and social media applications. History of excellent customer service. Commitment to bringing demonstrable value to and delivering measurable outcomes for the organization.

- Promoted to team lead within 4 months of hire
- Commitment to volunteering and community service

- Elected treasurer of Marketing Club
- Tripled Marketing Club's Twitter followers through collaborative efforts within 2 months at Mountain College

Education

2017–present	Mountain College — Springfield, WA GPA 3.75; completed 12 credit hours; major in Business Administration
2014–2015	Valley College — Hampton, OR GPA 2.6; completed 18 credit hours; coursework in Accounting, English
2014	River High School — Carlisle, OR

Relevant Experience

2016–present   *Team Lead* — All Things Tech
Promoted to Team Lead after 4 months of outstanding work and customer service. Supervise 3 technicians. Monitor and respond to customer feedback regarding repair services. Provide outstanding customer service to promote repeat business. Collaborate with store manager to increase social media presence for store.

2016   *Technician* — All Things Tech
Provided excellent customer service in repairing customer computers, mobile phones, and tablets. Applied extensive background and expertise with computer and phone hardware to efficiently complete assigned repairs.

2015–present   *Big Brother* — Big Brothers and Big Sisters of Central Washington
Serve as Big Brother to now 13-year-old boy. Meet regularly, 3–4 times per month, to play games, hang out, talk about challenges of school and friends. Provide regular support and mentorship.

2013–2014   *Server & Cook* — Neugent's Burger Stand
Performed duties of server and cook. Demonstrated strong customer service in taking orders. Supported coworkers in responding to customer complaints. Quickly learned tasks of line cook. Performed well in fast-paced and stressful environment during lunch and dinner rush. Recognized as employee of the month 3 times, August and December 2013, July 2014.

Find Job Opportunities

Once your résumé is ready to go, what's the next step? Search for open positions that interest you. Just as the word *search* implies, this is an active process that often requires patience and persistence. The good news is that there are employers out there looking to hire students and recent graduates.

Get Online. When employers have an open position to fill, they develop a description of responsibilities and qualifications the job requires. While few employers make use of newspaper classifieds in this digital age, some do list opportunities on online job boards like Monster.com, CareerBuilder, or Simply Hired.

If there are specific companies you'd like to work for, you might also look for job opportunities in the employment section of the organization's Web site. You can also check out the target company's Twitter account or Facebook page or look on LinkedIn. The federal government also advertises jobs online (www.usajobs.gov), as do some cities and states.

Use Campus and Community Resources. If your school has a career center, set up an appointment to get personalized guidance on your job search. Some college career counselors have vast networks of local and national hiring managers. They may be able to steer you toward specific companies or industries that are hiring. Additionally, your college career center may host on-campus interviews and have an online job search engine, free seminars on job search strategies, or other resources to help you in your job search.

Job fairs hosted by your school or in the community are another great place to network and learn about many open positions at once. When attending a job fair, dress professionally. This signals to recruiters that you're taking this process seriously and you want to make a good impression. In addition, print copies of your résumé on high-quality paper so you can provide them to employers whose opportunities interest you.

Join a Professional Association. Affiliation with a **professional association** is another good source of employment information. Professional associations are nonprofit organizations through which individuals who share a specific trade or job function can network, share best practices, and promote their profession and its interests. Student memberships in these organizations are generally quite affordable and provide access to job listings on members-only Web sites and listservs.

One way to identify appropriate professional associations is to consult your library's copy of *National Trade and Professional Associations of the United States*. You might also look for LinkedIn groups of professionals in your field, as this is another popular place to find job listings.

Network. Networking is really just about talking to people—everyone from fellow members of professional associations to instructors, classmates, friends, family members, neighbors, or those affiliated with your faith community, volunteer work, or recreational pursuits. Once you've identified the people you already know in your network, start contacting them. Explain that you're looking for a job, and be specific about what type of job or career field. Then ask them if they have any job leads or know anyone who could give you advice on following your chosen path. And don't forget: Networking is about establishing relationships with people, so be sure to follow up any meeting with an electronic or handwritten thank-you note.

Write a Cover Letter

Once you've identified an open position that interests you, it's time to work on a **cover letter** to accompany your résumé. Whereas your résumé can be somewhat generic, your cover letter should be highly tailored to the organization and position for which you're applying. This document is where you explain exactly how your previous experiences have prepared you to excel at the job in question.

As you can see in Figure 12.3, this document should be formatted like a formal

FIGURE 12.3   Sample Cover Letter

Marcus B. Student

2525 Market Street, #459
Springfield, WA 90546
marcus.student@email.com
403.555.1245

April 27, 2018

Madeline Iverson
Director of Human Resources
Techstar Inc.
45983 Ocean Drive
Springfield, WA 90546

Dear Ms. Iverson:

I am excited to apply for the Enterprise Solutions Account Manager position at Techstar Inc. I have admired the work of Techstar Inc. for the past few years, and I believe that I bring an optimal combination of experience, skills, and drive that will result in superb customer care and excellent sales within the division.

My past and current experiences are a strong match for the qualifications and skills you are seeking in your next Account Manager. As you can see from my résumé, I have a demonstrated history of providing excellent customer service, and I have placed customer service as my highest priority. I believe that when clients are satisfied they are more likely to return and they are our strongest advertisers to generate referrals and sales. I also possess the technical skills to excel in this position, evidenced by my experience in repair and now as the leader of a team of repair technicians. Further, I have a demonstrated history of exceeding expectations.

- Completed 78% of customer repairs on or under time, highest rate in the branch
- Tripled number of followers on Marketing Club Twitter account
- 3-time employee of the month

Thank you for taking time to consider my application. I am very excited about implementing my current skill set at Techstar Inc. and believe that as I complete my bachelor's degree at Mountain College, I will have even more to offer. If I can provide any additional information, please do not hesitate to contact me. I look forward to discussing this position further.

Sincerely,

Marcus B. Student

business letter, with your name and contact information at the top, followed by the date and the address of the company to which you're sending your application. If there's a contact person associated with the job posting, address that person by name. If no contact information is provided, you can use "To Whom It May Concern." In the first sentence of your letter, identify the position that you're applying for and comment on your excitement about the position. You might follow this with another sentence that elaborates on why you're interested in working for this organization and why you're a good fit for the job.

In the body of the document, zero in on specific aspects of the job description and draw connections to positions you've held in the past. This is the place to emphasize your transferable skills and demonstrate why they've prepared you to succeed in the post you're seeking.

In your conclusion, it's appropriate to thank the reader for his or her time and consideration. You might also summarize the reasons for your interest in the position and express your eagerness to discuss the opportunity further during an interview.

Interview Effectively

After you get an employer's attention with your résumé and cover letter, the next step is an interview. The employer's goal in interviews is to learn more about you and your qualifications, assess your interpersonal skills, and evaluate your fit with the job and organization.

Prepare for an Interview. To prepare for your interview, review the job description for the position you applied for, and do some research on the larger company itself. Does the organization have prominent competitors or established partnerships with other firms that you should know about? Are there trends and recent news related to that industry that you should be aware of? This level of research prepares you to speak from an informed position and signals to the employer that you're serious about joining their team.

It's also helpful to prepare responses for commonly asked interview questions. Be ready to walk the interviewer through your résumé and to tackle open-ended questions like "What can you tell me about yourself?" and "Why are you interested in the position?" (See also "Be Ready for Behavioral Interview Questions.")

Be Ready for Behavioral Interview Questions

In addition to standard interview questions, you may also be asked behavioral questions. **Behavioral interview questions** are designed to reveal information about how you act and react in certain types of situations. These questions usually begin with a phrase like "tell me about a time when . . . ," and the interviewer will then ask you to focus on the details of a past experience. For example, you might be asked to discuss a time you tackled a large, open-ended project or to describe how you handled a conflict with a classmate or coworker. In learning how you've handled challenging situations in the past, the interviewer will draw conclusions about how you'd conduct yourself as an employee in his or her organization. Behavioral interview questions are often more difficult to anticipate and prepare

for than the more standard interview questions, so it's wise to take a few seconds to think about potential responses and consider which will show you in the best light.

Once you've identified the example you'd like to share, it's important to tell the story in a clear way. The *STAR approach* — Situation, Task, Action, Result — is a great structure to use when answering behavioral questions.[6] After sharing the who, what, when, and where of the story (the situation), summarize the objective that you were aiming to accomplish (the task). Then provide a step-by-step description of how you proceeded (the action), and comment on the outcome (the result). The interviewer may ask follow-up questions during or after your story in order to thoroughly understand your thought process and actions.

Master Interview Etiquette. As important as your responses to interview questions will be, employers will also consider how you present yourself and draw conclusions about your interpersonal skills and level of professionalism. Be mindful of your dress and grooming, and err on the side of formality if you're unsure about the organization's dress code. On the day of the interview, aim to arrive a bit early and be sure to behave courteously toward the support staff and other people you meet in the building.

After the interview, it's customary to send a thank-you note to your interviewers. Handwritten notes are a nice touch, but e-mail is also an acceptable—and more timely—medium. In your note, thank the interviewer for his or her time, summarize what you learned during the interview about the organization and how you might fit in there, and reiterate your excitement about the position. Aim to send your thank-you note within twenty-four hours of your interview.

Typically, interviewers will let you know what their time line is for making decisions. If the interviewer says she will make a decision in two weeks, for example, expect to hear from her then and don't take further action after you send your thank-you note. But delays can happen, so if you haven't heard from the interviewer within the time specified, it's appropriate to reach out and ask about the status of your application. Not only does this provide you with peace of mind, it also signals your ongoing interest in the opportunity.

The Art of the Interview. Interviewing can be intimidating, but it's a skill you can get better at with practice. First, make sure you're prepared: Learn as much as you can about the company and practice answering questions about yourself and your experience. Then, when the big day comes, remember your interview etiquette: arrive early, look sharp, and be courteous. You've got this! Monkey Business Images/Shutterstock

End-of-Term Reflection: Assess Your ACES Progress

You've spent most of this chapter learning about yourself and considering your plans for the future—both academically and in terms of a career. In this final section, however, let's do something a bit different: Let's take a look back at how you've changed since this class began.

At the beginning of the term, you completed ACES, and in each chapter of this book you've had a chance to reflect on your scores and use them to target areas where you want to develop your skills. Now that you've reached the end of the term, it's time to revisit the ACES scales once more. This time, though, we're not the ones providing the results—you are! You'll assess how much you've progressed in the various skills during the term and use your assessment to celebrate improvement and identify areas for future growth. To do this, use Figure 12.4 as your guide and follow these steps.

1. Gather your ACES scores from the beginning of each chapter, or access your scores online using LaunchPad Solo for *Connections Essentials*.
2. On each scale in Figure 12.4, place an X where your corresponding ACES score falls. For example, if your Critical Thinking and Goal Setting score is 62 percent, mark the scale as follows.

Critical Thinking and Goal Setting

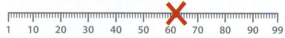

3. For each skill, ask yourself: Do I think my ability on this skill has improved since I took ACES at the start of the term? If so, what score would I give myself now? Do I think my ability is lower now than I thought it was at the start of the term? If so, what score would I give myself today?

4. Drawing on your honest responses to the questions in step 3, record a *new* score on each scale if you believe your abilities have changed or your original assessment was inaccurate. Place another X where the new score belongs.
5. For each skill, draw an arrow from your original score to your new score. For example, if you think that you've improved significantly in critical thinking and goal setting, you might mark the scale as follows.

Critical Thinking and Goal Setting

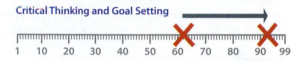

Resist any urge to rush through this activity. To really understand how your skills have changed, you need to trace what's happened over the term. For example, let's say that your initial score on the Reading scale was low. You weren't a confident reader when the term began, and you didn't enjoy reading. As time passed, though, you realized that you needed to read well in order to succeed in school, so you focused on improving. You previewed your reading materials before looking more closely at the content, and you mastered the art of crafting purposeful reading questions. Now you can feel good about giving yourself a higher score.

As another example, let's say that your original Organization and Time Management score was very high. At the beginning of the term, you were convinced that you were a time-management pro, but as the term progressed, you began to miss appointments and fall behind in your projects. As it turned out, managing your time was more challenging than you anticipated. Now that you've reached the end of the term, you realize that it's appropriate to give yourself a lower score

FIGURE 12.4 Self-Assessment of Change

Place an X on each scale to represent your corresponding ACES score from the beginning of the term. Then place another X on each scale to signify where you rate yourself today. Finally, draw an arrow on each scale from the first X to the second to get a visual representation of how you've improved or to identify the skills you might need to strengthen in the future.

Critical Thinking and Goal Setting

| 1 | 10 | 20 | 30 | 40 | 50 | 60 | 70 | 80 | 90 | 99 |

Motivation, Decision Making, and Personal Responsibility

| 1 | 10 | 20 | 30 | 40 | 50 | 60 | 70 | 80 | 90 | 99 |

Learning Preferences

| 1 | 10 | 20 | 30 | 40 | 50 | 60 | 70 | 80 | 90 | 99 |

Organization and Time Management

| 1 | 10 | 20 | 30 | 40 | 50 | 60 | 70 | 80 | 90 | 99 |

Reading

| 1 | 10 | 20 | 30 | 40 | 50 | 60 | 70 | 80 | 90 | 99 |

Note Taking

| 1 | 10 | 20 | 30 | 40 | 50 | 60 | 70 | 80 | 90 | 99 |

Memory and Studying

| 1 | 10 | 20 | 30 | 40 | 50 | 60 | 70 | 80 | 90 | 99 |

Test Taking

| 1 | 10 | 20 | 30 | 40 | 50 | 60 | 70 | 80 | 90 | 99 |

Information Literacy and Communication

| 1 | 10 | 20 | 30 | 40 | 50 | 60 | 70 | 80 | 90 | 99 |

Connecting with Others

| 1 | 10 | 20 | 30 | 40 | 50 | 60 | 70 | 80 | 90 | 99 |

Personal and Financial Health

| 1 | 10 | 20 | 30 | 40 | 50 | 60 | 70 | 80 | 90 | 99 |

Academic and Career Planning

| 1 | 10 | 20 | 30 | 40 | 50 | 60 | 70 | 80 | 90 | 99 |

for organization and time management than the score you had at the start of the term.

If you're uncomfortable at the thought of giving yourself a lower score, put your mind at ease: There are many logical reasons why your score might be lower now than it was at the beginning of the term. For example, you might have a more realistic understanding of yourself now than you did a few months ago. You've learned a lot about the attitudes and skills measured by ACES, so it's only natural that you're a better judge of your strengths and growth areas. Alternatively, maybe you misjudged the demands of college. You might have been a rock star at time management and organization in high school or at work, but now you need to step up your game in the more demanding college environment. So don't be afraid to lower your score if need be. Doing so shows that you're self-aware and allows you to more accurately gauge the progress you've made — or the skills you still need to strengthen.

After you complete Figure 12.4, you'll have a snapshot of the overall change in your skills from the start of the term to the end. To extract valuable insights from that snapshot, use these tips.

Keep Climbing toward Your Goals. In this class, you've had many opportunities to strengthen your self-awareness and build new skills. As you reflect on your ACES results, celebrate all that you've accomplished, and remember: Learning doesn't stop at the end of the term. Keep climbing toward your goals, one step at a time, and challenge yourself to master new skills and reach new heights. Philip & Karen Smith/Ascent Xmedia/CORBIS

- **Identify any patterns in your results.** For example, are the scales on which you made the most progress related to one another? What about the ones on which you made the least progress? And in the areas where you made the most progress, did you set and achieve SMART goals? Students often see the most improvement in areas where they establish goals to improve a skill, carry out their action plans, and achieve their desired results.

- **Celebrate the major improvements you've made.** You've worked hard, and you deserve to reward yourself. As you take more difficult courses and make tougher academic and career decisions in

upcoming terms, you can stay motivated by keeping your greatest successes in mind. And you can use the skills you've built to tackle each new challenge and make smart decisions.

- **Adopt a continuous-learning mind-set.** For skills in which you've made less progress than you'd hoped, remind yourself that it's hard to develop many different skills at the same time. As you progress through college and have more work experiences, you can keep striving to build certain skills. By taking this course, you've armed yourself with the tools you need to learn and improve in whatever areas you target. If you use these tools during the rest of your college journey, you'll continue to "move the needle" in a positive direction.

my personal success plan

ACADEMIC AND CAREER PLANNING

Are you inspired to set a new goal related to academic or career planning? If so, the Personal Success Plan can walk you through the goal-setting process. Read the advice and examples; then sketch out your ideas in the space provided.

LaunchPad Solo
macmillan learning

To access the Personal Success Plan online, go to LaunchPad Solo for *Connections Essentials*.

1 GATHER INFORMATION

Think about your strengths and weaknesses related to academic and career planning, and revisit your Academic and Career Planning score on ACES. What realistic goal will you set now that will help you achieve your longer-term goal of graduating and preparing for a rewarding career? Reread the relevant sections of this chapter if you need ideas.

2 SET A SMART GOAL

Use the information you've gathered to create a SMART goal, making sure to use the SMART goal checklist.

SAMPLE: I'll schedule an appointment with my adviser next week to discuss my course plan for next year.

3 MAKE AN ACTION PLAN

Outline the specific steps you'll take to achieve your SMART goal, and note when you'll complete each step.

SAMPLE: I'll e-mail my adviser on Monday and let her know when I'm free for an appointment.

4 LIST BARRIERS AND SOLUTIONS

Think about possible barriers to your action steps; then brainstorm solutions for overcoming them.

SAMPLE: If my adviser doesn't reply to my e-mail, I'll send a second e-mail and leave a message on her voice mail.

5 ACT AND EVALUATE OUTCOMES

Now that your plan is in place, take action. Record each action step as you take it. Then evaluate whether you achieved your SMART goal, and make any adjustments needed to get better results in the future.

SAMPLE: I got an e-mail back from my adviser, scheduled an appointment, and met with her. I'm really feeling good about my course plan for next year.

6 CONNECT TO CAREER

List the skills you're building as you progress toward your SMART goal. How will you use these skills to land a job and succeed at work?

SAMPLE: I'm not sure yet what career I'll pursue, but scheduling appointments, following up if there's no response, and living up to my commitments are skills I'll need in any career.

1 my
information

2 my
SMART
goal

☐ **S**PECIFIC ☐ **M**EASURABLE ☐ **A**CHIEVABLE ☐ **R**ELEVANT ☐ **T**IME-LIMITED

3 my
action
plan

4 my
barriers/
solutions

5 my
actions/
outcomes

6 my
career
connection

Chapter 12 Review

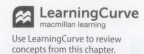

Use LearningCurve to review concepts from this chapter.

CHAPTER SUMMARY

- Understanding your interests, values, and skills helps you identify areas of study and lines of work that you may find rewarding.

- An academic plan is a roadmap showing the steps you'll take to complete a degree or certificate. Most academic plans involve declaring a major and completing both college major and general-education requirements. An academic adviser can review your plan and help you refine it as needed.

- To investigate potential careers, you can gather information using the O*NET; talk with career counselors and people working in jobs that interest you; and gain experience.

- A career search involves writing a résumé, finding job opportunities through research and networking, writing a strong cover letter, and interviewing effectively.

- By revisiting and reassessing your ACES results at the end of the term, you can celebrate improvement and target areas for future growth.

CHAPTER ACTIVITIES

Adopting a Success Attitude

PERSISTING IN THE FACE OF OBSTACLES

As you put your academic and career plans into action, what obstacles might you encounter? Might you have difficulty fulfilling the requirements for your chosen degree? Might you identify a career that seems perfect—except that few jobs will be available by the time you graduate? Identify three potential obstacles. Then, for each one, answer these questions:

1. What strengths do you have that will help you overcome this obstacle? What could you say to yourself to stay positive?
2. Who can support you or help you get past this obstacle? How?
3. What campus resources could help you deal with this obstacle? How will you connect with these resources? For example, is there a campus career center that you plan to visit? If so, where is it located?

Applying Your Skills

USING THE O*NET

Choose one occupation you'd like to learn more about. Then follow these steps to research that occupation on the O*NET:

1. Type "O*NET OnLine" into your Web browser or go to www.onetonline.org.
2. In the "Occupation Search" box, type the name of the occupation.
3. Click on the occupational title.
4. Of the tasks listed for this occupation, which do you find most appealing? Least appealing?
5. Scroll to "Skills." Which skills in the list do you already possess? Which skills would you still need to develop?
6. Scroll to "Interests." How does your Holland interest type (from your interest inventory) match the interest type or code for this occupation?
7. Scroll to "Work Values." How do your work values match those shown for this occupation?
8. Scroll to "Wages." What is the median annual wage (the middle number in a list of annual wages sorted from lowest to highest) for this occupation?
9. Select your state, and compare the national median annual wage for this occupation with the median annual wage for your state. Which is higher?
10. Based on what you've learned about this occupation, might it be a good match for you?

glossary

Academic Adviser/Counselor: A highly trained professional who can help you make effective academic decisions and refer you to valuable campus resources.

Academic Plan: A tool used by students and their advisers to plan and track a student's progress toward obtaining a degree or certificate.

Accountable: Responsible for completing tasks and meeting obligations.

Action Plan: A list of steps you'll take to accomplish a goal and the order in which you'll take them.

Active Reading: A reading strategy that involves engaging with the material before, during, and after reading.

Barrier: A personal characteristic or something in your environment that prevents you from making progress toward a goal.

Behavioral Interview Questions: Specific interview questions designed to reveal information about how you act and react in certain situations.

Budget: A plan that documents income and expenses for a specific period of time.

Career Counselor: A specially trained professional who uses career assessments and other resources to help students explore career options and make career decisions.

Chronological Résumé: A résumé that lists work and extracurricular experiences in reverse chronological order, with the most recent appearing first.

Cite: To give another author credit when you include his or her ideas in your paper or project.

Cloud: A place on the Internet where you can store your files.

College Major: A collection of courses that are organized around an academic theme.

Convergent Thinking: Thinking that involves determining the single best solution to a defined problem; uses a set of agreed-on processes, such as those required for higher-level thinking.

Cornell System: Method of note taking that organizes each page of content into sections: initial notes on the right, key points in a cue column on the left, and a summary section at the bottom of the page.

Cover Letter: A formal letter in which you introduce yourself, your interest in a job, and your appropriate skills and qualifications.

Critical Thinking: The ability to consider information in a thoughtful way, understand how to think logically and rationally, and apply those methods of thinking in your classes and your life.

Cumulative Exams: Exams that cover everything you've learned in the course up to that point in the term.

Discrimination: Treating people less favorably because of their membership in a particular group.

Divergent Thinking: Thinking that involves identifying multiple possible solutions to a defined problem; uses processes such as imagination, innovation, playfulness, openness to novelty, and curiosity.

Diversity: Characteristics or attributes that make us different from one another and that can be the basis for membership in a group.

Elaborative Rehearsal: The process of making connections between new ideas and other information already stored in your memory.

Emotional Intelligence: The ability to recognize, understand, and manage your own and others' emotions.

Empathy: The ability to understand another person's emotions.

Encoding: Taking in information and changing it into signals in your brain.

Extrinsic Motivation: Motivation that derives from forces external to you, such as an expected reward or a negative outcome that you want to avoid.

Fixed Mind-set: The belief that you cannot improve your talents, skills, and abilities.

Functional Résumé: A résumé that groups entries by skills and experiences.

General-Education Courses: A set of course requirements that gives all students a broad liberal education in the natural and social sciences, humanities, arts, and mathematics.

Goal: An outcome you hope to achieve that guides and sustains your effort over time.

Growth Mind-set: The belief that you can improve and further develop your skills.

Information Literacy: Finding information, evaluating its quality, and effectively communicating it to others.

Integrity: Being honest and displaying behavior that is consistent with your values.

Interpersonal Communication: An active exchange of information between two or more people.

Intrinsic Motivation: Motivation that stems from your inner desire to achieve a specific outcome.

Long-Term Memory: Memory that stores a potentially limitless amount of information for a long period of time.

Metacognition: Thinking about thinking or about learning.

Mnemonic: A learning strategy that helps you memorize specific material.

Multimodal Learner: Someone who uses different learning strategies to adapt to the situation at hand.

Paralinguistics: Changes in the voice (such as volume or pitch) that convey emotion.

Paraphrase: To restate information in your own words.

Personal Success Plan (PSP): A tool that helps you establish SMART goals, build action plans, evaluate your outcomes, and revise your plans as needed.

Plagiarism: When one person presents another person's words or ideas as his or her own.

Positive Psychology: A branch of psychology that focuses on people's strengths rather than on their weaknesses and that views weaknesses as opportunities for growth.

Prioritize: To give an activity or a goal a higher value relative to another activity or goal.

Procrastinate: To delay or put off an action that needs to be completed.

Professional Association: An organization through which individuals who share a trade or job function can network and promote the interests of their profession.

Purposeful Reading Questions: Specific questions you want to be able to answer when you've finished reading.

Resilience: The ability to cope with stress and setbacks.

Résumé: A document that lists your education, work experience, and extracurricular activities.

Self-Efficacy: Your belief in your ability to carry out the actions needed to reach a particular goal.

Sensory Memory: Process that uses information from the senses to begin creating memories.

Service Learning: Classes that combine classroom instruction with volunteer experience in the community.

Sexually Transmitted Infections (STIs): Illnesses, some treatable and some incurable, that are spread through the exchange of bodily fluids during sexual activity.

Short-Term Memory: Memory that stores a small number of items for a short period of time.

SMART Goal: A goal that is specific, measurable, achievable, relevant to you personally, and time-limited.

Supplemental Instruction: A student-led study program for especially difficult classes.

Test Anxiety: Nervousness or worry about performance on an exam.

Thesis: The main idea or argument of a paper or an essay.

Transferable Skills: Skills that can be applied in many different settings, such as work, home, and school.

Work Values: The aspects of your work or your work environment that you consider important.

Working Memory: The part of short-term memory that actively processes memories and information.

endnotes

Chapter 1

[1]"Educational Attainment," United States Census Bureau, accessed 9 May 2017, https://www.census.gov/topics/education/educational-attainment.html.

[2]C. L. Ryan and K. Bauman, "Educational Attainment in the United States: 2015," United States Census Bureau (March 2016). http://www.census.gov/content/dam/Census/library/publications/2016/demo/p20-578.pdf.

[3]J. Ma, M. Pender, and M. Welch, "Education Pays 2016: The Benefits of Higher Education for Individuals and Society," CollegeBoard (2016), https://trends.collegeboard.org/sites/default/files/education-pays-2016-full-report.pdf.

[4]A. P. Carnevale, N. Smith, and J. Strohl, "Recovery: Job Growth and Education Requirements through 2020," Georgetown University, accessed 9 May 2017, http://cew.georgetown.edu/recovery2020.

[5]Edward M. Glaser, *An Experiment in the Development of Critical Thinking* (New York: Teachers College, Columbia University, 1941).

[6] "The American Freshman: National Norms Fall 2012," Higher Education Research Institute at UCLA, Cooperative Institutional Research Program, accessed 19 June 2017, http://www.heri.ucla.edu/briefs/TheAmericanFreshman2012-Brief.pdf.

[7]A. M. Wood, P. A. Linley, J. Maltby, T. B. Kashdan, and R. Hurling, "Using Personal and Psychological Strengths Leads to Increases in Well-Being over Time: A Longitudinal Study and the Development of the Strengths Use Questionnaire," *Personality and Individual Differences* 50 (2011): 15–19; C. Proctor, J. Maltby, and P. A. Linley, "Strengths Use as a Predictor of Well-Being and Health-Related Quality of Life," *Journal of Happiness Studies* 12 (2011): 153–69.

[8]For more on positive psychology, see C. R. Snyder and Shane J. Lopez, eds., *Oxford Handbook of Positive Psychology*, 2nd ed. (New York: Oxford University Press, 2009); C. R. Snyder, Shane J. Lopez, and Jennifer Teramoto Pedrotti, *Positive Psychology: The Scientific and Practical Explorations of Human Strengths*, 2nd ed. (Thousand Oaks, CA: Sage, 2011).

[9]For more on resilience, see Jacqueline Aundree Baxter, "Who Am I and What Keeps Me Going? Profiling the Distance Learning Student in Higher Education," *International Review of Research in Open and Distance Learning* 13, no. 4 (2012): 107–29, http://www.irrodl.org/index.php/irrodl/article/view/1283; Robert Holloway, "From School to University: A Senior College Model," *Independence* 39, no. 1 (2014): 10–12; Steven M. Southwick and Dennis S. Charney, *Resilience: The Science of Mastering Life's Greatest Challenges* (Cambridge: Cambridge University Press, 2012); John W. Reich, Alex Zautra, and John Stuart Hall, eds., *Handbook of Adult Resilience* (New York: Guilford Press, 2010).

[10]C. R. Snyder, K. L. Rand, and D. R. Sigmon, "Hope Theory: A Member of the Positive Psychology Family," in *Handbook of Positive Psychology*, ed. C. R. Snyder and S. J. Lopez (New York: Oxford University Press, 2002), 257–76.

[11]C. R. Snyder, H. S. Shorey, J. Cheavens, K. M. Pulvers, V. H. Adams III, and C. Wiklund, "Hope and Academic Success in College," *Journal of Educational Psychology* 94 (2002): 820–26.

[12]S. A. Karabenick and R. S. Newman, *Help-Seeking in Academic Settings: Goals, Groups, and Contexts* (Mahwah, NJ: Erlbaum, 2006).

[13]"Top Ten Things Employers Look for in New College Graduates," Association of American Colleges & Universities, accessed 9 May 2017, http://www.aacu.org/leap/students/employerstopten.cfm; A. Willard, "Top Ten Skills Employers Seek," YouTube, accessed 9 May 2017, http://www.youtube.com/watch?v=ItL01G3Kovs.

[14]For example, "Employers: Verbal Communication Most Important Candidate Skill," National Association of Colleges and Employers, accessed 9 May 2017, https://www.naceweb.org/career-readiness/competencies/employers-verbal-communication-most-important-candidate-skill/.

Chapter 2

[1]Edward M. Glaser, *An Experiment in the Development of Critical Thinking* (New York: Teachers College, Columbia University, 1941).

[2]"Key Facts About Seasonal Flu Vaccine," Centers for Disease Control and Prevention, accessed 9 May 2017, http://www.cdc.gov/flu/protect/keyfacts.htm. See the Vaccine Benefits section.

[3]P. Kleiman, "Towards Transformation: Conceptions of Creativity in Higher Education," *Innovations in Education and Teaching International* 45, no. 3 (2008): 209–17; M. Fryer, "Facilitating Creativity in Higher Education," in *Developing Creativity in Higher Education: An Imaginative Curriculum*, ed. N. Jackson, M. Oliver, M. Shaw, and J. Wisdom (London: Routledge, 2006), 74–88.

[4]For more on cognitive development in an educational setting, see Julie Dockrell, Leslie Smith, and Peter Tomlinson, eds., *Piaget, Vygotsky, and Beyond: Central Issues in Developmental Psychology and Education* (London: Taylor & Francis, 1997).

[5]For example, B. S. Bloom, M. D. Engelhart, E. J. Furst, W. H. Hill, and D. R. Krathwohl, *Taxonomy of Educational Objectives: The Classification of Educational Goals. Handbook I: Cognitive Domain* (New York: David McKay, 1956); B. S. Bloom, "Reflections on the Development and Use of the Taxonomy," in "Bloom's Taxonomy: A Forty-Year Retrospective," ed. Kenneth J. Rehage, Lorin W. Anderson, and Lauren A. Sosniak, *Yearbook of the National Society for the Study of Education* (Chicago: National Society for the Study of Education) 93 (2).

[6]"Study Focuses on Strategies for Achieving Goals, Resolutions," Dominican University of California, accessed 9 May 2017, http://www.dominican.edu/dominicannews/study-highlights-strategies-for-achieving-goals.

[7]D. Morisano, J. B. Hirsh, J. B. Peterson, R. O. Pihl, and B. M. Shore, "Setting, Elaborating, and Reflecting on Personal Goals Improves Academic Performance," *Journal of Applied Psychology* 95 (2010): 255–64.

Chapter 3

[1]See Albert Bandura, *Self-Efficacy: The Exercise of Control* (New York: W. H. Freeman, 1997), 382.

[2]S. G. Rogelberg et al., "The Executive Mind: Leader Self-Talk, Effectiveness, and Strain," *Journal of Managerial Psychology* 28 (2013): 183–201; Christopher A. Wolters, "Self-Regulated Learning and College Students' Regulation of Motivation," *Journal of Educational Psychology* 90, no. 2 (1998): 224–35.

[3]J. D. Creswell, J. M. Dutcher, W. M. P. Klein, P. R. Harris, and J. M. Levine, "Self-Affirmation Improves Problem-Solving under Stress," *PLoS ONE* 8, no. 5 (2013), http://journals.plos.org/plosone/article?id=10.1371/journal.pone.0062593.

[4]A. Hatzigeorgiadis, "Instructional and Motivational Self-Talk: An Investigation of Perceived Self-Talk Functions," *Hellenic Journal of Psychology* 3 (2006): 164–75, http://www.pseve.org/journal/upload/hatzigeorgiadis3b.pdf.

[5]E. Kross, E. Bruehlman-Senecal, J. Park, A. Burson, A. Dougherty, H. Shablack, R. Bremner, J. Moser, and O. Ayduk, "Self-Talk as a Regulatory Mechanism: How You Do It Matters," *Journal of Personality and Social Psychology* 106, no. 5 (2014): 304–24.

[6]N. A. Vasquez and R. Buehler, "Seeing Future Success: Does Imagery Perspective Influence Achievement Motivation?," *Personality and Social Psychology Bulletin* 33, no. 10 (2007): 1392–405.

[7]C. S. Dweck, *Mindset: The New Psychology of Success* (New York: Random House, 2006).

[8]A. Kitsantas and B. J. Zimmerman, "College Students' Homework and Academic Achievement: The Mediating Role of Self-Regulatory Beliefs," *Metacognition and Learning* 4 (2009): 97–110.

[9]H. S. Waters and W. Schneider, *Metacognition, Strategy Use, and Instruction* (New York: Guilford Press, 2010).

Chapter 4

[1]For more about the research behind the techniques spotlighted in this section, see a recent comprehensive review of learning research published by psychologist John Dunlosky and his colleagues: J. Dunlosky, K. A. Rawson, E. J. Marsh, M. J. Nathan, and D. T. Willingham, "Improving Students' Learning with Effective Learning Techniques: Promising Directions from Cognitive and Educational Psychology," *Psychological Science in the Public Interest* 14 (January 2013): 4–58. There is also an informative article based on this review: J. Dunlosky, K. A. Rawson, E. J. Marsh, M. J. Nathan, and D. T. Willingham, "What Works, What Doesn't," *Scientific American Mind* 24, no. 4 (September/October 2013): 47–53.

For more on research-based learning strategies, including self-testing and interleaving, see also: P. C. Brown, H. L. Roediger III, and M. A. McDaniel, *Make It Stick: The Science of Successful Learning* (Cambridge: Harvard University Press, 2014). For more on these and other strategies (including dual coding and using concrete examples), see: M. Smith and Y. Weinstein, "Six Strategies for Effective Learning," The Learning Scientists, accessed 9 May 2017, http://www.learningscientists.org/blog/2016/8/18-1; and "Learn to Study…" posters from The Learning Scientists, accessed 9 May 2017, http://www.learningscientists.org/posters.

[2]A. S. Benjamin and J. Tullis, "What Makes Distributed Practice Effective?," *Cognitive Psychology* 61, no. 3 (2010): 228–47.

[3]Steven Pan recently described why this technique might be so effective: S. C. Pan, "The Interleaving Effect: Mixing It Up Boosts Learning," *Scientific American Mind* (August 4, 2015), http://www.scientificamerican.com/article/the-interleaving-effect-mixing-it-up-boosts-learning/.

[4]"Interleaving" definition, Dictionary.com, accessed 9 May 2017, http://www.dictionary.com/browse/interleaving.

[5]S. Bernard, "Neuroplasticity: Learning Physically Changes the Brain," *Edutopia* (December 1, 2010), http://www.edutopia.org/neuroscience-brain-based-learning-neuroplasticity.

[6]D. J. Menke and M. Pressley, "Elaborative Interrogation: Using 'Why' Questions to Enhance the Learning from Text," *Journal of Reading* 37, no. 8 (1994): 642–45.

[7]R. Azevado and V. Aleven, *International Handbook of Metacognition and Learning Technologies* 28 (2013): 1–16.

[8]A. Paivio, *Imagery and Verbal Processes* (New York: Holt, Rinehart, and Winston, 1971).

[9]J. D. Bransford, A. L. Brown, and R. R. Cocking, eds., *How People Learn: Brain, Mind, Experience, and School*, exp. ed., (Washington, DC: National Academy Press, 2000), 114–27, http://www.nap.edu/read/9853/chapter/8#116.

[10]V. Camos and S. Portrat, "The Impact of Cognitive Load on Delayed Recall," *Psychonomic Bulletin & Review* 22, no. 4 (August 2015): 1029. See also J. Sweller, "Cognitive Load Theory, Learning Difficulty, and Instructional Design," *Learning and Instruction* 4, no. 4 (1994): 295–312.

[11]The Royal Society, "Brain Waves Module 2: Neuroscience: Implications for Education and Lifelong Learning," (February 2011), https://royalsociety.org/~/media/Royal_Society_Content/policy/publications/2011/4294975733.pdf. See also

"Neuroplasticity: The Potential for Lifelong Brain Development," SharpBrains, accessed 9 May 2017, http://sharpbrains.com/resources/1-brain-fitness-fundamentals/neuroplasticity-the-potential-for-lifelong-brain-development/.

[12]R. Sylwester, "How Emotions Affect Learning," *Educational Leadership* 52, no. 2 (October 1994): 60–65, http://www.ascd.org/publications/educational-leadership/oct94/vol52/num02/How-Emotions-Affect-Learning.aspx.

[13]R. Curwin, "It's a Mistake Not to Use Mistakes as Part of the Learning Process," *Edutopia* (October 28, 2014), http://www.edutopia.org/blog/use-mistakes-in-learning-process-richard-curwin. See also D. R. Chialvo and P. Bak, "Learning from Mistakes," *Neuroscience* 90, no. 4 (June 1999): 1137–48, abstract available at http://www.sciencedirect.com/science/article/pii/S0306452298004722.

[14]R. Pekrun, T. Goetz, L. Daniels, R. Stupnisky, and R. Perry, "Boredom in Achievement Settings: Exploring Control-Value Antecedents and Performance Outcomes of a Neglected Emotion," *Journal of Educational Psychology* 102, no. 3 (2010): 531–49.

[15]H. Pashler, M. McDaniel, D. Rohrer, and R. Bjork, "Learning Styles: Concepts and Evidence," *Psychological Science in the Public Interest* 9, no. 3 (December 2008): 105–19.

[16]For more about the dimensions identified in the MBTI, see Isabel Briggs Myers and Peter B. Myers, *Gifts Differing: Understanding Personality Type* (Mountain View: CPP, 1995).

[17]N. D. Fleming and C. Mills, "Not Another Inventory, Rather a Catalyst for Reflection," *To Improve the Academy* 11 (1992): 137–55.

[18]National Survey of Student Engagement Report, *Engaged Learning: Fostering Success for All Students*, Annual Report (Bloomington: Center for Postsecondary Research, School of Education, Indiana University Bloomington, 2006).

Chapter 5

[1]T. Yu, "E-portfolio: A Valuable Job Search Tool for College Students," *Campus-Wide Information Systems* 29 (2012): 70–76.

[2]A. C. McCormick, "It's about Time: What to Make of Reported Declines in How Much College Students Study," *Liberal Education* 97 (2011): 30–39.

[3]N. J. Cepeda, N. Coburn, D. Rohrer, J. T. Wixted, M. C. Mozer, and H. Pashler, "Optimizing Distributed Practice: Theoretical Analysis and Practical Implications," *Experimental Psychology* 56 (2009): 236–46.

[4]M. Csikszentmihalyi, *Flow: The Psychology of Optimal Experience* (New York: Harper & Row, 1990).

[5]T. P. Rogatko, "The Influence of Flow on Positive Affect in College Students," *Journal of Happiness Studies* 10 (2009): 133–48.

Chapter 6

[1]R. Emanuel et al., "How College Students Spend Their Time Communicating," *International Journal of Listening* 22 (2008): 13–28.

[2]N. K. Duke and P. D. Pearson, "Effective Practices for Developing Reading Comprehension," in *What Research Has to Say about Reading Instruction*, 3rd ed., ed. A. E. Farstrup and S. J. Samuels (Newark, DE: International Reading Association, 2002), 205–42.

[3]V. S. Gier, D. Herring, J. Hudnell, J. Montoya, and D. S. Kreiner, "Active Reading Procedures for Moderating the Effects of Poor Highlighting," *Reading Psychology* 31 (2010): 69–81.

[4]J. Retelsdorf, O. Koller, and J. Moller, "On the Effects of Motivation on Reading Performance and Growth in Secondary School," *Learning and Instruction* 21 (2011): 550–59.

Chapter 7

[1]N. D. Rahim and H. Meon, "Relationship between Study Skills and Academic Performance," *AIP Conference Proceedings* 1522 (2013): 1176–78.

[2]V. Slotte and K. Lonka, "Review and Process Effects of Spontaneous Note-Taking on Text Comprehension," *Contemporary Educational Psychology* 24 (1999): 1–20.

[3]P. A. Mueller and D. M. Oppenheimer, "The Pen Is Mightier than the Keyboard: Advantages of Longhand over Laptop Note Taking," *Psychological Science* 25 (2014): 1159–68.

[4]D. Cohen, E. Kim, J. Tan, and M. Winkelmes, "A Note Re-structuring Intervention Increases Students' Exam Scores," *College Teaching* 61 (2013): 95–99.

[5]B. Christe, "The Importance of Faculty-Student Connections in STEM Disciplines: A Literature Review," *Journal of STEM Education: Innovations and Research* 14 (2013): 22–26.

Chapter 8

[1]R. C. Atkinson and R. M. Shiffrin, "Human Memory: A Proposed System and Its Control Processes," in *The Psychology of Learning and Motivation: Advances in Research and Theory*, vol. 2, ed. Kenneth W. Spence and Janet Taylor Spence (Waltham, MA: Academic Press, 1968), 89–195.

[2]I. Winkler and N. Cowan, "From Sensory to Long-Term Memory: Evidence from Auditory Memory Reactivation Studies," *Experimental Psychology* 52 (2005): 3–20.

[3]N. Cowan, "The Magical Number 4 in Short-Term Memory: A Reconsideration of Mental Storage Capacity," *Behavioral and Brain Sciences* 24 (2000): 87–105; Y. Kareev, "Seven (Indeed, Plus or Minus Two) and the Detection of Correlations," *Psychological Review* 107 (2000): 397–402.

[4]Y. Hu, K. A. Ericsson, D. Yang, and C. Lu, "Superior Self-Paced Memorization of Digits in Spite of a Normal Digit Span: The Structure of a Memorist's Skill," *Journal of Experimental Psychology* 35 (2009): 1426–42.

[5]W. Klimesch, *The Structure of Long-Term Memory: A Connectivity Model of Semantic Processing* (Hoboken: Taylor and Francis, 2013).

[6]S. D. Gronlund and D. R. Kimball, "Remembering and Forgetting: From the Laboratory Looking Out," in *Individual and Team Skill Decay: The Science and Implications for Practice*, ed. Winfred Arthur Jr., Eric A. Day, Winston Bennett Jr., and Antoinette M. Portrey (New York: Routledge/Taylor and Francis, 2013), 14–52.

[7]N. J. Cepeda, N. Coburn, D. Rohrer, J. T. Wixted, M. C. Mozer, and H. Pashler, "Optimizing Distributed Practice: Theoretical Analysis and Practical Implications," *Experimental Psychology* 56 (2009): 236–46.

[8]C. Gillen-O'Neel, V. W. Huynh, and A. J. Fuligni, "To Study or to Sleep? The Academic Costs of Extra Studying at the Expense of Sleep," *Child Development* 84 (2013): 133–42.

[9]G. D. Hendry, S. J. Hyde, and P. Davy, "Independent Student Study Groups," *Medical Education* 39 (2005): 672–79; Donita J. Shaw, "Promoting Professional Student Learning through Study Groups: A Case Study," *College Teaching* 59, no. 2 (2011): 85–92.

[10]P. Wilhelm and J. M. Pieters, "Fostering Effective Studying and Study Planning with Study Questions," *Assessment and Evaluation in Higher Education* 32 (2007): 373–82.

[11]P. Baghaei and J. Cassady, "Validation of the Persian Translation of the Cognitive Test Anxiety Scale," *Sage Open* 4 (2014): 1–11.

[12]J. C. Cassady, "The Influence of Cognitive Test Anxiety across the Learning-Testing Cycle," *Learning and Instruction* 14 (2004): 569–92.

[13]D. W. Nelson and A. E. Knight, "The Power of Positive Recollections: Reducing Test Anxiety and Enhancing College Student Efficacy and Performance," *Journal of Applied Social Psychology* 40 (2010): 732–45.

[14]M. Mavilidi, V. Hoogerheide, and F. Paas, "A Quick and Easy Strategy to Reduce Test Anxiety and Enhance Test Performance," *Applied Cognitive Psychology* 28, no. 5 (2014): 720–26.

Chapter 9

[1]"Michael Gorman vs. Web 2.0," *Chronicle of Higher Education* 53 (2007): B4.

[2]"Wikipedia: Wikipedia Is a Volunteer Service," *Wikipedia*, accessed 9 May 2017, https://en.wikipedia.org/wiki/Wikipedia:Wikipedia_is_a_volunteer_service.

[3]B. Burnsed, "Wikipedia Gradually Accepted in College Classrooms," *U.S. News* (20 June 2011), http://www.usnews.com/education/best-colleges/articles/2011/06/20/wikipedia-gradually-accepted-in-college-classrooms.

[4]R. T. Kellogg, "Attentional Overload and Writing Performance: Effects of Rough Draft and Outline Strategies," *Journal of Experimental Psychology: Learning, Memory, and Cognition* 14 (1988): 355–65.

[5]Hart Research Associates, "It Takes More than a Major: Employer Priorities for College Learning and Student Success," *Liberal Education* 99, no. 2 (2013): 22–29.

[6]C. B. Pull, "Current Status of Knowledge on Public-Speaking Anxiety," *Current Opinion in Psychiatry* 25 (2012): 32–38.

Chapter 10

[1]"Build Better Listening Skills," National Education Association, last modified 2015, http://www.nea.org/tools/build-better-listening-skills.html.

[2]Emotional intelligence has been defined in various ways by different people. Our definition and model of emotional intelligence is a synthesis of the following works by Mayer and Salovey: J. D. Mayer and P. Salovey, "Emotional Intelligence: New Ability or Eclectic Traits?," *American Psychologist* 63, no. 6 (2008): 503–17; J. D. Mayer and P. Salovey, "What Is Emotional Intelligence?," in *Emotional Development and Emotional Intelligence: Educational Implications*, ed. P. Salovey and D. Sluyter (New York: Basic Books, 1997), 3–31.

[3]Mayer and Salovey, "Emotional Intelligence," 503–17.

[4]A. Nerurkar, A. Bitton, R. B. Davis, R. S. Phillips, and G. Yeh, "When Physicians Counsel about Stress: Results of a National Study," *JAMA Internal Medicine* 173, no. 1 (2013): 76–77.

[5]R. S. Mohd, "Life Event, Stress, and Illness," *Malaysian Journal of Medical Sciences* 15, no. 4 (2008): 9–18.

[6]Ibid.

[7]M. Bayrami, "Effect of Assertiveness Training on General Health in the First Year of Students of Tabriz University," *Psychological Research* 14, no. 1 (2011): 47–64.

[8]J. Darrington and N. Brower, "Effective Communication Skills: 'I' Messages and Beyond," *Families and Communities*, April 2012, Utah State University Cooperative Extension.

[9]S. Miller and P. A. Miller, *Core Communication: Skills and Processes* (Evergreen, CO: Interpersonal Communication Programs, 1997).

[10]J. Wang and J. Shively, *The Impact of Extracurricular Activity on Student Academic Performance* (Sacramento: California State University, Sacramento, Office of Institutional Research, 2009).

[11]A. W. Astin, *Achieving Educational Excellence: A Critical Assessment of Priorities and Practices in Higher Education* (San Francisco: Jossey-Bass, 1985).

[12]Ibid.

[13]S. Uusiautti and K. Maatta, "I Am No Longer Alone—How Do University Students Perceive the Possibilities of Social Media?," *International Journal of Adolescence and Youth* 19, no. 3 (2014): 293–305.

[14]S. R. Ennis, M. Rios-Vargas, and N. G. Albert, "The Hispanic Population: 2010," *2010 Census Briefs*, U.S. Census Bureau (May 2011), http://www.census.gov/prod/cen2010/briefs/c2010br-04.pdf.

[15]"Gender," World Health Organization (2017), http://www.who.int/gender-equity-rights/understanding/gender-definition/en/.

[16]"Guidelines for Psychological Practice with Lesbian, Gay, and Bisexual Clients," *American Psychologist* 67 (January 2012): 10–42.

[17]Ibid.

[18]American Psychological Association, Task Force on Socioeconomic Status, *Report of the APA Task Force on Socioeconomic Status* (Washington, DC: American Psychological Association, 2007).

Chapter 11

[1]Mayo Clinic Staff, "Chronic Stress Puts Your Health at Risk," accessed 9 May 2017, http://www.mayoclinic.org/healthy-living/stress-management/in-depth/stress/art-20046037.

[2]Ibid.

[3]F. J. He, C. A. Nowson, M. Lucas, and G. A. MacGregor, "Increased Consumption of Fruit and Vegetables Is Related to a Reduced Risk of Coronary Heart Disease: Meta-analysis of Cohort Studies," *Journal of Human Hypertension* 21 (2007): 717–28.

[4]ChooseMyPlate.gov, "MyPlate Tip Sheets," United States Department of Agriculture, accessed 9 May 2017, http://www.choosemyplate.gov/ten-tips.

[5]"Eating Disorder Statistics," National Association of Anorexia Nervosa and Associated Disorders, accessed 9 May 2017, http://www.anad.org/get-information/about-eating-disorders/eating-disorders-statistics/.

[6]H. W. Bland, B. F. Melton, L. E. Bigham, and P. D. Welle, "Quantifying the Impact of Physical Activity on Stress Tolerance in College Students," *College Student Journal* 48 (2014): 559–68.

[7]World Health Organization, *Global Recommendations on Physical Activity for Health* (Geneva: WHO Press, 2010).

[8]O. Pikovsky, M. Oron, A. Shiyovich, Z. Perry, and L. Nesher, "The Impact of Sleep Deprivation on Sleepiness, Risk Factors, and Professional Performance in Medical Residents," *Israel Medical Association Journal* 15 (2013): 739–44.

[9]M. T. Trockel, M. D. Barnes, and D. L. Egget, "Health-Related Variables and Academic Performance among First-Year College Students: Implications for Sleep and Other Behaviors," *Journal of American College Health* 49 (2000): 125–31.

[10]National Alliance on Mental Illness, *College Students Speak: A Survey Report on Mental Health* (Arlington, VA: National Alliance on Mental Illness, 2012).

[11]"The Core Alcohol and Drug Survey," Core Institute, Southern Illinois University, accessed 9 May 2017, http://core.siu.edu/results.

[12]"Contraception," Centers for Disease Control and Prevention, accessed 9 May 2017, http://www.cdc.gov/reproductivehealth/unintendedpregnancy/contraception.htm.

[13]American Psychological Association, *Stress in America: Paying with Our Health* (Washington, DC: American Psychological Association, 2014).

[14]"Characteristics of Postsecondary Students," National Center for Education Statistics, last updated April 2017, http://nces.ed.gov/programs/coe/indicator_csb.asp.

[15]National Center for Education Statistics, *Undergraduates Who Work while Enrolled in Postsecondary Education, 1989–1990* (Washington, DC: National Center for Education Statistics, 1994).

[16]"Fast Facts: Financial Aid," National Center for Education Statistics, accessed 9 May 2017, http://nces.ed.gov/fastfacts/display.asp?id=31.

Chapter 12

[1]J. L. Holland, *Making Vocational Choices: A Theory of Vocational Personalities and Work*, 3rd ed. (Odessa, FL: Psychological Assessment Resources, 1997).

[2]Based on O*NET Work Values: "Browse by O*Net Data," O*Net OnLine, updated April 18, 2017, http://www.onetonline.org/find/descriptor/browse/Work_Values/.

[3]H. J. Yoon, H. In, S. G. Niles, N. E. Amundson, B. A. Smith, and L. Mills, "The Effects of Hope on Student Engagement, Academic Performance, and Vocational Identity," *Canadian Journal of Career Development* 14, no. 1 (2015): 34–45.

[4]"The Game Changers: Systemic reforms. Significant results. More college graduates," Complete College America (2014), http://completecollege.org/the-game-changers/#clickBoxGreen.

[5]J. Gault, E. Leach, and M. Dewey, "Effects of Business Internships on Job Marketability: An Employer's Perspective," *Education + Training* 52, no. 1 (2010): 76–88.

[6]For more information on the STAR approach to behavioral interviewing, see: M. Barbeau, "Be a 'STAR' Interviewer," iGrad (4 August 2010), http://www.igrad.com/articles/behavioral-interviewing-and-the-star-approach.

index

A

Abbreviations, in note taking, 110, 119
Abstinence, 194
Abstracts, in journal articles, 98, 99–100
Academic accommodation, 65
Academic advisers
    academic planning and, 210
    reading help from, 100
    resources, acting as, 10, 25
Academic and Career Excellence System (ACES)
    academic and career planning and, 204
    connecting with others and, 164
    critical thinking and goal setting and, 14
    identifying strengths and weaknesses with, 6
    information literacy and communication and, 148
    learning preferences and, 50
    memory, studying, test taking and, 126
    motivation, decision making, personal responsibility, and, 34
    note taking and, 106
    organization and time management and, 70
    personal and financial health and, 186
    progress assessment with, 221–23
    reading and, 88
Academic plans, 203–11, 224–26
    definition of, 208
    developing, 208–10
    milestones in, 210
    Personal Success Plan for, 224–25
    self-knowledge for, 205–7
    voices of experience on, 211
Academic success
    critical thinking and, 3, 13–32
    different learning environments and, 63–65
    goals in, 24
    hope and, 9
    personal responsibility for, 10
    strengths and weaknesses and, 5
Academic values, 206–7
Accommodations, 65
    note taking and, 110
Accuracy, in note taking, 121
ACES. See Academic and Career Excellence System (ACES)
Achievable goals, 22–23, 28, 32
Achievement, as value, 206
Acronyms, as memory aids, 131
Acrostics, as memory aids, 131
Action plans, 33
    decision making and, 40, 41
    flexibility in, 28
    goal setting and, 23–24
    Personal Success Plan and, 27–28, 30
Active learning, 42–44

Active listening,
    understanding and improving, 165–66
    while note taking, 108–9
Active reading, 89
    definition of, 89
    focus in, 92–96
    note taking and, 108–9
    preparation for, 89, 90–91
    review in, 89, 97
Addiction, 192
Adrenaline, 187
Advocacy, diversity and, 181
Age diversity, 178, 179
Agency, 9
Aggression, 171–72
AIDS, 193
Alcohol abuse, 192
Al-Kachak, Amni, 80
All-nighters, 52, 189
"All of the above" answers, 139
Analysis, in Bloom's taxonomy, 19, 20, 21
Annotating, while reading, 92, 93
Anorexia nervosa, 189
Anxiety
    about tests, 125, 135–37, 138
    mental health and, 192
APA style guide, 155, 162
Appearance, for presentations, 159
Application
    Bloom's taxonomy and, 19, 20, 21
    memory and, 128
    reading and, 94–95
Archives, as information sources, 150
Argument, critical thinking and, 21
Artistic interests, 205
Assertiveness, 171–72, 173, 176, 181, 184
Associate's degrees, 195, 208
Associations, as memory aids, 131
Attention to detail, 121
Attitude
    evaluating, 48
    motivation and, 37
    success and, 12, 32, 48, 68, 86, 104, 124, 146, 162, 184, 202, 226
    transferable skill and, 11
Audience, for presentations, 158
Aural learners, 58
Author credibility, evaluating, 151

B

Baby boomers, 179
Bachelor's degrees, 195, 208
Backing up documents, 72

Bandura, Albert, 35
Barriers
    achieving goals and, 25, 27–28, 30, 32
    communication and, 165, 166
    motivation, decision making, personal responsibility, and, 46–47
    Personal Success Plan and, 30
Baskin, Brittnee Nicole, 62
Behavioral interview questions, 219
"Being a doormat," 172
Bias
    about differences, 180
    information sources and, 151
Bibliographies, 156
Birth control, 193, 194, 202
Birth control pill, 194
Bloom, Benjamin, 19
Bloom's taxonomy, 19–21, 140–41
Body language, 159, 165, 168
Body posture, 165, 166
Books, as information sources, 149
Boredom, 55, 96
Brain
    dual coding theory on, 54
    learning disabilities and, 65
    learning research and, 55
    memory and, 127
Brainstorming ideas, 154
Branches, in mapping, 118
Breakfast, 188, 190
Breathing, for relaxation, 136, 169
Briggs, Katharine, 56
Browsers, computer, 142
Budgets, 195–96, 202
Bulimia nervosa, 189

C
Caffeine, 189
Calendars, time tracking with, 73–74
Campus clubs, 175
Campus engagement, 207
Campus resources. See Resources
Career
    college success and, 11
    connecting goals to, 28, 30
    critical thinking and success in, 13
    finding your purpose and, 7
    goal setting, 30
    investigating potential, 212–14
    planning. See Career planning
    valuing a meaningful, 4
Career advisers, 25
CareerBuilder, 217
Career centers, 10, 217
Career planning
    investigating career options in, 212–14
    job searches and, 215–20
    Personal Success Plan for, 224–25
    self-knowledge for, 205–7
    your skills and, 207
    your values and, 206–7
Certificates, choosing, 208
Chapter summaries, reading, 90
Charting, for note taking, 115, 124

Cheating, 142
Chlamydia, 193
Choices
    academic and career, 38, 40–41, 75, 205, 208–10, 212
    health, 188, 192
Chronological résumés, 215, 216
Citations, 151, 154, 155, 156
Classes. See Courses
Classmates
    clarifying confusing material with, 95
    comparing notes with, 111
    connecting with, 174
    learning strategy help from, 65
    resources, acting as, 10
Clues, in test questions, 139
Coaching for success, 5–6, 12
Cognitive overload, 54
College, differences between high school and, 44
College Board, 2
College success, 1–12
    career success and, 11
    decision making and, 33, 40–41
    finding your purpose and, 7
    learning about yourself and, 3–6
    motivation in, 33–39
    organization and, 69
    personal responsibility and, 33, 42–45
    positive psychology and, 8–10
    reading for, 87–104
    reasons to attend college and, 2
    transition to college life and, 44–45
Color-coding documents, 72
Comfort dogs, 192
Comfort zone, 2
Common ground, finding, 173
Communication, 147–62
    assertive, 171–72, 173, 176, 181, 184
    better speaking for, 166
    conflict resolution and, 171, 174
    embracing diversity and, 178–81
    emotional intelligence and, 167–70
    enhancing skills in, 165–66
    information and, 149
    interviews and, 220
    listening in, 165–66
    Personal Success Plan for, 160–61
    presentations and, 158–59
    as a transferable skill, 11
    writing, 152–56
Community engagement, 2, 175
Comparing and contrasting
    definition and example of, 16
    writing and, 154
"Complete" folders, 72
Comprehension
    Bloom's taxonomy and, 19
    computer vs. pen-and-paper notes and, 111
    reviewing after reading and, 97
Compromises, 171, 173
Computers, for note taking, 107, 111
Concentration. See also Focus
    improving for reading, 95–96
    note taking and, 108

Conclusions, writing, 155, 158
Conditional language, 139, 140
Condoms, 193, 194
Conferencing tools, 159
Confidence
    conflict resolution and, 172
    reading and, 94, 124
Conflict resolution, 171–73, 176
Confusing content, clarifying while
        reading, 95
Connections
    between classes, 43–44
    health and, 185–202
    importance of, 1
    making during study, 53–54, 131–32
    with others, 163–84
    Personal Success Plan for, 182–83
Context
    distributed studying and, 53
    self-explanation and, 54
Continuous-learning mind-set, 223
Conventional interests, 205
Convergent thinking, 18
Co-op programs, 214
Core courses, 209
Cornell system of note taking, 116–17, 124
Cortisol, 187
Counseling centers, 10
Counselors, 210
    career, 212, 214, 217
Course reserves, as information sources, 150
Courses. See also Majors; Online courses
    attitude toward, 37
    getting involved in, 43
    motivation for, 36, 38–39
    online, managing time for, 77
    participating in, 108–9
    presentations in, 158–59
    scheduling, 75–77
    selecting, 209–10
    self-efficacy and difficult, 8
    strengths and weaknesses and, 5–6
    your interests and, 4
Cover letters, 217–19
Cramming, 53, 130, 134, 189
Creative thinking, 18
    conflict resolution and, 173
    self-talk and, 37
    writing and, 154
Credit cards, 199, 202
Credit reports, 199
Credits, course, 209
Critical thinking, 13–32
    ACES score on, 14
    building skills in, 15–18
    creative thinking compared with, 18
    definition of, 3, 15
    diversity and, 178, 180–81
    goal setting and, 22–25
    levels of learning and, 19–21
    making memory connections and, 131–32
    to overcome procrastination and distractions, 81
    Personal Success Plan and, 27–30
    reading and, 89, 92–95

test taking and, 140, 143
    track time and, 73
    as transferable skill, 11
    writing and, 152–53, 154
    yourself, regarding, 3–6
Cue column, in notes, 116
Cues
    Cornell system of note taking and,
        116
    note taking and, 108–9
    reading and, 96
    verbal, about important material, 109
Culture
    diversity and, 179
    nonverbal communication and, 165–66
Cumulative exams, 134
Currency, of information sources, 151

D

Databases, as information sources, 150
Deadlines
    goal setting and, 24
    online classes and, 77
Debt
    credit card, 199
    student loan, 197–98
Decision making, 33, 40–41
    examples of processes in, 41
    Personal Success Plan for, 46–47
    process for, 40–41
    reflecting on, 34
    transition to college life and, 44–45
Deducing, definition and example of, 16
Definitions, noting while reading, 92, 93
Degrees
    choosing, 208
    income and, 195
Depression, 190, 202
Designated drivers, 192
Diagrams, 98
Diet, healthy, 188–89
Differences, embracing, 178–81
Directions, reading, 138
Disabilities, note taking and, 110
Disability services offices
    reading help from, 100
    resources of, 10
Discrimination, 178, 180, 181
Discussion sections, in journal articles,
        99, 100
Distractions, 55
    minimizing, 82
    note taking and, 108
    reading and, 89, 96
Distributed studying, 53
Divergent thinking, 18
Diversity, embracing, 178–81
Doctoral degrees, income and, 195
Documentation, 156, 162
Documents, organizing, 71–72
Dogs, comfort, 192
Doormat, being a, 172
Drafts, writing first, 152, 153–55

Drug abuse, 192
Dual coding, 54
Dweck, Carol, 42

E

Earplugs, 82
Eating disorders, 189, 190
Eating right, 188–89
E-books, marking text in, 101
Education
    earning and unemployment rates and, 195
    history of, on résumés, 215
    value of, 2
    valuing, 4
Education level
    income and, 2, 195
    statistics on, 2
Efficiency, in reading, 95–96
Elaborative interrogation, 53–54
Elaborative rehearsal, 131–32
Elective courses, 209
Electronic document storage, 71–72
E-mail
    as distraction, 82
    etiquette, 174–75
    staying connected through, 176
    thank-you notes via, 217, 220
Emotional intelligence, 167–70
    building, 184
    definition of, 167
Emotions. *See also* Stress
    ability to learn and, 55
    anxiety about tests, 125, 135–37, 138
    conflict resolution and, 171–73
    feeling overwhelmed and, 82
    managing, 168–69
    in online classes, 156
    recognizing, 169–70
    suppressing, 170
    understanding, 168–69, 173
Empathy, 168–69, 176, 178
Employment
    college success and, 11
    critical thinking and success in, 13
    education level and, 2
    getting experience and, 214
    goal setting and, 30
    social media photos and, 192
Encoding, in memory, 127, 129
Encoding failure, 129
Encouragement, in communication, 166
Encyclopedias, as information sources, 150
Engagement, 207
Enterprising interests, 205
Entertainment
    presentation purpose, 158
    writing purpose and, 152
Environments, learning, 63–65
Equations, note taking and, 119, 120
Equifax, 199
Essay questions, 140–41
    anticipating, 146
    critical thinking and, 140

Ethnic diversity, 178, 179
Etiquette
    e-mail, 174–75
    interview, 220
Evaluating
    action plan results, 28
    after tests, 143
    Bloom's taxonomy and, 19, 21
    critical-thinking skills and, 15, 16, 17
    decision making, 40, 41
    definition and example of, 16
    information, 149, 150, 153
    online information, 150–51
    outcomes in goal setting, 25
    Personal Success Plan outcomes, 30
    self-talk in, 37
    while reading, 92–95
    your change progress, 221–23
    your learning, 45
Evidence, in writing, 154, 155
Examples, generating, 54
Exam taking. *See* Test taking
Exercise, 185
    importance of, 189
    scheduling time for, 78
    stress and, 189
    test preparation and, 134
Expectations
    of college, 2, 43–44
    reframing, 82
Expenses
    budgets and, 195–96
    reducing, 196
Experian, 199
Experts, career advice from, 212, 214
Expressive writing, 152
Extracurricular activities, 175
Extravert/Introvert dimension, 56, 58
Extrinsic motivation, 38
Eye contact, 165–66

F

Facebook, 19, 176
FAFSA. *See* Free Application for Federal Student Aid
    (FAFSA)
Failure
    learning from, 26
    reflecting on past, 6
Family and friends
    conflict resolution and, 171–73
    connecting with, 163–84
    growing and sustaining healthy relationships with,
        174–76
    resources, acting as, 10
    scheduling time for, 77
    staying connected with, 176–77
    time-management priorities and, 75
Feedback
    communication barriers and, 166
    diversity and, 181
    during communication, 165–66
    on your note taking, 97, 111
    on your writing, 155, 157

Feeling/Thinking dimension, 57, 58
Fight-or-flight response, 187
Files
    backing up, 72
    naming and labeling, 72
Fill-in-the-blank questions, 140
Financial aid, 9, 197–99
    keeping, 198
    learning about, 202
Financial aid offices, as resource, 10
Financial health, 185–86, 195–99
    credit cards and, 199
    financial aid and, 197–99
    Personal Success Plan for, 200–201
Fixed mind-set, 42
Flash cards, 51–52, 98
Fleming, Neil, 58
Flow state, 83
Focus
    active reading and, 92–96
    during listening, 165, 166
    note taking and, 108–9
    test anxiety and, 135
    time-management priorities and, 75, 80
Folders, naming and labeling, 72
Follow up, after tests, 143
Food choices, 188–89
Forced completion exams, 142
Forgetting, 129
Formatting, 155
Formulas
    note taking and, 119, 120
    studying, 133
Free Application for Federal Student Aid (FAFSA), 197, 198
Functional résumés, 215

G

Gender diversity, 179
General-education courses, 209–10
Generation X, 179
Genital herpes, 193
Goals
    academic plans and, 210
    assessment of progress toward, 221–23
    barriers to achieving, 25, 26, 27–28, 30, 32
    career, 208–9
    choosing a major and, 208–9
    interests and, 4
    learning, setting, 45
    long-term, 22, 36
    reading, setting, 96
    reflection on setting, 3
    short-term, 22
    SMART, 22–23, 30, 32
    staying motivated for, 35–38
    values and, 3
    weak, 22–23
    work-related, 30
Goal setting, 13–32
    ACES score on, 14
    action plans for, 23–24
    benefits of, 24
    critical thinking for, 22–25

Personal Success Plan and, 27–30
    reflection on, 3
    skills for, 11
    steps for, 22–25
    value of for careers, 30
    voices of experience on, 26
Gonorrhea, 193
Google Scholar, 59
Grades, healthy behavior and, 190
Grants, 197
Group work, 63–64, 68
Growth mind-set, 42

H

"Happy" (Williams), 8
Hate crimes, 181
Hatzigeorgiadis, Antonis, 37
Headings
    purposeful reading questions based on, 91
    reading, 90
Health, 185–202
    education level and, 2
    exercise and, 78, 134, 185, 189
    financial, 185–86, 195–99
    grades and, 190
    Personal Success Plan for, 200–201
    physical and mental, 188–92
    reflection on, 186
    sexual, 193–94
    sleep and, 134, 185, 189
    stress and, 170, 187
    test taking and, 134
    voices of experience on, 191
Higher-level thinking skills, 15–18. *See also* Critical thinking
Highlighting, while reading, 92, 93
    online texts, 101
High school, differences between college and, 44–45
Historical documents, as information sources, 150
HIV, 193
Holland, John, 205
Holland's interest inventory, 205–6
Homework. *See also* Reading
    personal responsibility for, 43
    planning for large projects, 86
    scheduling time for, 77
Honesty, 142
Hope, 8, 9
Human papillomavirus (HPV), 193
Humor, coping with stress using, 202
Hypotheses, 98

I

Identity, vocational, 207
Immune system, stress and, 170
Income
    boosting, 197
    budgets and, 195–96
    education level and, 2, 195
Independence
    transition to college life and, 44–45
    as a value, 206
Independent learners, 43

Information
    applying in critical thinking, 17
    for budget creation, 195–96
    citing sources for, 156, 162
    communicating in writing, 152–56
    for decision making, 40
    about diversity, 180–81
    evaluating critically, 15, 16, 17
    finding, 149–50
    gathering, 17
    for goal setting, 22
    included in note taking, 109–11
    overload of, 55
    Personal Success Plan and, 28, 30
    transforming through note taking, 121
    verbal, 54
    visual, 54
Informational interviews, 214
Information literacy, 147–62
    definition of, 147
    developing, 149–51
    Personal Success Plan for, 160–61
    presentations and, 158–59
    reflection on, 148
    writing and, 152–57
Informing
    as presentation purpose, 158
    as writing purpose, 152
"In Progress" folders, 72
Instagram, 19
Instructors
    asking for help from, 119
    clarifying confusing material with, 95
    connecting with, 174–75
    following up with after tests, 143
    getting feedback on notes from, 111
    learning strategy help from, 65
    preparation for test taking and, 135
    as resources, 10, 25
    verbal and nonverbal cues from, 109
Integrity, 142
Interest inventories, 205
Interest rates, 198, 199
Interests
    exploring, 205–6
    following your, 4
    occupational searches based on, 212, 213
Interleaved practice, 53
Internet
    career information on, 205, 213, 215, 226
    connecting with others on, 176
    evaluating information on, 150–51
    job searches on, 217
    occupation information on, 226
    online tests and, 142
    reliability of sources on, 95
Internships, 214
Interpersonal communication, 165
Interviews
    behavioral questions in, 219
    informational, 214
    for jobs, 219–20
    on-campus, 217

Intrauterine devices (IUDs), 194
Intrinsic motivation, 38–39
Introductions
    in journal articles, 98, 100
    reading, 90
    writing, 153, 154
Introvert/Extravert dimension, 56, 58
Intuitive/Sensing dimension, 56–57, 58
Investigative interests, 205
Involvement, in classes, 43
"I" statements, 172, 176, 184

J
Jackson, Russell, 7
Jean, Thamara, 26
Job fairs, 217
Jobs
    during college, 197, 198
    college success and, 11
    critical thinking and success in, 13
    education level and, 2
    getting experience in, 214
    note taking at, 104, 121
    scheduling time for, 77
Job searches, 215–20
    cover letters for, 217–19
Journal articles
    as information sources, 150
    reading, 98–100
Journalists' questions, 15, 104
Journals, worry, 136
Judging/Perceiving dimension, 57, 58
Jung, Carl, 56

K
Kao, Tony, 211
Key points, identifying, 124
Key terms
    purposeful reading questions based on, 91
    reading, 90
Khan Academy, 133
Kinesthetic learners, 59
Knowledge
    applying in critical thinking, 17
    audience's, 158
    in Bloom's taxonomy, 19
    prior, 20

L
Labeling
    of documents, 72
    while note taking, 107, 109
Large class assignments, planning for, 86
Leadership skills, 175
Learning, 49–68. *See also* Education
    the brain in, 54
    from computer vs. pen and paper notes, 111
    levels of, 19–21, 140–41
    lifelong, 55
    love of, focus on, 35
    making it personal, 56–61
    online, time management for, 77

reflecting on, 50
research on, 51–55
thinking about, 45
Learning assistance centers, 100
Learning disabilities, 65
Learning environments, 63–65
Learning preferences, 49
group work and, 63–64
identifying your, 56–61
Personal Success Plan and, 66–67
research on, 56
Learning science, 51
Learning strategies, 43–45
changing up material, 53
distributed studying, 53
evaluating, 45
making connections, 53–54
multimodal, 54, 64
self-testing, 51
voices of experience on, 62
Leisure
scheduling time for, 78
tracking time for, 73–74
Library research, 149–50
Lifelong learning, 55
LinkedIn, 19, 176, 215, 217
Listening, 109, 165–66, 173, 176. *See also* Active
listening; Communication as transferable skill
Lists, to-do, 78
Literary genres, 104
Loans, 197–98, 199
Long-term memory, 128, 129

M

Magazines, as information sources, 150
Majors
attitude and, 37
selecting, 208–9, 211
values and choosing, 4–5
Mapping, in note taking, 116, 118, 124
Master's degrees, 195
Matching questions, 139–40
Math classes
note taking for, 119, 120, 124
reading for, 98, 99
studying for, 132–33
test taking in, 141
MBTI. *See* Myers-Briggs Type Indicator (MBTI)
Measurable goals, 22–23, 27, 32
Memorizing terms, 98
Memory, 125–29
forgetting and, 129
long-term, 128, 129
making connections between, 131–32
Personal Success Plan for, 144–45
sensory, 127
short-term, 128, 129
study strategies and, 130–33
Mental diversity, 179
Mental health, 190, 192
Mentors, 33
Metacognition, 45, 49, 110
Methods sections, in journal articles, 98, 100

Milestones, in planning, 210
Millennials, 179
Mind-sets
continuous-learning, 223
growth vs. fixed, 42
Mistakes, learning from, 26, 55, 143
MLA style guide, 155, 162
Mnemonics, 131
Monster.com, 217
Motivation, 33–39
decision making and, 40–41
evaluating, 48
extrinsic, 38
interests and, 4
intrinsic, 38–39
Personal Success Plan for, 46–47
procrastination and, 81
for reading, 95
reflecting on, 34
setting goals and, 3
stress as, 35
to study, 146
as transferable skill, 11
voices of experience on, 39
Movement
overcoming procrastination through, 81
reading concentration and, 96
Multidimensionality of people, 178
Multimodal learning strategies, 54, 64–65
Multiple-choice questions, 138–39
Muscle relaxation techniques, 136
Myers, Isabel, 56
Myers-Briggs Type Indicator (MBTI), 49, 56–58
MyPlate, 188

N

Napping, 189
National Center for Education Statistics, 197
*National Trade and Professional Associations of the
United States,* 217
Networking, 217
Newspapers, as information sources, 150
Nodes, in mapping, 116
Nonverbal communication, 165–66. *See also* Body
language
Nonverbal cues, 109
Note taking, 105–24
computer vs. pen and paper, 111
getting feedback on, 97
improving skills in, 124
for math and science classes, 119, 120
methods for, 112–18
for online classes, 119–20
online tests and, 142
in online texts, 101
Personal Success Plan for, 122–23
plagiarism and, 156
reading and, 92
reflection on, 106
strategy for, 107–11
voices of experience on, 114
as work skill, 121
Nutrition, 134, 188–89

O

Objectivity, in information sources, 151
Obstacles, persisting in the face of, 226
Offensive language, 181
Office hours of instructors, 135
Office space, organizing, 71
O*NET, 205, 212, 213, 226
Online communities, 176
Online courses
    communicating with instructors of, 135
    note taking in, 119–20, 124
    reading for, 100–101
    reading for, marking up, 92, 101
    studying for, 133
    test taking, 141–42
    time management for, 77
    writing posts in, 156
Online posts
    responding to, 101
    writing, 156
Online presentations, 159
Online study groups, 133
Open mind, critical thinking and, 17
Open posture, 165, 166
Options, for decision making, 40, 41
Organization, 69–86
    of documents, 71–72
    in essay questions, 141
    of notes, 107, 111
    Personal Success Plan for, 84–85
    reflection on, 70
    of study space, 71
Outcomes, evaluating, 25, 30
Outlining
    for note taking, 112–13, 114, 124
    for writing, 153, 154
Overdoses, 192
Overwhelmed feelings, 82

P

Panic attacks, 192
Paper document storage systems, 72
Paragraphs, structure of, 155
Paralinguistics, 168
Paraphrasing
    during communication, 166
    in note taking, 110, 111
Participating in class, note taking and, 109
Passion, motivation and, 39
Passivity, 171
Patch, birth control, 194
Pathways, 9
PDF format, 101
Peer-reviewed journal articles, 150
Perceiving/Judging dimension, 57, 58
Perfectionism, 82
Persistence, 217, 222
Personal growth, 42
Personal responsibility, 8, 10, 33, 42–45
    evaluating, 48
    learning strategies and, 65
    Personal Success Plan for, 46–47
    reflecting on, 34
    transferable skills in, 11

Personal Success Plan (PSP)
    for academic and career planning, 224–25
    for connection skills, 182–83
    creating, 27–30
    examples of, 29
    for information literacy and communication, 160–61
    for learning preferences, 66–67
    for memory, studying, test taking, 144–45
    for motivation, decision making, and personal responsibility, 46–47
    for note taking, 122–23
    for organization and time management, 84–85
    for personal and financial health, 200–201
    for reading, 102–3
Personal supports, 12. See also Support systems
Perspectives, understanding others', 169, 173, 178
Persuasion
    as presentation purpose, 158
    as writing purpose, 152, 154
Physical ability, diversity in, 179
Physical health. See Health
Plagiarism, 155, 156
Planning. See also Schedules; Time management
    academic, 203–11, 224–26
    career, 203–11, 208–20, 224–26
    for reading, 90
    for writing, 152–53
PLUS loans, 198
Pop-ups, browser, 142
Positive psychology, 8–10
Positive self-talk, 37
Positivity
    in conflict resolution, 173
    power of, 8–10
    in reading, 89
    self-talk and, 37
    studying and, 146
    test anxiety and, 136
    as transferable work skill, 11
    writing and, 162
Posture, 165, 166
PowerPoint slides, 108, 159
Practice
    interleaved, 53
    for presentations, 159
    in problem solving, 132–33
Practice tests, 132. See also Self-testing
    to manage test anxiety, 136
Prefaces, reading, 90
Preferences. See Learning preferences
Preparation
    for interviews, 219–20
    for note taking, 107–8
    for reading, 89, 90–91
    for test taking, 134–37, 143
    for writing, 152–53
Presentations, 158–59
Previewing
    for note taking, 107
    questions on tests, 138
    before reading, 90
Prezi, 159

Prioritizing
    defending, 86
    definition and example of, 16
    goal-setting action steps, 24
    time management and, 69, 75
Private loans, 198
Problem solving, practicing, 132–33
Procrastination
    goal setting and, 22
    overcoming, 81–82
Productivity
    distractions and, 82
    time tracking and, 73
Professional associations, 217
Progress, monitoring, 45, 48
Project plans, 79, 86
Proofreading
    essay question answers, 141
    written work, 155
Psychology, positive, 8–10. *See also* Positivity
Public speaking, 158–59
Punctuality, 159
Purpose
    finding your, 7
    in presentations, 158
    in reading, 104
    in writing, 152
Purposeful reading questions, 91, 93, 97, 132

Q

Questions
    asking in class, 43, 110
    behavioral interview, 219
    in critical thinking, 15
    essay, 140–41, 146
    fill-in-the-blank, 140
    follow-up, 166
    journalists', 15, 104
    making learning connections with, 53–54
    matching, 139–40
    multiple-choice, 138–39
    purposeful reading, 91, 93, 97, 132
    true/false, 140
    unanswered, bringing to class, 108
Quotations, avoiding plagiarism with, 156

R

Racial diversity, 179
Reading, 87–104
    active, 89
    asking for help with, 100
    benefits of, 95
    different types of materials, 98–101
    embracing, 89
    focus in, 89, 92–96
    gaining confidence in, 94
    importance of, 87, 89
    out loud, 155, 156
    Personal Success Plan for, 102–3
    preparation for, 89, 90–91
    review in, 89, 97
    success attitude toward, 104
Read-Write learners, 59

Realistic expectations, 82
Realistic interests, 205
Receiver, in interpersonal communication, 165
Reciting, after reading, 97
Reference lists, 156
Reflection
    on barriers to goals, 32
    on connecting with others, 164
    in critical thinking, 17
    goal setting and, 3
    on information literacy, 148
    on learning preferences, 50
    on motivation, decision making, and personal
        responsibility, 34
    on note taking, 106
    on organization and time management, 70
    overcoming procrastination through, 81
    personal, 12
    on personal and financial health, 186
    on reading, 88
    on strengths and weaknesses, 5
    on test performance, 143
    on thinking and learning, 45
    on your progress, 221–23
Reframing
    expectations, 82
    test anxiety and, 136
Rehearsal, memory and, 128, 131–32
Relationships, 163–84
    communication skills and, 165–66
    conflict resolution and, 171–73
    emotional intelligence and, 167–70
    growing and sustaining healthy, 174–77
    Personal Success Plan for, 182–83
    reflection on, 164
    as a value, 206
    voices of experience on, 177
Relaxation techniques, 135–36, 138, 159
    for managing emotions, 169
    for sleep, 189
Relevance
    of goals, 22–23, 27, 32
    motivation and, 35–36
Religious diversity, 179
Research
    evaluating information in, 150–51
    finding information in, 149–50
    for writing, 152–53
Resilience, 8–9, 11
Resources, 10, 25, 100, 155. *See also* Support
        systems
Respect, for differences, 178, 180
Responsibility. *See* Personal responsibility
Results sections, in journal articles, 99, 100
Résumés, writing, 215–16
Retrieval failure, 129
Retrieving memories, 127
Review
    in active reading, 89, 97
    notes, 111
    of previous tests, 134
    for test taking, 134
Review sheets, 132
Rewards, scheduling time for, 78
Roark, James L., 110

S

Safe Zone Training Program, 181
Schedules. *See also* Time management
    building, 75–78
    flexibility in, 78
    note taking and, 107
    for online courses, 100
    for sleep, 189
    time tracking and, 73–74
Schneider, Mathew, 191
Scholarships, 197, 202
School events, scheduling time for, 77–78
Science classes
    note taking for, 119, 120
    reading for, 98–100
    studying for, 132–33
    test taking in, 141
Self-awareness, 49
Self-direction, 49
Self-efficacy
    building, 8
    homework and, 43
    motivation and, 35
    as transferable skill, 11
Self-explanation, 54
Self-knowledge
    in academic and career planning, 205–7, 226
    for decision making, 40, 41
    and diversity, 180
    finding your purpose, 7
    gaining, 3–6
    and interests, 4
    and strengths and weaknesses, 5–6
    and values, 3–4
Self-questioning, 53–54
Self-talk, 37
Self-testing, 51–52
Sensing/Intuitive dimension, 56–57, 58
Sensory memory, 127
Sentences, writing complete, 156
Service learning, 175–76, 214
Sexual health, 193–94, 202
Sexually transmitted infections (STIs), 193–94, 202
Sexual orientation diversity, 179, 180
Short-term memory, 128, 129
Simply Hired, 217
Skills
    building new, 6
    communication, 165–66
    conflict resolution, 173
    critical thinking, 11, 15–18
    exploring your, 207
    growth mind-set about, 42
    note taking, 121
    reading, 89
    strengths and weaknesses, 5–6
    transferable, building, 36
    transferable to work settings, 11
    waypower and, 9
Skimming, 96
Skype, 159
Sleep, 134, 185, 189

SMART goals, 22–23, 27
    constructing, 32
    examples of, 23, 29, 46, 66, 84, 102, 122, 144, 160, 182, 200, 224
    for motivation, decision making, and personal responsibility, 46–47
    for the Personal Success Plan, 30
    self-efficacy and, 35
Smith, Erin, 39
Snapchat, 19
Snyder, Charles, 9
Social interests, 205
Social media
    connecting through, 176
    critical thinking about, 19
    as distraction, 82
Social support networks, 174–77
Socioeconomic status, diversity in, 179
Sources
    citing, 154, 155, 156, 162
    quality of, 150–51
Space, in note taking, 119, 120
Speaker, in interpersonal communication, 165, 166
Specific goals, 22–23, 27, 32
Spending, reducing, 196–97
Stereotyping, 178
STIs. *See* Sexually transmitted infections (STIs)
Storage systems, 71–72
    in memory, 127, 129
Strengths
    goal setting and, 14
    learning your, 5–6
Stress
    health and, 185
    humor in coping with, 202
    impact of, 187
    motivation from, 35
    self-talk and, 37
    suppressing emotions and, 170
    voices of experience on, 191
    work–school balance and, 197
Student engagement, 207
Student loans, 197–98
Study groups, 130–31, 133, 143
Study guides, comparing notes to, 111
Studying
    changing up material in, 53
    connections, making during, 53–54
    creating space for, 71
    distributed, 53
    flexibility in plans for, 28
    learning how and what to focus on for, 2
    for math and science classes, 132–33
    motivation for, 146
    for online courses, 133
    overcoming procrastination and distractions and, 81–82
    personal responsibility for, 43
    Personal Success Plan for, 144–45
    scheduling, 75–78
    strategies for, 130–33
    tracking time for, 73–74
Study space, 71
Study tools, 132

Stumberg, Samuel Caleb, 177
Style guides, 155
Subsidized loans, 198
Substance abuse, 192
Success
    attitude, 12, 32, 48, 68, 86, 104, 124, 146, 162, 184,
        202, 226
    observing in others, 35
    personal responsibility and, 43
    reflecting on past, 6
    self-efficacy and, 35
    setting yourself up for, 43
    visualizing, 48
Summaries, reading, 90
Summarizing
    in Cornell system of note taking, 116
    in note taking, 116
    reading and, 97
Supplemental Instruction, 130–31
Support systems
    finding and recruiting, 10
    healthy relationships in, 174–77
    learning disabilities and, 65
    personal, 12
    self-efficacy and, 35
    self-talk and, 37
    as a value, 206
Suppressing emotions, 170
Syllabi, 72, 134
Symbols
    in mapping, 118
    in note taking, 110
    studying math and science, 133
Synthesizing
    in Bloom's taxonomy, 20–21
    definition and example of, 16
Syphilis, 193

T

Tables of contents, reading, 90
Teachers. *See* Instructors
Teamwork
    ensuring positive experiences in, 68
    learning preferences and, 63–64
    as transferable skill, 11
Technology
    as distraction, 82, 174
    for communication, 156, 176, 215, 217
    for study and work help, 100–101, 119–20
Television, as distraction, 82
Test anxiety. *See* Anxiety, about tests
Test formats, 134
Test questions
    Bloom's taxonomy and, 21
    essay, 140–41, 146
    fill-in-the-blank, 140
    matching, 139–40
    practice, 132
    true/false, 140
Test taking
    anxiety about, 125, 135–37, 138
    following up after, 143
    integrity in, 142

levels of learning and, 20, 21
    in math and science classes, 141
    online, 141–42
    Personal Success Plan for, 144–45
    preparation for, 134–37
    scheduling time for, 77
    self-tests, 51–52
    strategies for, 138–42
    voices of experience on, 137
Textbooks
    marking notes in your, 93, 97
    previewing material in, 90
    purposeful reading questions and, 91
    reading science, 99
    studying, 132, 133
Texting, 176
Thank-you notes, 217, 220
Theorems, reviewing, 133
Thesis statements, writing, 153–54, 158
Thinking/Feeling dimension, 57, 58
Time-limited goals, 22–23, 28, 32
Time management, 69–86
    building schedules and, 75–78
    goal setting and, 22
    growth mind-set and, 42
    identifying priorities and, 75
    for large class assignments, 86
    for online learning, 77
    organization and, 71–72
    overcoming procrastination and distractions in, 81–82
    Personal Success Plan for, 84–85
    for presentations, 159
    reading and, 90
    reflection on, 70
    steps in, 73–79
    for studying, 130
    in test taking, 138, 141
    tools for, 80
    tracking progress in, 78–79
    tracking time for, 73–74
    voices of experience on, 80
To-do lists, 78
Tolerance, 178
Topic selection, 153
Tracking, in time management, 73–74
Transferable skills, 11, 121, 207, 209–10, 219
Transferring, 208–10
Transition words, 155
TransUnion, 199
True/false questions, 140
Tutoring centers, 10
Tutors
    learning strategy help from, 65
    for online classes, 133
    as resources, 25
    in revising writing, 155
Twitter, 19, 176, 215, 217

U

Unconditional language, 139, 140
Underlining, while reading, 92, 93
Unemployment, education levels and, 195
Unsubsidized loans, 198

U.S. Department of Agriculture, 188
U.S. Department of Education, 197
U.S. Department of Labor, 195, 202, 212, 213

V

Vaginal rings, 194
Values
    definition of, 3
    exploring your, 206–7
    learning your, 3–4
    work, 206–7
VARK (Visual, Aural, Read-Write, and Kinesthetic) model, 49, 56, 58–61
    questionnaire, 59–61
Verbal cues, 109
Verbal information, 54
Veteran services offices, 10
Viewpoints, understanding others', 173
Visual aids, 158–59
Visual information, 54
Visualization
    for motivation, 38–39
    before presentations, 159
    for relaxation, 135, 136
    of success, 48
Visual learners, 58, 62
Vocabulary, 89, 95, 167
    for math and science classes, 133
    memorizing math/science terms and, 98
Vocal inflections, 172
Vocational identity, 207
Voice, emotions conveyed by, 168
Voices of experience
    on finding your purpose, 7
    on goal setting, 26
    on learning strategies, 62
    on maintaining relationships, 177
    on motivation, 39
    on note taking, 114
    on reading, 94
    on selecting a major and classes, 211
    on staying healthy and coping with stress, 191
    on tests and test anxiety, 137
    on time management, 80
    on writing, 157
Voice volume, 159

W

Waypower, 9
Weaknesses
    goal setting and, 14
    identifying your, 5–6
WebEx, 159
Web sites
    currency of, 151
    evaluating untrustworthiness, 150–51
    social media, 82, 156, 215, 217
    as source of practice math problems, 132
Weight management, 189
"Why?", asking, 53–54
Wikipedia, 151
Willey, Ashley J., 157
Williams, Nicole S., 114
Williams, Pharrell, 8
Willpower, 9
Work during college
    to boost income, 197
    exploring careers through, 214
    scheduling, 76, 77
Working conditions, 206
Working memory, 128, 129
Work values, 206–7
Worry journals, 136
Writer's block, 162
Writing, 152–57
    cover letters, 217–19
    e-mail, 174–75
    first drafts, 153–55
    preparing for, 152–53
    résumés, 215–16
    voices of experience on, 157
Writing centers, 10, 155, 156

Y

Young, Stephanie, 137
Yourself, learning about, 3–7
Yousafzai, Malala, 36

Z

Zuckerberg, Mark, 19